Creative Soc

Leadership for a H

Kathryn Goldman Schuyler has curated a fierce, brave book that offers immense hope whilst looking our future square in the eye. The voices presented in this book embody a powerful, inspiring collaborative effort that harnesses a diversity of wisdom traditions to urge a return to wholeness, relatedness, inclusivity, and interdependence. It calls for us to detox and heal ourselves and our world as we, as ancestors of the future, imprint our stewardship on this planet.

— Dr Chellie Spiller, Associate Dean Maori and Pacific, University of Auckland Business School

This book throbs with the aliveness of wise thinking, deep questions, exciting narratives, and innovative global change projects for generating a more healthy and sustainable world. Reading it gave me hope, enthusiasm and new ideas for practical actions I can implement within my own leadership and organisations. Kathryn Goldman Schuyler has skillfully edited a collection of the most profound and powerful thinking, dialogue, and guidance; especially for those in leadership positions. I cannot recommend this book highly enough for anyone wanting to assure their own wholeness alongside a genuine legacy of making the world a better and healthier place to live, work and lead in.

— Dr Lynne Sedgmore CBE, Former Chief Executive of 157 Group, Centre for Excellence in Leadership UK, Debretts 500 list, UK, 2015

What is our vision of a healthy person, organization, or world? How do we dream together a world both economically sound and spiritually profound? *Leadership for a Healthy World* is a valuable and timely resource for leaders, educators, activists, and visionaries dreaming together the new story for an interdependent world. No longer solving isolated problems, this book ushers in a deeper conversation about where we are going as a species and how we can be in a new relationship with the land, with nature, community and our own highest self.

— Alan Briskin, PhD, author of The Stirring of Soul in the Workplace, Daily Miracles, *and* The Power of Collective Wisdom

We have the technology to create a healthy world. Now we stand at the precipice of the last, great frontier in making this happen — our relationships with one another. This wonderfully insightful and actionable book helps all of us to make the leap.

— Chris Ernst, Changemaker, Bill and Melinda Gates Foundation and Author, Boundary Spanning Leadership

21st century enterprises are awakening to a simple fact of modern life: achieving commercial success without preserving the health and well-being of our world is a fool's errand. Leaders who want to confidently embrace this challenge of building a truly healthy world should carefully read Dr. Schuyler's book.

— Michael Carroll, Author of Awake at Work *and* The Mindful Leader

This book combines and offers elegant theory, hard-earned wisdom, and real-life solutions in the service of transforming complex systems from pathology to health. As I have worked in leadership development in South Africa for more than 25 years (a country with its own share of shame, pain and hope, and a host of wicked problems), I am skeptical when I open a new leadership book. My skepticism faded as I read, as I encountered ideas and shared experiences that deepened my thinking and stirred new creative impulses. If enough leaders embrace the thinking and practical possibilities described here, then the vital attitude of simultaneously caring for our psyches, our communities, and our one precious planet may become a mainstream way of being.

> — *Hélène Smit, Author of* Beneath — Exploring the Unconscious in Individuals and Depth Leadership

This book is a must read for all leadership students, professors, and consultants. Thoughtful, provocative and deeply meaningful work!

> — *Prasad Kaipa, CEO Advisor and Coach, and Co-Author of* From Smart to Wise *(with Navi Radjou) and* You Can *(with Meera Shenoy)*

At a time when people know what must be done, but the deeper issue is how to make it happen, this guide to deep change does not offer the definitive answer, but rather experiences, models, and actions that can help us look at our own communities and make a difference. I find this a rich and wonderful toolbox that I can continually dip into to help open myself up to the work that I need to do. Thank you.

> — *Dennis T. Jaffe, Ph.D., Wise Counsel Research*

Creative Social Change is an inspiring book that brings together an amazing group of thought leaders to reimagine leadership in building a healthy, sustainable, and equitable world for all — humans and other living creatures. The journey towards a healthy world is both an inner journey for leaders and a necessity for us all, as the book makes clear. That journey starts with self-awareness, purpose, and insight, because leaders need to become much more aware of their power and their impacts than they currently are. Leadership then becomes an outer journey that reshapes our major institutions so that they support what gives life and vitality, not merely what is 'efficient' and profitable. Using the ideas and insights of big systems thinkers, the book focuses on what gives life, inspiration, and imagination to organizations, societies, and, indeed, the world as a whole. It helps us all to imagine a better world, a balanced, vital, and healthy world that supports human beings without the destruction inherent in far too many of today's business and societal practices. The authors recognize the inherent interconnectedness of life and of us all, and of our deep connection to the natural world around us. Thus, the book argues that leaders need to approach our organizations and our world mindfully, aware of the impacts of their decisions and actions and aware of the need to shape our world for the better. With insights on mindfulness practices, the role of women, indigenous perspectives, the arts, communities, and sustainability thinking, this book is a valuable and much needed resource for all of us.

> — *Sandra Waddock, Galligan Chair of Strategy and Professor of Management, Boston College*

Creative Social Change

Leadership for a Healthy World

Edited by

Kathryn Goldman Schuyler
Alliant International University; Coherent Change, San Francisco, CA, USA

John Eric Baugher
Goucher College, Baltimore, MD, USA

Karin Jironet
InClaritas Foundation, Amsterdam, The Netherlands

International Leadership Association

Emerald

United Kingdom – North America – Japan
India – Malaysia – China

Emerald Group Publishing Limited
Howard House, Wagon Lane, Bingley BD16 1WA, UK

First edition 2016

British Library Cataloguing in Publication Data
A catalogue record for this book is available from the British Library

ISBN: 978-1-78635-146-3
ISSN: 2058-8801 (Series)

ISOQAR certified
Management System,
awarded to Emerald
for adherence to
Environmental
standard
ISO 14001:2004.

Certificate Number 1985
ISO 14001

INVESTOR IN PEOPLE

Contents

List of Contributors

John, Lord Alderdice	House of Lords, London, UK; Centre for Democracy and Peace-Building, Belfast, UK; Centre for the Resolution of Intractable Conflict, Oxford, UK
John Eric Baugher	Goucher College, Baltimore, MD, USA
Carolina Bown	Salisbury University, Salisbury, MD, USA
Riane Eisler	Center for Partnership Studies, Pacific Grove, CA, USA
Kathryn Goldman Schuyler	Alliant International University; Coherent Change, San Francisco, CA, USA
Susan Amber Gordon	Artist, Alexandria, VA, USA
Steadman Harrison III	Global Outreach International, Tupelo, MS, USA
Jill Hufnagel	Cambridge Leadership Associates, New York, NY, USA
Karin Jironet	InClaritas Foundation, Amsterdam, The Netherlands
Max Klau	City Year, Inc., Boston, MA, USA
Jane McCann	McCann Consulting Ltd., Wellington, New Zealand
Walter Osika	Karolinska Institutet, Stockholm, Sweden
Charles J. Palus	Center for Creative Leadership, Greensboro, NC, USA
Joshua J. Prasad	Michigan State University, Lansing, MI, USA

Robert E. Quinn	University of Michigan, Ann Arbor, MI, USA
Karl-Henrik Robèrt	Blekinge Tekniska Högskola, Karlskrona, Sweden
Otto Scharmer	MIT Sloan School of Management, Cambridge, MA, USA
Ed Schein	Professor Emeritus, MIT, Cambridge, MA, USA
Peter Senge	MIT Sloan School of Management, Cambridge, MA, USA
Barbara Rose Shuler	Writer and Broadcaster, Pacific Grove, CA, USA
Éliane Ubalijoro	McGill University, Montréal, Canada
Bagwiza Jacqueline Uwizeyimana	McGill University, Montréal, Canada
Marilyn Verghis	McGill University, Montréal, Canada
Patricia A. Wilson	University of Texas, Austin, TX, USA
Samuel G. Wilson	Swinburne Leadership Institute, Swinburne University of Technology, Hawthorn, Australia
Margaret Wheatley	Consultant and Speaker, Provo, UT, USA

Foreword

These are complex times for studies in leadership. In the past, it was much more straightforward. Leaders were recognized, elected, or appointed, and then once in place the main challenge was usually from rivals for the position. The mass of people generally accepted that it was for some to be leaders, but for most people to be followers. All that changed, perhaps most notably a century ago with the Great War, as it was called at the time. During World War I, there was, for perhaps the first time, serious regular criticism of the military leadership on all sides. Many of the leaders were in place through accident of birth rather than by popular demand or obvious skill and ability. The massive losses of life, the legacy of terrible injuries, and the sense that even the victors were diminished by the outcome ensured that all the traditional social and political leadership were damaged. The result was the collapse of the whole imperial order in Europe, with repercussions all around the world. This was followed by an unprecedented extension of democracy and, as the 20th century passed, an increasing and eventually almost universal rejection of the principle that foreign powers, or domestic leaders could legitimately take or hold power in a country by physical force.

After World War II, the process of decolonization gathered pace and elections increasingly became the principal mechanism by which changes of government and power could take place without a violent revolution. The social structure also changed with an appreciation that every individual should have the right to follow their own beliefs, ambitions, and way of life without restriction other than the avoidance of harm to others. There was also an increasing belief that anyone could achieve almost anything if they set their mind to it with sufficient commitment. Such was the dramatic and optimistic vista these changes appeared to open up that as the people pulled down the Berlin Wall with their own hands in 1989, Francis Fukuyama famously declared the triumph of western liberal democracy and the endpoint of humanity's sociocultural evolution — "the end of history" as he described it.

However, as is always the case, even the best-informed foresight cannot discern with certainty what is beyond the horizon of time, and the decades since Fukuyama's assertion have seen dramatic changes resulting from the continuing loss of deference and even respect for traditional forms of leadership, the exponential development of information and communication technology, and a new social order characterized more by constantly evolving networks than by hierarchies and bureaucracies.

The dawn of the new millennium has now seen something quite unexpected. While in areas like healthcare and technology there really is progress ever onward and upward, instead of a greater sense of freedom, stability, and prosperity we see a regression from the aspiration for a world of freedom-loving, free-wheeling, healthy egalitarian individuals, and the development of a patch-work of more anxious, inward-looking communities of people, fearful that while I can with pleasure travel to other people's countries, they can now with ease come to mine and perhaps change its culture in ways that I find uncomfortable and unwelcome. In addition, not only can new fashion, new social trends, and remarkable new devices arrive in my community, but so can terrorists and drones. States that appeared to be on the road to democracy have imploded and been replaced with domination by fundamentalist warlords. War itself is no longer something that happens elsewhere, but is an unwelcome visitor on my own home territory, and if that were not enough, even our environment cannot be depended upon to stay stable, and is changing in ways which may threaten the continued welfare or even existence of some of our communities and even small countries.

The results of these changes, at once exciting and frightening, are paradoxical. Everyone feels they can be a leader, seeking out followers by broadcasting their thoughts in blogs and social media. No one gives much respect to those appointed or elected to leadership, and those who find themselves in such positions are unable to deliver the illusions of progress and prosperity which they had to offer in order to be elected. At the same time, there is a frenetic searching for those who through their ideas, inspiration, and charisma may provide new forms of leadership — thought leaders, agents of social change, and inspirational models who need to be able to convey their ideas and philosophy, if not in the 140 characters of Twitter, then in 15 minutes of video on a TED Talk.

Into this complex and uncertain context, the International Leadership Association gathers colleagues to bring their experience and expertise, addressing the challenges of leadership as it affects our environment, health, the arts, women, first nation people, ethics, and the United Nations and a clutch of other topical challenges and put it to paper in their Building Leadership Bridges series.

The most critical and difficult thing facing our path to a better future is determining how to change our culture, our way of being in the world in a community. How do we change our way of being in the world so that it accommodates to the new world? We can check off certain boxes in problem solving exercises, but can we change our culture? If we don't change our way of being, as a whole community, we will die. In this volume, *Creative Social Change: Leadership for a Healthy World*, it is the editors' and authors' wish, coming as they do from different backgrounds and life experiences, to address the current challenges with a positive health-promoting and affirming mode of thinking, focusing less on the problems and what doesn't work, but rather seeking out stories, models, and inspirations that can help us see how to change our way of being and contribute to a healthier world and better future.

When a group of us from Northern Ireland traveled to South Africa to meet with Nelson Mandela, he told us, "I'm not here to tell you how to solve your problems, but what I can do is tell you our story. And, if there are parts of that story that resonate for you, that help you in your journey, then that's a useful thing for all of us and it's good for us to have met." Between the covers of this volume of papers, meet these ideas, let the authors lead your thinking into new paths and be excited by the possibilities.

John, Lord Alderdice
House of Lords, London, United Kingdom

Acknowledgments: From the Editorial Team

This book could only have been created with the participation in many ways of many people. We appreciate them and their varied and important contributions so very much!

One person has a special place on our team and in our hearts. Lena Lid-Falkman worked with us initially as editor and chose to withdraw to focus her full attention on her young son and now baby daughter. This was not an easy choice for any of us, but it so embodies what we mean by making good choices in life that promote health. We missed her contributions and hope to work with her again.

Deep thanks go to Peter Senge, whose thoughtful reflections on our previous book prompted our decision as a team to write this one. His views helped us "raise the bar" on ourselves and choose to focus on what we otherwise may have deemed too large a topic.

The editorial team thanks Debra DeRuyver, Communications Director of the ILA — always accessible, a source of good ideas, a friendly sounding board, and a great communicator. We also thank the ILA for their faith in us and support for our work. Shelly Wilsey, Chief Operating Officer, and Bridget Chisholm, Director of Conferences, are a pleasure to work with. They, and the rest of the ILA staff, have supported the creation and promotion of this book in too many ways to mention; we love being on their team.

We deeply appreciate the ongoing care, thought, and hard work of all of those who contributed chapters and artwork: writing about the topics included here has not been easy for any of us. We so value having you on this journey with us. We also wish to thank all who submitted proposals for this volume and who are not in it; we value that you too care for these important questions, wish we could have included you, and hope that writing for us helped you take your plans and dreams a bit further.

And from each member of the team individually:

Kathryn thanks Mary Fambrough, who took time when she was particularly busy to read large portions of the manuscript and offer her always-insightful suggestions. And my deepest thanks go to my two colleagues, Karin and John. This virtual team has still never met physically in one room, but our virtual meetings are so alive and nourishing. Each of you has gone so far beyond what you expected to commit in terms of time and thought. Together, despite the challenges of a difficult year, we have, I believe, done all we hoped to and more in creating this book. Special thanks to my sister, who gave copies of our last book to people she knew throughout her local government: what a gift to them and to me — and what an inspiration! Finally: Sky — your presence and interest nourish me in so many ways, far beyond what I know that I know. Your music, creativity, wise technology support, and love keep me able to smile and continue working on tasks like this book!

John thanks Kathryn and Karin for their unique gifts and for the joys of working together through all the unfolding of this project. And on the deepest level, I thank Andrea Mortello and a vast web of support — seen and unseen — that sustained me in every sense while working on this project. May the healthful aspirations of all who contributed to this volume and all who read it be attained!

Karin thanks Inga-Britt Ahlenius and Jan Eliasson, as well as Lena Lid-Falkman who through their generosity in sharing very personal ideas, impressions, and experiences imparted unique insight into the United Nation's organization and inspired me in writing the chapter on ethics in the UN. Over the years, my appreciation for Kathryn and John (and Lena) and our way of working together has deepened and moved from the initial phases of appreciation and curiosity to deeply felt respect. Kathryn patiently and masterfully created space for our individual expertise to serve the purpose of the book. John, with scrutinizing honesty, persisted in letting the call for presence resound. I would not have wanted to miss one single hour with you. Harry Starren, who not only read and helped me revising the UN chapter, and whose erudite genius took me through long nights of reading, reflecting, and commenting on other chapters of the book, most of all, brought light, joy, and a sense of fascination with life.

1 Introduction

Kathryn Goldman Schuyler

There is something deeply nourishing about focusing attention on creating a healthy world. In the face of any human or cultural tendencies to focus on what doesn't work, we can choose to contribute to what does, to planting seeds for the future. Perhaps this is core to health: finding ways to appreciate the current moment while contributing to people and actions that we sense to be toward life, rather than focusing on making do, making money, or doing what we believe to be required of us. Both the "moving towards" and the awareness of connection with the natural world seem essential in appreciating the nature of health. This book is intended to create dialogue about together creating a healthy society — a healthy world. It is grounded in a question we can each ask ourselves: What is my role in creating healthy organizations and a healthy world?

It's refreshing to know that research suggests that most people wish to contribute to the world they live in (see Singer, 2015; Vaillant, 2012). A recent survey of U.S. adults found that 90% of those asked agreed that "It is important for me to leave this world better than I found it," and 95% agreed that "My efforts are motivated by a desire to help humanity in some way" (see Lee, Poloma, & Post, 2013. Quotes are from personal communication, Lee, July 22, 2015)

I open with a personal story, because our stories are the soil from which we create the new. What becomes a framework, a profession, a book ... starts somewhere much earlier, in the experiences that kindle within us something that we may not even know is there, nor realize how this invisible seed connects with later actions in life. As I thought about how to describe the sources of this book, I asked myself how I became interested in healthy organizations and started to remember experiences from many years ago.

"L'Imagination au Pouvoir!"

My interest in creating healthy organizations in a healthy society is not new: It goes back to my experiences of campus and societal change in the 1960s as a graduate student during the Vietnam War. I was in Paris on a year of Fulbright study when students and workers took to the streets and almost brought the entire country to a halt in dramatic protests typically referred to as *les évènements* (the events). This experience was so vivid that it has colored much of my life since then. It was important on several levels:

Cognitively I learned that we could completely invert what I had always thought to be true about the relationship of hopes and "reality." I had been taught in the 1950s and early 1960s that one had to look around, see what was possible, and then make a choice among those options. Very reasonable. That was how life worked. Then, in the heady weeks and months leading up to *les évènements*, huge posters appeared throughout Paris, emblazoned on the walls, crying *"L'imagination au pouvoir!"* (Power to the imagination!) I discovered that humans could imagine what might be possible and aim to create it, to make it real. I saw that the power to create the new could come from our visions of what was possible, rather than from slight adaptations of what already existed.

Although this is not what I felt happened during this "mini-revolution" at my institution, l'Ecole Pratique des Hautes Etudes (6éme section — the school of arts and sciences), where I was studying the sociology of knowledge, this experience profoundly impacted my thinking about the nature of change. What could be created no longer depended upon what existed, but upon what could be thought and imagined and sensed as possible. In some ways, this was like discovering that gravity had changed and was no longer as heavy — as though I'd traveled to a new planet, where it worked differently.

Emotionally, I felt a changed relationship to power, both the power of authority and of the past, and also instinctively knew that I could not be and had no desire to be a revolutionary. To live in the Latin Quarter of Paris in May 1968 was to be in the middle of constant activity, fast-moving crowds uprooting and throwing *pavés* (small cobblestones) and even burning cars, and rows on end of police armed with helmets, large clear plastic shields, and *matraques* (batons). It was a world of self-organizing committees at the university making decisions that evaporated as soon as those making them went to sleep for a few hours, replaced by others who didn't know of the decisions and so made others. It was also a world where the famously unfriendly French were warm, friendly, and inclusive of everyone. Being of Jewish heritage, growing up with a father who was not only an M.D. but also a psychoanalyst in New York City, I'd previously thought that the police were there to help me, but it took no experience at all to realize this was an entirely different world. No one had to tell me to cross the street and stay out of the way. It was obvious. The police were not the friends of students, not then.

At a gut level, I realized that as wild as this was, it was calm compared to a "real" revolution involving mass violence and killing. I saw the physical power of the police and later experienced bureaucratic power, as these "events" transitioned into change committees at the university that met all day, day after day, making a great many small procedural decisions that changed the life of the younger faculty but impacted me as a student not at all. The beautiful sunny June that followed the upheavals of May was spent entirely indoors, in committees that were planning change, but types of change that had little to do with imagination or the dreams of the students and workers in the streets. So I saw raw power and bureaucratic power — and realized that neither was what drew nor enlivened me.

Finally, at a personal level, I realized that I would go home to the United States and figure out where I belonged — how I could be part of the change that I did want to see emerging in the world, but without blood or excessive bureaucracy. Somehow, despite the state of the United States at the time, with the Vietnam War, race riots, and the assassinations of Robert F. Kennedy and Martin Luther King, Jr. that year, I began to sense that the United States had some kind of potential and possibility that I could not describe or identify, but only feel.

This led to my interest in organizational and societal health. I came out of my life in somewhat revolutionary Paris knowing that people spent most of their lives at work in communities, and that if these were healthy, the people could be nourished by them, and if they were not, they became deadening, constricting the sense of possibility that can be felt when one is very young, surrounded by love, or in a community or workplace that helps one feel whole.

Those experiences sourced my professional life of research and practice and this book. I believe in studying what you know and care deeply about and encourage students to do the same. When seeking to understand how to create a healthy society or world, behavioral science research, embodiment, and ancient spiritual traditions are all invaluable (see Goldman Schuyler, 2004a, 2004b). Training in somatic (embodied) learning with Dr. Moshe Feldenkrais (1972, 1979) gave me a profound approach to health: the notion that a healthy person is one who lives their avowed *and unavowed* dreams fully. Feldenkrais was renowned globally for working with the body, yet his definition of health focused on action and awareness, not on the physical *per se*. Seeking further deep roots for transformation, I explored how the Dalai Lama and other Tibetan Buddhist master teachers brought traditions of non-Western, disciplined practices for opening awareness about life (Goldman Schuyler, 2004a, 2007). These had been passed down directly from one master teacher to another for hundreds of years, ensuring that no confusing elements were brought in by those who might write about them without having experienced them. While other indigenous wisdom traditions have also been passed down in similar ways, this particular one intrigued me from a leadership perspective, because of the role of the Dalai Lama as a global thought leader (Goldman Schuyler, 2012).

Our Shared Dream

This book highlights current ways of thinking and projects to create a healthy world: a place that nourishes humans and all other living beings. The dream of the editorial team is of a place where humans recognize and live in reciprocity with one another and other forms of life, where the human capacity to use tools and our minds to transform our environment not only does not destroy it (as seems a distinct possibility to many), but instead contributes to the flourishing of all humans, excluding none. A home for all nationalities, for women and men, for animals, for the vast varieties of species of plants — without using them up in service of just our dominant species. A home that respects differences of values and culture without presuming that one's own approach is better or higher than that of others. A home in the full meaning of the word: a place that we think of with love, which gave us birth, and where those we love reside.

We in the editorial team have no illusion or delusion of being complete or providing "the answer" to these important questions. Our intention is to foster conversation within the world of social science on the notion of a healthy society and the role of leadership and healthy organizations in such a world. There did not seem to be any way to have the book fully represent the efforts taking place around the world in service of our goals, as the task would be too vast. Given the vastness of the topic, we chose to present fundamental conceptual themes and perspectives and then shine light on seeds that are being planted by many people around the world, as symbolized by those included in the book.

In the 2014 Building Leadership Bridges volume, *Leading with Spirit, Presence, and Authenticity*, we as an editorial team presented authors from around the world who had focused on developing leaders' inner wisdom (Goldman Schuyler, Baugher, Jironet, & Lid-Falkman, 2014). This book builds on that context: the path from inner development to impact in the world. In this second volume we seek to address, with humility, the omnipresent task of generating a healthy society and world.

As Editor Karin Jironet describes her experience of our work together in creating this book:

> We live in different parts of the world, in different time zones and cultures, and with different biographies, educations and professions. Yet, we have a common mindset and close affinity with the leadership field. The medium — online conversations — seems to create a liminal space of sorts; it is not a professional meeting yet not a social meeting but a base for sharing our personal stories within the professional framework.

The team began this undertaking with the same members as for *Leading with Spirit, Presence, and Authenticity*, but life intervened. In creating the last book, we had a relatively easy time, although we had to learn to be at ease stating views in the face of a colleague's strong disagreement. That process established a fundamental trust in ourselves and one another. This time, our work was longer and more challenging, perhaps because of the scope of the topic we chose, or perhaps simply because there is actually increasing turmoil and change in many people's lives. Somehow we felt how health can silently reverberate in the background, amidst all the chaos, suffering, and noise — things that we too, as individuals, experienced in our lives over the 20 months that we worked together virtually to co-create this book.

Much as Lena Lid-Falkman wished to work with us, she withdrew for personal reasons — and now has a beautiful baby daughter. We miss her endless good will and abundant energy. John Eric Baugher continues to bring his superb editing skills, his broad sociological perspectives, his commitment to social change, and his deep involvement with the role of suffering as a source of transformation. Karin Jironet is our "wise woman": Her insights about people and interpersonal dynamics combine with her knowledge of philosophy, Jungian psychology, and religion to help us incorporate perspectives that might otherwise be neglected. And Debra DeRuyver, who transitioned into the more expansive role of Communications Director at the International Leadership Association, continues to support us graciously with respect to logistics, good humor, and all the many invisible details involved in getting a book created and complete.

The Design of This Book

Creative Social Change: Leadership for a Healthy World is composed of three parts:

(1) **The Ground: Foundations from Thought Leaders** provides the rich thinking of key social science contributors to our growing understanding of how to create organizational and societal health,

(2) **Air and Water: What Flows Lives** offers nourishment from contributors who enrich our thinking about what it is to be a cultivator of health as a leader,

(3) **Seeds and Plants: Local Case Studies** includes case studies about bringing such ideas to life in various parts of the world, on many continents.

The **ground** is set primarily by the thinking of eminent social scientists who have been addressing leadership and health over the last several decades: Robert E. Quinn, Otto Scharmer, Ed Schein, Peter Senge, and Margaret Wheatley. Each of these scholars and consultants has made major contributions to thought and action in the area of systemic and transformational change. We chose them because of their interconnections and the breadth of what they bring, as foundational action-oriented organizational scholar-practitioners.

In addition, we sought contributions that address key topics in this vast global process, which we consider to be **air and water** or nutrients. Riane Eisler, distinguished award-winning author and activist for partnership in society since the 1980s, brings her powerful distinction between partnership and domination as an underlying framework of societies throughout human history. She alludes to the importance of measuring the components of a healthy society and leadership that is conducive to it, which is further discussed by leadership scholar Samuel G. Wilson in his chapter on developing indicators of societal health, with a focus particularly on leadership for the greater good, for which he developed and beta-tested an indicator in Australia. Sociologist Baugher, neuropsychiatrist Walter Osika, and MD and founder of The Natural Step Karl Henrik Robèrt enable us to look at the science behind *sustainability* in the context of the shift in moral needed for any significant change to take place. Psychoanalyst, theologian, and executive guide Karin Jironet reflects on how a personal leadership ethos forms the basis for the United Nation's work for a healthy world. In the final chapter of this section, Charles J. Palus, Steadman Harrison III, and Joshua J. Prasad of the Center for Creative Leadership explore the theoretical foundations of their leadership development work and how this has been used in Africa, which facilitates a transition in the book from thought to case studies of action.

The third part consists of a selection of case studies that we think of as **seeds or young plants**: efforts to take steps toward wholeness in different communities, cultures, and parts of the world. We are delighted that this selection brings in experiences from many parts of the world of attempting to bring about healthier organizations and communities. Patricia A. Wilson, professor of international development, public participation, and conflict resolution, describes action research in peri-urban Mexico that led not only to community change but also to the development of new university programs. Researcher Carolina Bown recounts the unique ways that indigenous women are developing as leaders in Ecuador, based on a study she conducted over a three-year period in a number of Andean communities, drawing upon local *Kichwa* concepts about life. Consultant Jane

McCann had been observing public chief executives in New Zealand for decades and was inspired by the call for this book to write about her observations and the implications. Barbara Rose Shuler, a music journalist with extensive involvement in the Carmel California Bach Festival, explores how this festival, designed 80 years ago to nourish its community, has built on this foundation over the many decades and how its current leader is initiating projects that honor the broadest community bases for the arts, creating a reciprocal benefit between the community and the arts. Max Klau and Jill Hufnagel, both of whom are deeply trained in Ron Heifetz's adaptive leadership approach, analyze how it has been used in the very diverse settings of the state of Kansas (the United States) and Bangladesh. Finally, Éliane Ubalijoro, Bagwiza Jacqueline Uwizeyimana, and Marilyn Verghis bring their experiences about how women in Rwanda have, through their leadership, been healing the deep wounds of the horrific genocide that took place there in 1994. In their case studies, these contributors touch on themes that are core issues for leadership and organizational studies: the role of women, the importance of sustainability, the complexity of leadership development, the importance of cultural competence, and the interdependent nature of practice-based learning and scholarly research in expanding our collective wisdom.

We believe that art and creativity are essential components for addressing global problems and opening people to new perspectives. As such, each part of the book opens with an original piece of art created by Susan Amber Gordon to express that part's theme. We hope you will give time to thoughtfully consider each piece, moving beyond words into the image-making regions of your mind before and after reading each part. Finally, in selecting contributors and topics, we as editors knew we could never be comprehensive; we hope we are raising core questions with enough varied voices to catalyze both dialogue and action. May the work of all our contributors help build a body of knowledge across disciplines, in different cultures, and over time about what works in nourishing a healthy world.

References

Feldenkrais, M. (1972). *Awareness through movement*. New York, NY: Harper and Row.

Feldenkrais, M. (1979). On health. *Dromenon*, 2(2), 25–26.

Goldman Schuyler, K. (2004a). The possibility of healthy organizations: Thoughts toward a new framework for organizational theory and practice. *Journal of Applied Social Science, 21*(2), 57–79.

Goldman Schuyler, K. (2004b). Practitioner – Heal thyself: Challenges in enabling organizational health. *Organization Management Journal, 1*(1), 28–37. doi:10.1057/omj.2004.9

Goldman Schuyler, K. (2007). Being a bodhisattva at work: Perspectives on the influence of Buddhist practices in entrepreneurial organizations. *Journal of Human Values, 13*(1), 41–58.

Goldman Schuyler, K. (2012). *Inner peace—Global impact: Tibetan Buddhism, leadership, and work*. Charlotte, NC: Information Age Publishing.

Lee, M. T., Poloma, M. M., & Post, S. G. (2013). *The heart of religion: Spiritual empowerment, benevolence, and the experience of god's love*. New York, NY: Oxford University Press.

Singer, P. (2015). *The most good you can do: How effective altruism is changing ideas about living ethically*. New Haven, CT: Yale University Press.

Vaillant, R. (2012). *Triumphs of experience: The men of the Harvard grant study*. Cambridge: Belknap Press.

The Ground: Foundations from Thought Leaders

Susan Amber Gordon. *Mountain Magicity*. 2014. Digital mixed media, 24″×18″. Private collection

The Ground: Foundations from Thought Leaders

Kathryn Goldman Schuyler

F ocusing on organizational and societal health brings life into leadership and organizational development. Some use the term organizational *effectiveness*, but the word *effective* suggests something that works really well, like a machine or computer, and not a living presence with heart. What seems more fitting for our humanly constructed societies are communities with heart and consciousness. In this perspective, leadership becomes the art and skill of focusing people's attention on how to sustain and nourish such dynamic living systems. No one would wish for ineffective action or leadership, but effectiveness on its own does not source a vital, dynamic human world.

We open the dialogue with the perspectives of five eminent social scientists who have been thought leaders for many decades on the nature of organizational and societal development. These interviews took place between December 2014 and May 2015, via virtual technology or in person, so that we could talk informally, as though we were together, even though we were geographically far apart. This part of the book introduces the fundamental issues and questions we seek to raise by writing this book, then introduces the five leading thinkers, presents the interviews where we talked together about organizational health, summarizes their key points, and finally weaves together the main implications and a foundation for the rest of the book. We begin with their current thinking to bring you up to date on their views and present a virtual dialogue among these distinguished scholars and authors who have in many ways laid the foundations for social science work toward creating healthy organizations in a healthy world.

Background: Organizational Health as Seen in the Social Sciences

Early in the life of the field of organization development (OD), the term *health* was often used to describe the goals of the profession, in addition to the term *effectiveness* (See, for example, Beckhard, 1969). The words health or healthy appear repeatedly in Richard Beckhard's (1969) opening description of "What is OD?", and his discussion of definitions of the leading thinkers of the time (Ed Schein, John W. Gardner, Matthew B. Miles) shows that they too used the term when describing the focus of OD. Beckhard was not simply one of many scholars, but was one of the leading pioneers in the creation of OD as a professional field and founder of the main professional organization, the OD Network. His statement that the goal is "to increase organization effectiveness and health" has been referenced by most who teach about the field (p. 9). He seemed to find it normal to use both terms next to one another — *effective* and *healthy* — as though to him they simply went together.

Chris Argyris's (1958) study of a manufacturing plant appears to be the earliest empirical study focused explicitly on organizational health. According to Argyris (1958), a healthy organization is one that *enables mature human functioning*. This is the most succinct statement of the value of healthy organizations that I have found, since others tend to be descriptive, providing details rather than conveying the essence of their value to societies. He concluded that organizational health was more complex than it appeared to many, because what was labeled "healthy" in fact produced immature behavior as a "logical result of an organizational pattern which places the employee in such a submissive, dependent position — an organizational pattern typical of the great majority of our business enterprises today" (p. 116). Although the workforce has changed in many ways since the 1950s, allegedly giving people roles that value independent thinking and action (as the percentage of knowledge workers increases in the workforce), the data continue to show disengagement. As Argyris hypothesized,

> It is as if the employee says to himself: "I want to be a healthy, creative human being; I cannot be and still produce what I am required to produce. Therefore I will say

to hell with my total personality and place the emphasis on money." (p. 116)

Argyris believed that this type of hierarchical, quiet domination in the workplace would be harmful for democracy, as he saw this as a source of atrophy over time for individuals, organizations, and even the nation.

In seeking a model or criteria, I found that 50 years ago Ed Schein (1965) described five criteria for a healthy organization. It would be able to (1) sense environmental change, (2) get information to the right places, (3) digest and utilize information, (4) adjust and transform itself without destruction, and (5) get feedback on consequences of transformations. The notion of adaptability is core to these criteria: Healthy organizations are those that can identify the need to change and act on this successfully. Argyris' research and writings (1958, 1960, 1964) suggest two additional requirements: Healthy organizations are those that provide for their employees (1) a sense of meaning and direction and (2) tasks that are challenging and possible to do well.

Then, in the 1990s, Peter J. Frost and Sandra Robinson introduced the importance of the ongoing elimination of toxins. As Schein (2000) wrote in an interview about Frost's work, "Some level of toxicity is normal. That really has to be hammered home rather than thinking of toxicity as abnormal. The body is producing toxins all the time" (p. 36). This implies that health is not an end state, something to achieve and enjoy, but instead an ongoing capacity to remove toxins from a living system, whether a person or an organization, and it exists always in process on a continuum, rather than being a dichotomous variable. There is something far more comfortable about this, as one no longer is pressured to strive for the seemingly unattainable, but simply to keep on breathing, being present to what is actually taking place, and seeing how to remove whatever is most harmful. Sociologist John G. Bruhn (2001) attempted to enrich the social science conversation on organizational health by bringing in the notion of *spirit* and how it "is the core or heart of an organization, ... what makes it vibrant, and gives it vigor" (p. 147), using the WHO's definition of health, but I haven't seen writings other than mine that build on his approach, despite the potential it offers.

Toward the end of his life, Beckhard (1996) returned to the topic of healthy organizations, referring to this as one of the main themes of his work. "I have spent a major part of my professional life exploring the nature of the health of organizations ...." and he concluded that the same criteria could be applied to individual and organizational health (p. 951). However, Beckhard's concepts remained general and did not convey the heart of the matter in the way that Argyris' approach did, with its focus on nourishing mature functioning. I was intrigued by his statement that "It is not illusionary to see, in the far future, a 'sick' society where the 'oddball' is truly healthy but will be locked up because there is no way of knowing that it is the majority who are ill" (Argyris, 1958, p. 107). This is not what I expect to see in the *Harvard Business Review* of the 1950s! His capacity to see through superficial pictures of so-called *health* to its dysfunctional nature is impressive, as is the clarity of his analytical discovery process. Such innovative thinking about health, society, and the individual is why Argyris has had such a lasting influence on so many researchers and practitioners across the social sciences for decades. In my own case, I have drawn upon Argyris and others' thinking on organizational health for much of my research and practice, as I have often focused explicitly on holistic ways to conceptualize and generate health (Goldman, 1979; Goldman Schuyler, 2004a, 2004b; Goldman Schuyler & Branagan, 2003).

However, many contemporary OD texts either omit the term from the definition they use and regard the field as addressing organizational effectiveness (Cummings & Worley, 2015) or mention Beckhard's definition and then remove the term in the definition they develop (Anderson, 2015). At least one mentions health several times, but opts not to use the concept in his definition, because the concept "health" is regarded as coming from a medical model that is not appropriate to use with organizations (McLean, 2006, p. 6). There has not been a great deal of focus on organizational health outside of one major consulting firm that has done considerable research over the past 12 years using its own way of measuring health, which regards health as "the ultimate competitive advantage" (Bazigos, De Smet, & Schaninger, 2015; De Smet, Schaninger, & Smith, 2014; Keller & Price, 2011). They affirm that considering both health and performance combined appears to make the most significant difference in customary business outcome measures, as a survey that they conducted in 2010 "… of executives at companies undergoing transformations revealed that organizations focusing on both performance and health rated themselves as nearly twice as successful as those focusing on health alone and nearly three times as successful as those focusing on performance alone" (Keller & Price, 2011, p. 5). Their work emphasizes the overall, quantifiable "health" of a given organization using a proprietary index of organizational health and suggesting that following one of four "recipes" is the best pathway to health as they conceptualize it, but does not look at organizational health in the context of its impact on its natural and built environments or the surrounding culture, which is our perspective in this volume.

Providing Roots for the Dialogue

It seems like it ought to be easy to describe a healthy organization, community, and world — these should be almost common sense notions, that all would agree on. However, people have been striving to create these throughout history, and the world as a whole does not seem to many like a very healthy place. Some say that we, as humans, are doing better than we have at any time in history, based on relatively new indicators of happiness and societal wellness (see Chapter 6 for references) and a thorough philosophical and statistical analysis of a wide range of data (Pinker, 2011). Whatever such indices may show, genocides have taken place on three continents during my lifetime, billions of people do not have enough to eat or are ill through lack of clean water, and women are still considered to be property in many countries — in other words, billions of people lack key fundamentals of what most in many parts of the world would agree to be a good life.

Aiming to revitalize global interaction about how healthy organizations and communities can be developed and are essential for a healthy world is a huge undertaking — one in which this book is one of many initiatives. We want to till the soil by encouraging each person who reads this to reflect on your own story that catalyzed your interest in this theme. We also want to give the conversation deep roots, and the contributions by the thought leaders included here bring in their unique blends of scholarship and action, over many decades. The Quakers have a term for people of substance. A "weighty" Quaker is one with a deep spiritual life whose insight into events is highly valued and deemed "weightier" as compared with others who are younger in their understanding of life. These interviewees are indeed "weighty" social scientists, and we are delighted to bring them together for the conceptual grounding of our collective exploration of organizational and societal health.

What is a healthy world? Perhaps it is easier to comprehend what a healthy community or organization is, as they are closer to us, more concrete, and probably more achievable. Rather than try to answer this question and bring early closure, we want to open up thinking and questions, so as to nurture dialogue on this theme among those who teach and lead. We hope to encourage an explicit focus on this topic in a wide variety of courses and leadership development programs. Now that an initial agreement has been reached about climate change, there are grounds for reaching an actionable consensus regarding what constitutes a healthy society and healthy world. Divergent thinking is highly appropriate for such a broad question at this stage. But if we never converge on the basics, the outcome may be a planet unsuitable for human life ....

References

Anderson, D. A. (2015). *Organization development: The process of leading organization change.* Los Angeles, CA: Sage.

Argyris, C. (1958). The organization: What makes it healthy? *Harvard Business Review, November-December,* 107–116.

Argyris, C. (1960). *Understanding organizational behavior.* Homewood, IL: Dorsey Press.

Argyris, C. (1964). *Integrating the individual and the organization.* New York, NY: Wiley.

Bazigos, M., De Smet, A., & Schaninger, B. (2015). Securing lasting value through organizational health. *People & Strategy,* 1(38), 24–29.

Beckhard, R. (1969). *Organization development: Strategies and models.* Menlo Park, CA: Addison Wesley.

Beckhard, R. (1996). The healthy organization. In J. Gallos (Ed.), *Organization development.* San Francisco, CA: Jossey-Bass.

Bruhn, J. G. (2001). *Trust and the health of organizations.* New York, NY: Kluwer Academic/Plenum Publishers.

Cummings, T. G., & Worley, C. G. (2015, 2009). *Organization development and change.* Stamford, CT: Cengage.

De Smet, A., Schaninger, B., & Smith, B. (2014, April). The hidden value of organizational health—and how to capture it. *McKinsey Quarterly,* (2), 69–79.

Frost, P., & Robinson, S. (1999). The toxic handler. *Harvard Business Review,* 77(4), 96–107.

Goldman, K. L. (1979). *Organizations and autonomy: An exploration of the relationship between organizational openness and personal autonomy in American community colleges.* Ph.D. dissertation, Department of Sociology, Columbia University, New York, NY. Retrieved from ProQuest.

Goldman Schuyler, K. (2004a). The possibility of healthy organizations: Thoughts toward a new framework for organizational theory and practice. *Journal of Applied Social Science, 21*(2), 57–79.

Goldman Schuyler, K. (2004b). Practitioner – heal thyself: Challenges in enabling organizational health. *Organization Management Journal, 1*(1), 28–37. doi:10.1057/omj.2004.9

Goldman Schuyler, K., & Branagan, L. (2003). The power line: A model for generating a systemic focus on organizational health. *Sociological Practice, 5*(2), 77–88.

Keller, S., & Price, C. (2011, June). Organizational health: The ultimate competitive advantage. *McKinsey Quarterly,* (2)94–107.

McLean, G. N. (2006). *Organization development: Principles, processes, performance.* San Francisco, CA: Berrett-Koehler.

Pinker, S. (2011). *The better angels of our nature: Why violence has declined.* New York, NY: Penguin.

Schein, E. H. (1965). *Organizational psychology.* Englewood Cliffs, NJ: Prentice-Hall.

Schein, E. H. (2000). The next frontier: Edgar Schein on organizational therapy. *Academy of Management Executive, 14*(1), 31–48.

2

Visions of a Healthy World: Views from Thought Leaders

Kathryn Goldman Schuyler, with Margaret Wheatley, Otto Scharmer, Ed Schein, Robert E. Quinn, and Peter Senge

S ome see organizational health as a way of measuring the capacity of an organization to function profitably, but in this book we consider health more broadly, looking at both organizations and their influence on society and the planet. Our interest is in how to develop organizations that enable a rich quality of human life without degrading the planet on which this takes place. This connects organizational and societal health with one of the most widely used definitions of sustainability from the Brundtland Report: "… development that meets the needs of the present without compromising the ability of future generations to meet their own needs" (The World Commission on Environment and Development, 1987, p. 41). Stated more boldly: How can we foster organizations and work that contribute to there being a high variety of types of human societies, while increasing biodiversity and the longest term viability of the planet we call Earth? That makes the context for this book the interconnection of leadership, sustainability, and organization development, as three arenas of research and action that can, in combination, influence the course of events globally.

Underlying Questions and Frameworks

Underlying this chapter is my belief that humans can act together to create a world that endures and nourishes not only our species, but all life. This is fed by threads from spiritual traditions, philosophy, and systems thinking (as manifested in organization development and change). Systems thinking increasingly is understood to underlie most thinking in sociology, organizational psychology, and organization development.

The philosophical and historical underpinnings of this approach have been addressed quite thoroughly, in very different ways, by Eisler (1987), Senge, Smith, Kruschwitz, Laur, and Schley (2007), Scharmer and Kaufer (2013), and Singer (2015), so I will not attempt to do so here. A large and complex body of thinking has been growing across the social and behavioral sciences on the nature of living dynamic systems since von Bertalanffy's (1968) pioneering work in this area, developed between the 1930s and 1960s, plus (among others) very widely referenced contributions by scholars such as Katz and Kahn (1966), Ackoff (1974), and Laszlo (1996). In addition there are ancient spiritual teachings about the interconnectedness and interdependence of all life from all of the religious and philosophical sources, as well as philosophical reflections and analyses from many cultures, that offer a value basis for creating "truly healthy organizations," as described by Kriger and Hanson (1999, p. 302). The current thinking in the social sciences that is described in the introduction to this part of the book has been sourced by vast grounds in human awareness over centuries.

It seems as though increasing electronic interconnectedness, giving ready access to others' thinking, publications, and conversations, may be reinforcing awareness of the many lines of thought about the interdependence of life. For example, never before in history have so many people been familiar with what are considered to be the highest spiritual teachings of various cultures, such as the Dzogchen and Vajrayana teachings of Tibet which were, until recently, known only by hundreds or thousands of people at a time, all within Tibet. Now, whether or not students practice with a depth of understanding, these teachings are available all over the world, in print and electronically. Instead of teaching to small groups of students in one locale, master teachers have centers in many countries, and people of all ethnicities participate together in deep spiritual retreats — some in person and some virtual, with participants from around the world.

This suggests that although, as many people have been pointing out, the current focus on mindfulness and consciousness continues to be expressed mainly at the individual level (e.g., a focus on "my" awareness), there are increasing calls for awareness of the social field. For examples, see Otto Scharmer's thinking in *Theory U* (2009) and John Eric Baugher's (2014) thoughts about mindfulness in societies. Most practices and action paths currently seem to be grounded in individual perceptions and needs — what Scharmer would refer to as the ego level of seeing and listening (see Scharmer & Kaufer, 2013, as well as the archived online course). However, Scharmer and others are creating spaces for people to explore a collaborative kind of listening, thinking, and taking action that could be considered to come from evolving people's awareness of interdependence and mutuality — a level of listening and action that Scharmer calls *eco*.

In this context, healthy organizations and societies might be places that provide enough nourishment of all types needed by humans (e.g., physical, emotional, interpersonal, intellectual, and spiritual) so that they can thrive and create, while living aware of interdependence with other beings and the planet, so as to contribute to them as well. Our intention in this book is to create a foundation for scholars and practitioners from across the various social sciences and social science-based arenas of practice to explore and build on these possibilities. These are the deeper, underlying issues upon which the interview questions were developed. It was for this reason that the book is grounded in interviews with these five eminent thought leaders, juxtaposing their perspectives. We decided to ask each the same questions and encourage them to let the conversation go where it needed to, given their interests, in order to provide a glimpse of their current perspectives on these questions of organizational and societal health.

All were asked this simple set of questions.

(1) What is "a healthy organization" — what must it have?
(2) What is leadership in this context, and what is its role in creating and sustaining such organizations?
(3) Where do we see this today? Is it increasing? If so, what nourishes this; if not, what gets in the way?
(4) Is this a critical component of creating a healthier world? What do you see as the key factors for there being a healthy world in 50 years?
(5) What do we need in leadership education/leadership development in order for these fields to contribute significantly to moving the world in healthy directions?
(6) What do we see you doing? Some snapshots of you in action .../writing — moods — coaching/areas of focus

(7) What other questions should I be asking? Comment on them, please!

Although I asked everyone the same questions, I intentionally allowed the conversation to go where each person took it. This created an intriguing fabric, with overlaps and distinct differences. Each interview lasted 60–90 minutes and was transcribed in full. I then created an edited version of each, since I wanted to convey the quality of spoken speech, yet also have clarity and focus. In order to enhance the readability, I slightly modified the wording or added a few bridging phrases, removing the filler words that we often use in spoken language and do not typically use in print. These interviews were shared with the interviewees, so they could revise and have the interview express what they wished to have represent them on this topic, as of this point in time.

Originally, I imagined that I might weave short extracts from the interviews into one narrative, but as I attempted to implement this notion, I found that it lessened each one's clarity of voice. There are similar concepts behind their work, yet each has a very different flavor, taste, or tone. Among us as a group, we don't necessarily agree with all that appears in the various interviews. What is said may at times seem messy, as I was not seeking convergence. To retain and showcase their uniqueness, each speaks for him or herself, with his or her own voice. Following this, I looked across all five to discern commonalities and implications, and in the end, actually did see a shared model emerging.

This is written from my own experience. It represents a part of my "learning journey" that is ongoing. I selected these authors to spark dialogue in the fields of leadership studies and organization development because each has been important to large numbers of people across the planet, as well as to me personally. I hope you will feel as though you are getting to know them, rather than staying in an analytic, cognitive space as you read and think about the questions we raise. In fact, I invite you in as I would to a virtual salon, where we share a space together, focusing on questions and issues of great concern to us all, and where you can write notes to yourself and to us to join this dialogue. Since this volume is developed by the International Leadership Association, with thousands of members around the world leading companies, consultancies, and university programs, it is intended to be part of an ongoing dialogue that continues off the pages of the book, in small and large conferences, on websites, and in classrooms.

The Contributors: Wise Voices from the Social Sciences

I discovered **Margaret Wheatley** as a person and thinker with the publication of *Leadership and the New Science* (1992), but she had been consulting since 1973. *Leadership and the New Science* has great power and has been very influential: Wheatley was the first to develop the implications of the 20th century's new scientific perspectives for organizational studies. As she describes this book in her website bio, she showed "an orderly universe where relationships are the basis of everything, a world that organizes itself according to unchanging laws that modern humans hope to ignore" (n.p.). Since then, I have often used another of her books, *A Simpler Way* (Wheatley & Kellner-Rogers, 1996), in courses on personal and professional development for new organizational consultants; in it, she combines photos and words to convey the ways people can live more simply, beautifully, and at ease with underlying patterns of life. Wheatley has written additional books on building community and persevering in the face of obstacles at the personal, organizational, and global levels. Recently, her experience and writing has focused on the contributions of ancient wisdom traditions (2012, 2014). She has been a full-time professor and has served as advisor to leadership development programs in the U.S. military, major corporations, and to leadership development in Europe, Africa, Asia, and Australia. She has come to value the contribution of deep, silent retreat, and makes space in her life to do a three-month contemplative retreat every year.

Otto Scharmer brings his German education as an economist to the practical and broad context of systems theory. He offers readers an overview of the social and economic development of societies through four stages that lead to a possible desirable future: an eco-based economy that transcends the notion that having stakeholders collaborate across separate interests is the best humanity can do (Scharmer & Kaufer, 2013). He invites people around the world, from business, government, and not-for-profits, to develop platforms for communicating across existing organizations and to train themselves to listen deeply to one another. One example of such a platform is his MIT edX MOOC (Massive Open Online Course), which he offered twice in 2015, connecting over 50,000 people from 191 countries in an exploration of their own values and what they are doing to bring these alive, with support from a team that included professors, social activists, and corporate leaders. He aims to nourish a "revolution in learning and leadership" (http://www.huffington-post.com/otto-scharmer/mooc-40-the-next-revoluti_b_7209606.html) that generates a global action research university. He is an eloquent and articulate advocate for leadership development that includes spirit, purpose, and social action (Scharmer, Saxena, & Goldman Schuyler, 2014). And the next contributor, Ed Schein, was one of his main teachers and mentors at MIT.

Ed Schein has been a founding and highly influential contributor to many discourses within organizational studies: the field's focus on organizational culture came out of his contributions (1985/2004). His discussions of how to help others (*Helping*, 2009/2011; *Humble Inquiry*, 2013), grounded in his pioneering development of process consulting (1988, 1999), have been foundational in creating a skillful, compassionate, and open way of consulting that might not have existed without him. To experience him in action with a group of students is an experience in seeing a master at work, as he delves into a comment made by a member of the group in ways that open up what really happened for the person, what he or she really wishes to understand, learn, or do that he or she initially did not fully recognize. His teaching and mentoring influenced the development and actions of both Otto Scharmer and Peter Senge, as all were colleagues at MIT: Including all three in this exploration of organizational and societal health brings into book form a conversation that has been taking place among them for years. He has not written explicitly about organizational health since 2000 (Schein, 2000), when he commented on an article by Frost and Robinson (1999).

Robert E. Quinn has helped to initiate a major discourse related to the topic of organizational and societal health: the focus on positive organizational studies and its grounding in individual reflection and change. I first used Quinn's best-selling *Deep Change* (1996) in 2001 in a course for masters students on personal and professional development. We read and discussed it to catalyze exploration of the values of each student and how they were living these, day to day. His books on positive organizations have been key factors in the huge growth of this perspective, from the appearance of *Positive Organizational Scholarship: Foundations of a New Discipline* (Cameron, Dutton, & Quinn, 2003) through his most recent book *The Positive Organization: Breaking Free from Conventional Cultures, Constraints, and Beliefs* (Quinn, 2015). Co-founder and Director of the Center for Positive Organizational Scholarship at the University of

Michigan, Quinn and his colleagues aim to build on Seligman's (1999) desire to create an emphasis on the positive, both individual and collective (Seligman & Csikszentmihalyi, 2000), within the field of psychology.

Comparable to the way that Wheatley opened the conversation about the "new science" and ways of organizing, Schein opened conversations about organizational cultures, and Quinn opened conversations on positive organizations, **Peter Senge** gave legitimacy to discussing the importance of inner development for leaders in describing self mastery and reflection on mental models as two of the core disciplines in *The Fifth Discipline* (1990, 2006). This book gained huge attention among executives: it has often been handed out by the CEO to all members of a corporate executive team before a strategic thinking retreat, as I experienced with several corporations in the 1990s. Referred to often as one of the top 25 business books of the 20th century, *The Fifth Discipline* created a huge space for organizational consultants to address questions of deeper personal development in the context of leadership and organizational performance. As Senge gained influence, he chose to focus his practice on areas that he felt would have the most importance for the development of human society and the planet: in particular, large cross sector collaborations to work on complex problems like global food systems and the future of primary and secondary education — rather than continuing, as many consultants do, to focus on large business clients (Senge, 2012). In place of interpreting influence or importance based on economic return, as contemporary cultures tend to do, he makes choices for his own actions based on his analysis of the systems involved in planetary change.

The next portion of the book contains the interviews with each of these thought leaders, so that you can see the varied ways that our conversation flowed, even when grounded in the same set of questions. Following the interviews, I share what I see as the main themes, as well as the implications and the questions that they raise — questions that are then addressed by the other contributors to this book.

Margaret Wheatley: Healthy Organizations Rely on the Human Spirit

Kathryn Goldman Schuyler: What do you see as a healthy organization?

Margaret Wheatley: One of the things I've most enjoyed about the whole science of living systems is that it's scale independent. If I think about what is a healthy individual, what is a healthy life, I can freely apply that at another level of scale to the organization. That makes it a much more interesting question, because being healthy doesn't mean that you always feel well, it means that you know how to overcome your dilemmas and challenges.

This connects health directly with sustainability. One of the newest definitions of sustainability that I really like comes from an author who's written on the collapse of complex civilizations: Sustainability is not an ecological issue of simply using up fewer resources. We build sustainability with the quality of how we solve our problems. We build sustainability by knowing how to come together and how to deal with our challenges, which is also core to my definition of healthy. This is what makes for a sense of well-being: that we can make it through whatever we need to face. It works organizationally, nationally, or individually.

In an organization, this leads to the question of "How do we solve problems? What do we do when something goes wrong?" We're abysmal at this right now. So one of my conditions for a healthy organization is being one that knows how to solve its problems and challenges and recover from them. For me, that has to be participative, has to be engaging relevant parts of the system, has to create full and honest information that's available to be used in solving the problem.

And also the criteria of time to think! The most significant liability we have right now is we're no longer thinking about our problems — we're no longer thinking, period. So a healthy organization (like a healthy individual) takes time for assessing, going into the complexity of an issue, takes time for reflection, takes time for letting in intuition and such.

A healthy individual is not someone who feels great all the time: it's someone who knows what to do when they don't feel great, knows how to handle crises, and knows how to maintain a sense of equanimity in dealing with the great challenges. There's a quality of stability of mind in individuals that can be present in organizations too. But with the tyranny of time taking over, everything needs to be done instantly or just not done at all because we don't have time for it. I think one of the qualities of health at these different levels of scale is that we know when we need time. We need time for rest, we need time for reflection, we need time for problem solving, and we know what well-being feels like. The really good organizations, and there are far too few of them these days — they feel different. There truly is an *esprit de corps*, and people don't worry about taking risks, it's not even an issue, actually. They're more experimental and creative because they're in this together, and they take time, and they use thinking once again.

HEALTH AND WHOLENESS

The other thing about health that I would bring in is the definition, or the etymology of the word itself, which is that it comes from the word for *wholeness*, which comes from the word for *holiness*. Like any living system, our health is predicted by the number and quality of our interconnections. So a healthy organization is one that knows that it's a complex interconnected system and uses that well.

Kathryn Goldman Schuyler: That's beautiful. So what is leadership and what is its role in creating and sustaining such organizations?

Margaret Wheatley: I feel increasingly that people are more and more anxious, fearful, overwhelmed, overworked. There is an essential role for leaders now, which is to really show the way, but they have to radiate a quality of "we're in this together and we can get through this," which means they have to be the kind of leader who knows that they are hosting other people's potential, they're not heroically jumping in to save the day or telling people what to do.

It goes back to the qualities of leaders and the conditions that they establish, and those conditions have to be giving people time and resources to think, to work together, to slow things down, to not be badgered by constant demands from a leader or above the leader, where they're just constantly asking for more and more, or "Do this, no — do this, no — do this" and "Give me this information — it's essential I have it, and I need it in 24 hours."

Leaders can do the most good in creating an organization that is healthy by creating the conditions for people to come together and be thoughtful again. The other role for leaders is to play defense against the incessant demands from above. This is harder and harder work. The political environment for so many leaders now is impossible, and I'm not just talking about people who are in government agencies, but people who are in non-profits, people who are in health care. The demands are reaching the breaking point for some of the leaders that I support. And so I know that as leaders we must play defense and keep the beasts at bay.

On the other hand, I'm increasingly in conversations with the senior leaders that I support about "How much longer can I take this?" I'm in that question with them; I don't know the answer. Some of them have a finite term of service, and so they know how much longer they can take it, but for others retirement appears more and more necessary in order to preserve their sense of well-being. It is a highly stressful time for leaders.

"I WANT LEADERSHIP TO BECOME A NOBLE PROFESSION AGAIN"

Kathryn Goldman Schuyler: What is needed then, Meg, both from leadership education, meaning the programs that train people in universities, and leadership development, what's being done out in corporations, non-profits, and government? Many members of the International Leadership Association are in these fields. What do we need from them?

Margaret Wheatley: I think they're very good at featuring the new leaders who can deal with chaos, who thrive on adrenalin and the thrill of the hunt, and who deal well with 24/7 demands. That seems to be the focus of a number of leadership development programs: How do you work well in a chaotic environment. That's all well and good, but what's missing is "What's the purpose of your work, what are the values you're trying to work from, what is the definition of integrity?"

I want leadership to become a noble profession again. I don't want it to be as instrumental and self-serving as it currently is. I don't want people to be taught how to create an organization, be a great entrepreneur, and then sell it for a lot of money and go onto the next one. I want there to be far more connection now between hearts and minds. Why would anyone want to be a leader these days? It's increasingly difficult to be a leader who knows to maintain their integrity and values.

Kathryn Goldman Schuyler: Please go into this, Meg. Where do you see this kind of leadership, this kind of organizational health? Can you give us a few snapshots of where you see it happening?

Margaret Wheatley: I never name organizations because they break your heart. As soon as one leader is gone, the organization retreats into some very bad behaviors. One of the leaders I support, who runs a very large organization, is telling all her staff now, "We do good work because we do good work, that's what we're here for, that's what we do, that's what we are. It doesn't matter if we get the grants, if we get the awards, if others take over our territory, we're doing this work because this work has value and we know that." Still it is very stressful for her to deal with the political environment. So when this CEO says "We do good work because we do good work," she is reminding everyone why they're there, independent of the craziness around them. We're here to serve these populations of people. It's a recall to mission and to values, but it's highly personal, it's not redoing the mission statement or letting PR back in to frame a great mission statement. Those are easy, but the hard work is reconnecting people at a personal level to their own sense of purpose and thereby giving them the strength to persevere throughout.

There's another kind of leadership I've seen that I think is very important. I was just in the presence of a woman leader, and she called it optimism, but I don't think that's the right word. She meets with staff, and people are very troubled and upset. They're in doomsday scenarios, which are I think pretty realistic these days, but they are just overwhelmed by despair and cynicism. She then places the meaning and purpose of the organization in the larger context, but from a perspective of "This is what people need from us, this is why people love us, this is why people appreciate us, so we have to work for those people." So, again, it's reconnecting to mission and purpose, but in this case in the larger context where there is quite a large level of public support for what they're doing. She's not cheerleading: She's actually basing what she says on fact. She's creating a different understanding of the broader context than staff have available to them, because they're so overwhelmed.

Let's go back to the individual — to me. No matter what, I know the work I'm engaged in is the work I want to be engaged in, and even if it doesn't yield great results, I'm committed to doing that work because it's the right work for me to be doing. I feel that's what I'm describing in these organizations. The leaders have to find a purpose that transcends current craziness, where we're doing this work because it's the right work for us to be doing, and we're doing it as best we can, it's important that we do it, and we don't know the future, period. We don't know whether it will work well or not, but we know we're going to be wholehearted about doing it.

Kathryn Goldman Schuyler: So how would you describe or define the work that you're engaged in? What is your work?

WARRIORS FOR THE HUMAN SPIRIT

Margaret Wheatley: I'm quite clear about this lately. My work is calling forth the warriors for the human spirit, the people who want to stay and be available as these times become more and more distressing and destructive. I'm focusing now on "What is the human spirit, who is it?" I meet a lot of people who are in this question. What does it mean to be fully human? Can our work create experiences where we experience the fullness and richness of our humanity, which includes our creativity, our generosity, our kindness, our ambition? And then it includes the dark side of what happens when we get greedy and grasping and fearful.

I have really narrowed my work now too, because I do see this very clearly as a need: Who's going to champion people? I say this all the time. Are you going to stand up and be the champions for the human spirit, or are you going to continue to be complicit with these conditions, which are truly degrading human capacity and destroying people's spirits? Are you going to stand up and do what you can to really support people to know that even in the midst of terrible circumstances, we human beings can experience that rare quality called true joy?

This is something I learned many, many years ago from being with people post natural disaster and talking to them about their experiences, and I had this experience a few weeks ago in Christchurch, New Zealand, which has gone through terrible earthquakes. People describe the experience of rescue and rebuilding as the most joyful times of their life. That used to be a puzzle for me, but now I realize that's the essence of our experience here: When we are truly together, we feel we're of one mind and heart. As we do work that's filled with tragedy, that's filled with grief and loss, still we experience joy. This is so far from our current quest for happiness.

Humans can get through anything as long as we're together. My work going forward is to focus on the people who really want to take on this very challenging role of standing up, knowing what they stand for, supporting other people who are fearful and exhausted and somewhat terrorized at the future. This kind of work of warriorship requires a lot of training, a lot of discipline. I see it in myself. The more I'm out in the world, the more I'm open to what's going on in the world and the incredible levels of suffering; I know what it takes to keep myself grounded, stable, peaceful, and present. It takes a lot of work.

My work going forward is to work with these people, across cultures — people who are willing to undergo the discipline and training that's required so we don't get caught up by anger and aggression and fear.

Kathryn Goldman Schuyler: What is the discipline and training that's required of the leaders?

Margaret Wheatley: I think it's broad based and very deep. One is stability of mind, that's probably the biggest one, and that involves a lot of different dimensions. One is knowing how to not be triggered; that, of course, goes back to stability of mind. Another is just knowing you're part of a group of people and that we truly have each other; we have one another's back.

And it's that *esprit de corps* which I have found in the military and among nuns, but I haven't found it elsewhere. I work deeply with both of those groups, so I know what I've learned from both of them. There's a constant question of "What else do I need to know, what skills do I need?" I think skills of discernment, of understanding issues at their deepest causes. I think using one's intuition, using one's prescience, using one's ability to imagine and to vision. These are all things that at one level may sound familiar, but then put them in the context that we're working in organizations that are deteriorating, and my clear sense is that historically this is not going to turn around.

In human history, when times get tough we usually become very barbaric, we turn on one another. You can see that happening around the whole immigration issue everywhere. We're turning on the stranger and making them the victim of our rage and fear. I want more people to know that we can be really glorious in difficult times; we have the dark and the light side of our human natures, and I want to work as hard as I can to create the conditions for people to experience the glorious side of human nature, not the barbaric.

Kathryn Goldman Schuyler: I know that you've chosen retreat as a big component for your own development. How do you see this for the top leaders in organizations? Do you see us asking them to be in retreat some of the time, or what aspects of that ....

Margaret Wheatley: I don't know the answer to that. I don't actually think warriors for the human spirit will be formal leaders. They may be former formal leaders. I do know that Parker Palmer's work with leader education is all about finding time for reflection. I know my own life and my own personality and my own karma make long retreats the most potent form of development for me, but I'm in a rare position. I'm not asking for retreat *per se*, but "How do you process what's going on? What are your ways of gaining the big picture? What are your practices for restoring a sense of peace and possibility within you?" We don't find these answers in the outer world; we do find them in the inner world.

Fortunately, it's becoming more common to speak about inner work now. I think that's a very important trend, but for me it's the inner work so I can do the outer work, but outer work that benefits the world, not that just creates these weapons of mass distraction, as Charlie Rangel once named Google's products, despite how much they are into mindfulness!

So it's all about purposeful organizations that can contribute, truly contribute, not to profitability and growth, but to human welfare and well-being. I don't know what it will take for the current crop of formal leaders to wake up to the need to work on themselves internally, but I certainly know that reflection and meditation are the most potent ways to do that.

PREVENTING A DOWNWARD SPIRAL

Kathryn Goldman Schuyler: It seems to come down to a combination of "What does it mean to be fully human?" and "How does that relate to having a healthier world?"

Margaret Wheatley: Well, if we were actually aware of who we are and who we can be and who we become in difficult times, that would go a long way to preventing this downward spiral we're on, which is degradation and destruction of the better human qualities.

We're driving people more and more like machines. When a lot of current leaders approach scaling up, they just write a bigger number on a piece of paper or spreadsheet. "Okay, we have 500 clients in this field, we need to go to 2,500," and that's scaling up for them. It's this imaginary world they live in, where if they put it down on paper or a spreadsheet their work is done. We're driving people into breakdown, and I've been seeing this for years.

Kathryn Goldman Schuyler: Say a little bit more about that, Meg, because I don't know that everybody agrees ....

Margaret Wheatley: Look at the indicators, look at days lost for mental health reasons, which are about a third of the days lost in the United States and Canada. Look at the kinds of physical ailments we have that can be related to stress; look at growing health problems in general; look at the level of exhaustion, which is profound at this point. When we insist on more and more tasks, what we're doing is moving up to a very superficial level of the functioning brain. We lose all the deeper gray matter capacities of memory and visioning and imagination and caring and judgment.

That's what we're doing right now: We push people for more and more tasks that have less and less meaning. When you're in a task list and you're just ticking it off, there's no question of meaning. When humans work in a meaning-poor or meaningless environment, it's incredibly demoralizing and de-energizing, because we are meaning seeking creatures. The meaning then that comes into our lives is more about consumption, fun, and just having a good time. But in the workplace, I find people are horribly demoralized and exhausted. You can talk about a new project to them, and they just kind of look at you like these very tired little donkeys who are already carrying much too much weight and have no interest in it. So when I say we're at the breaking point, I've been watching things for about five years, and we're getting very close to where people just say, "Enough." Now, I want them to say "Enough" and push back.

Kathryn Goldman Schuyler: Do you see a movement among young people toward work with meaning? I know when I talked with Otto Scharmer for his chapter in *Leading with Spirit, Presence, and Authenticity* (Scharmer et al., 2014) a couple of years ago, he saw this. He was talking about how much young people are looking for work with ....

Margaret Wheatley: They're *looking* for work with meaning. Are they going to find it? Well, they find it in a few places, but even more and more of them are going into entrepreneurship. That is *the* trend right now in business schools and in younger people, because they don't want to participate in the large bureaucracies of corporations, or they're going into social entrepreneurship and really wanting to do good work with their creativity and passion. But getting that work done in this current larger system is not happening.

If you look at the course of history, we're not turning this around. That's why I want people to be prepared with their own levels of warriorship. The work I do with younger people now is about shifting your identity from a social activist to a spiritual activist. What does it take for you to keep going? What does it take for you not to withdraw? Because I've seen this over and over go into just bitterness and anger.

People in government will say, "We have no idea what to do," but that's not true, we know how to solve these problems if we go into root causes and have moral will, but it's not happening. And it's not happening because other dynamics are at play here, including the emergence of an elite group that doesn't care, that's taking everything for themselves.

I want to work with those younger people, but not from a sense of "they're the hope of the future." I want to work with them so their energy, passion, and idealism and connection to the best in people can bear fruit, can be nurtured, but it's not about being successful about changing the world anymore.

Kathryn Goldman Schuyler: What haven't I asked that I should ask you?

Margaret Wheatley: I don't know. These are good questions. They obviously spurred a lot in me, and they felt refreshingly different.

Kathryn Goldman Schuyler: We started with a healthy individual and a healthy organization. What's a healthy world?

Margaret Wheatley: It's one that never existed, seriously. You've read the doctrine on human rights, that's a description of a healthy world, but it's never existed. I'll just close with this, which is one of my current bugaboos. As I study more and more history of the human species and complex civilizations, what seems hilarious at this point is our belief, as Americans, that the world is changeable, and we're the ones to do it.

All this current work on us discovering mindfulness, working with the mind, all ways in which we truly as individuals do evolve, has switched to another level where we're saying in America that with sufficient numbers we are going to transform the human species, we're undertaking conscious evolution. I just got invited to speak at a conference called *Conscious Evolution*. Through our own waking up to what's possible with mind, we're going to transform the human species.

That has finally struck me, and why I think it's funny? It's an essentially American idea that whatever we get, whatever we understand, whoever we are, that we will change the whole world for the better. Do you think when Tibetans or Hindus or indigenous wisdom keepers knew how to work not only with their mind but also with the elements, do you think they thought they were going to transform humanity? It just strikes me as so unimaginably ridiculous an idea.

And the Puritans' ideal: *We shall be as a city on a hill; the eyes of all nations shall be upon us.* That's in our founding energy. But it's this craziness that everyone wants to be like us, so that now that some of us are becoming "mindful" this bodes well for human evolution. It's such an ahistorical narcissistic point of view, so I'll leave it at that.

Otto Scharmer: Health Is Always a Question of "Whose Health?"

Kathryn Goldman Schuyler: What is a healthy organization?

Otto Scharmer: A healthy organization is an organization that is enhancing health for all of its stakeholders: the internal and also the external stakeholders. If we double-click on this, the question becomes, "What do we mean by health?" There are different levels of health and well-being: a material level, plus the social dimension of connecting with the quality of relationships that you have with the community around you, and a spiritual dimension, which is connecting to the deeper or emerging capacities and dimensions of yourself. All of that would be part of a holistic concept of health.

The word health has the same root as the word *whole*, and both are actually coming from the same root as *holy*. So health is inherently a balance, a wholeness, a *making whole*. All its components are on the one hand, differentiated (all the organs) and yet, also integrated in a whole, which again is integrated into a larger whole, as in the systems concept of nested wholes.

This relational capacity and this capacity of making whole is at the root of creating healthy organizations. The problem of organizations is that they are too small for the big problems and too big for the small problems. The issues that we face in society and business today are often issues that deal with the larger systems, or ecosystem issues, where a single organization cannot make any difference alone, where they need to team up with other organizations. So this question of wholeness and how to move from the isolation, or the war of the parts, to something that's more coherent and more whole is really at the very heart of leadership challenges today.

Therefore, I think a healthy organization is an organization that is cultivating the capacity of making whole on all of its different levels: the individual, the team, the organization level, and also the whole system level. It's an organization that is dealing with its ecological, cultural, or spiritual environment in a way that contributes to bridging the divides that I described in my recent book (Scharmer & Kaufer, 2013).

Kathryn Goldman Schuyler: It sounds wonderful to be moving through this war of the parts to wholeness. How do you see leaders doing this?

START WITH YOURSELF

Otto Scharmer: As a leader, you have to start with yourself. I think the post-modern reality is really that the whole no longer holds together, and it's falling apart. We see that in societies. Societies falling apart, countries falling apart, ecosystems falling apart. We see it all over. We also see this on the human development dimension. It's communities falling apart and families falling apart and individuals falling apart. So, I as a person or citizen am much more disintegrated. Technology has a big play here, so more and more, I am basically just responding, reacting, to external stimuli. This disintegration, or this post-modern condition, of the world we are living in and of the economy we are living in is the challenge that we have today.

So, as a leader, how do I make an impact? By embodying health, first and foremost myself. Health not just in absence of sickness, but health defined on these deeper levels. The first levels would be the absence of sickness and presence of functionality: Our bodily functions perform to a normal standard, so to speak. On a deeper level, health has to do with creating well-being by tapping into the deeper sources of my own creativity: Connecting with my own purpose, which in a more holistic point of view, I should say, really is the core of health. Rather than just avoiding sickness, really connecting with your own essence and strengthening that is the source of your own well-being and happiness.

Being a leader in a healthy organization means that you embody these principles despite the environment of the post-modern condition that we operate in. You begin to re-integrate these more and more disintegrating parts, role-modeling the quality of attention, of well-being, and of conduct or leadership around you. I think such cultivation of your own self is the first principle of a health-based leadership. To the degree that you can embody this, you have a foundation to actually reshape and further evolve the environments around you and the relationships we have with others.

Kathryn Goldman Schuyler: If we look at today's world, we see people who lead large groups of people who believe that they're doing good, yet are pitted against one another. We have Christians seeing themselves as right. We have Muslims seeing themselves as right. We have political groups in many countries seeing themselves as right and others as wrong. I keep wondering, how do we expand the group of people that we include in our "own group," so that those who are already leading people to fight one another start instead to listen to their own listening and to their deeper selves? I don't know how to transcend our current situation of the war of the parts!

Otto Scharmer: You are right. If you look around, there are many instances of framing of ideologies and of viewpoints that put themselves into the center and then tend to frame themselves and their own truth with a capital T and no space around them. In that way, they do not embody a healthy ecosystem because in their view, there is no space for others. It's just about them. There is no space for other access points to the divine, to the inner dimension that other wisdom traditions may have, or that people may have directly from their life experience, without being mediated by religion.

We see a lot of fundamentalisms around us, not only in religions and faith communities, but also in other fields of society. That's what I try to describe with the distinction between presencing and absencing; basically we live in a time of disruption where we see both phenomena at the same time. There's an enhanced presence of absencing, which basically means we freeze in old patterns that fight each other for supremacy. Yet at the same time, often not that loud and not as well-represented in public media, we see also the other social field that I refer to with the term presencing, which basically means the cultivation of a social field that allows people to connect with deeper sources of knowing, being, creativity, and self.

I think that's where we are. We see both presencing and absencing, and only one of them gets amplified through public media (absencing). The other one is more quiet (presencing). Leadership means that when you get stuck in some patterns from the past that may have been appropriate in some past period but currently no longer are, you let go of that and reconnect with your real intention. You focus on connecting with the whole and with ecosystems that are inclusive of the other rather than excluding them. You could say the leader's new work is about realigning attention with intention: realigning what we pay attention to with our intention, with what we want to create with our life and with our work going forward.

The tension that you mentioned, I experience, and I think that's our condition. We all live in the stretch where sometimes we are in one world and sometimes we are in the other world. Human and leadership development basically means to strengthen the capacity to make the choice in which world we end up, operating more and more intentionally and less and less randomly.

Kathryn Goldman Schuyler: That's a good one, Otto. How do you see this as a component of creating a healthier world?

Does the world become healthier over time, do you think? Can it become healthier or does it just stay in this tension? Is that human existence?

DOES THE WORLD BECOME HEALTHIER OVER TIME?

Otto Scharmer: I think you can make both cases. From a material point of view, if you look at the arc of the past 200 years, we are on an upward slope. Many things have been much improved, like the progress on the Millennium Development Goals (MDGs) which is not something to disregard. On the social side, however, I think that's where we still have a long way to go. It's difficult to say whether we are moving backward or forward. Probably both things at the same time. There's still a lot of progress to be made, particularly in addressing needs that are presently unmet for a large part of the global population. If you flip to the inner side and to the quality of life, we're living longer, but what's the quality of your life? How much can you really connect with your own deeper sources of meaning in what you do?

The biggest part that's unaddressed is the inner dimension. Rather than fighting the symptoms of sickness, how can we strengthen the inner sources of health? That has everything to do with our educational system. It has to do with the model of learning, where we are just at the very, very beginning. It's exciting because this is an area of development that if we go down that path, it allows us to enhance the quality of life without wrecking the planet.

Health is always a question of "Whose health?" There's the health of me, as an individual, and my family. Then, there is my community, my organization, my country. Then there's society and planet earth. The way we define health in most cases is to look at the material aspect of health, rather than the inner aspects. We also focus too much on just the human dimension of health, rather than including our ecosystems into that.

Coming back to the framework that Katrin Kaufer and I put forth in our most recent book (2013), I could then define the capacity that leaders need to develop in order to lead health-enhancing organizations. That would be the capacity to bridge the ecological, the social, and the spiritual divide. That's essentially what we are talking about. It's not enough to connect just with yourself. It's not enough to connect just with the other stakeholders around you. You also need to do your share to reconnect with planet earth and create models that enhance well-being in our ecosystems, rather than destroying them.

One interesting indicator is the HPI, Happy Planet Index, developed by the New Economics Foundation in the United Kingdom, which assesses well-being divided by ecological footprint. It shows how much nature you use and consume in order to create well-being in your community, on a global scale. The two worst areas are sub-Saharan Africa, because so many people are suffering there, and the United States, because its high GDP comes at the expense of environmental destruction. So one way of looking at the health of organizations and society from a more holistic point of view, is from the viewpoint of the three divides: ecological, social, and spiritual, taking into account something like the Happy Planet Index, which looks at the well-being that we create relative to our ecological footprint. This isn't ideal, but it's a step in the right direction. If you look at economies from this viewpoint, it's a very different list than the list of GDP per capita. Many of the top ten countries in that list are from Latin America. Then, if you look across the globe, there's a middle band of countries around the equator that goes from Central America and the northern part of South America all the way to Bhutan and Indonesia, so it's these countries. It's not the north, the far north, not the south, but it's the area in-between that tends to scores highest.

Kathryn Goldman Schuyler: Not Scandinavia?

Otto Scharmer: Scandinavia is pretty high, but the ecological footprint is significantly higher in Scandinavia than it is in Costa Rica, perhaps because of the need for heating. If you look only at well-being, Scandinavia, particularly Denmark, is very much at the top, and at the same time, these countries are also more advanced in their sustainability practice, if you compare them with the United States or many other European countries. Still, the ecological footprint is not insignificant.

MOOCs, EDUCATION, AND TRANSFORMATION

Kathryn Goldman Schuyler: How do you see what you're doing with the global MOOCs you conducted on *Transforming Business, Society, and Self*, in relation to some of these questions about leadership, education, and health at a societal level?

Otto Scharmer: The MOOC that we've created is an experiment. It's a leadership and innovation platform that's basically a hybrid between education and movement-building. The education part is that there are methods, tools, new learning environments, basically, that in part are online and supplied by

MITx/edX and the Presencing Institute. The movement-building aspect is that this is designed to activate initiatives by local communities: We designed the MOOC to support individuals who activate the dormant potential to self-organize in existing communities, organizations, and networks. You see the activation level in over 50,000 registered participants from 191 countries, 350 self-organized Hubs around the world, and about 1,000 coaching circles across the two MOOCs. Since it is an action learning process, people prototype their projects: They sense and actualize something they really care about. Based on our earlier discussion, this meets the definition of health. So, it's at the root of health. The viewpoint of the U-Lab is to bring together science or methods on the one hand and profound social change on the other hand with a third force: the evolution of consciousness. We are helping these tens of thousands of participants see that the cultivation and shift of their own consciousness is a key leverage point in shifting a social field and helping social systems to evolve.

Today in the world of leadership, the world is full of methods and tools and examples of how mindfulness is successfully applied to health, to neuroscience, to education, as well as to social-emotional learning. But what we and business leaders are missing is the application of mindfulness onto transforming the collective, by which I mean generating profound shifts in how a social field is operating. That's what we try to address with the U-Lab platform. We believe that developing open, free, and very accessible platforms of learning that bring together very diverse groups across sectors and cultures is a great opportunity, because fundamentally the underlying problem is the same. The core of the developmental change that we face today in health, in education, in business, in government, and also in civil society and all the NGO organizations is all the same problem.

Kathryn Goldman Schuyler: Are you picturing an extension of these same processes in leadership education, leadership development, to significantly help the world move in this direction that you're describing? Obviously as large as the MOOC is, it's still small compared with the scope of the problems. It's not large enough to move the world yet ....

Otto Scharmer: I totally agree. It is tiny as compared with the size of the problems that we face. Yet, look at nature. How does the new come into being? Look at the seed. The seed is tiny. You can't even see it, and where does it grow? In the midst of the old and yet, it has the capacity for a whole new organism. Look at history. It's said that the Renaissance effectively was brought about by not more than 300 people. Now, in the MOOC, we are already a lot more than 300! I'm not saying that our current situation is exactly like the conditions during the Renaissance, but I am saying that this is how change works. We know that from organizations and so on. You don't need 100%. You need a very committed core of people who are completely aligned around the same intention and who are really pulling together, opening up a field. A core that is able to catalyze the potential of change that many people feel exists today and yet, often we don't see really fully realized. I think that's the situation we are in.

Many people feel the need for change. They also think it's possible, yet they don't know how. That's where we try to contribute our unfolding story, contribute with small-scale experiments that maybe if we are lucky, if we are successful, will really help us to move in this direction more intentionally, creatively, and collectively. That's exactly what's necessary today. And I feel, I know that the size of the problems and challenges that we face today very much outsize our currently existing capacities, but we also know that human beings are amazing. So, when you really look into the abyss, there's this saying from Holderlin that where the danger is, the saving power also grows. That is a poetic way of articulating a principle that I have experienced many times. When you face a severe situation, having the courage to face it, not driven by fear and avoiding it, is actually the source of connecting with deeper sources of help, energy, and guidance.

Kathryn Goldman Schuyler: Is there anything that we haven't touched on that you think is really important for this larger question about helping to stimulate health for the planet and society?

Otto Scharmer: One thing that's more like a comment in passing. If I reflect back, I define organizational health and a healthy organization in terms of the capacity to cross the ecological, the social, and the spiritual divide for its members and for its stakeholders, so basically bridging these divides. If you look into the methods and tools, then I would say Ed Schein with his process consultation and with his book *Helping* really offered a wonderful methodology for crossing these self-other divides. That's a very practical tool-kit. When I look at his work on organizational culture, the different levels that he describes of culture (the tangible, the artifacts, and the espoused values and taken-for-granted assumptions), what is that? If you look at this in terms of methodology, it helps you look at the contradictions across these levels and then use these contradictions, focusing consciousness leadership on them as a developmental intervention to generate healthy organizations.

So making taken-for-granted assumptions visible and conscious, making them focus of leadership development on a collective level enables the confrontation of self with self. It is like Chris Argyris' work, and organization learning work in general: looking at how the organization is enacting its assumptions in embodied behavior. If you take this and Peter (Senge's) work with children and education, we're focusing on sustainability. What is sustainability? It's basically the ecological divide, figuring out how we can be more inclusive of that dimension in management and leadership. I'm thinking that if you use these distinctions, frameworks, and bodies of theory that your other interviewees bring, they seem to complement one another.

Kathryn Goldman Schuyler: My own research has gone in this direction too, Otto. This week I'm working on a paper with a young woman in Finland whom I've never met in person, but connected with through my research on moments of being suddenly "present" at work, about the implications of this research for sustainability. In our data, it appears that often when our participants became really present, either they did so in nature or they then started to be very aware of the importance of nature.

Otto Scharmer: Yes, and the other way around, right? It is particularly evident in Scandinavia. For many years, I went to Finland, and I noticed that in Finland parents were treating their children quite differently, with much more listening to each other and respect than I would have seen in other countries. I asked my host in Finland, "How come?" She said, "Well, you need to know. Here in Finland, when you're young, your parents take you into the woods and then, they teach you to listen to the woods." It's that kind of connection with nature which facilitates the real connection to yourself. I think we all have experienced that, but if you can experience that early-on, that's a real gift, and even though some of us have experienced that once in a while, we tend to lose touch with it.

Kathryn Goldman Schuyler: That's what we've seen too. As we develop our action research projects about systemic health, we may see that there are countries like Finland that have a deeper knowledge of such things.

Ed Schein: Health, Cultures, and Relationships

Kathryn Goldman Schuyler: We're discussing organizational health and societal health, and how it's grounded in the individual. You can take answers any direction you want. You don't need to feel bound by exactly what I ask, but I'll just start out by saying so what is a healthy organization? Is that the level to start out going from organization or do you want to start at the individual? You tell me.

Ed Schein: When I first got interested in organizational psychology, I thought that we had to start with a systems point of view: even the individual is a complex system. I translated that into systemic health rather than individual organizational or group. What should a system be to function healthily and be viewed as healthy by others? The first idea that appealed to me was something that Warren Bennis had gotten from the mental health literature. He said that when you look at all the different criteria for mental health, the things that fall out are a sense of identity, knowing who you are, the ability to live in a real environment, the ability to see the environment, and the ability to learn from what you see. On a systemic level, you could also add a fourth criterion, which would be internal integration; most systems have subsystems in them that should be aligned.

If you're looking at the organizational level, you would say, "If an organization has a lot of departments, and each department knows what it's doing, but they're all fighting with each other rather than collaborating, then you have healthy subsystems but an unhealthy total organization." You could then expand this to the relation between the individual and the group and say, "Does an individual to be healthy not only have those criteria of identity, and an ability to learn, but have to have some connection to the group or groups in which that individual exists, in the sense that that group is a core identity building reference point, what we used to call reference groups or identity groups?"

I've always believed that the human personality is an amalgam of all the different selves that you have learned in all the different groups in which you have existed. You have the self you were as a child. You have the self you were in your peer groups. You have the self that you were in school and so on. The person is a multilayered set of identities, and we draw out these identities in different situations according to our perception of what the situation requires.

"THE HUMAN BEING IS NOT A BIOLOGICAL ISLET"

The human being is not a biological islet. The human being is by definition a member of a group, and that group might initially just be the parent, the mother, but humans don't spring into existence without starting with contact with another human being. You could say that that's basically how society got built.

Maybe the word "health" itself is a social construct because we define it not by survival but by acceptance of the group. When we think of someone as unhealthy, we either hospitalize them or do something to bring them back. I've always believed in Erving Goffman's notion that what really happens in therapy, and especially when you're hospitalized, is you're retrained in how to get along with people. It's not some deep psychological process. It's basically if you want to get out of this hospital, you'll learn how to eat, and talk properly, and get along with people. That's one way of seeing what health is.

Kathryn Goldman Schuyler: What happens at the societal level?

Ed Schein: The thing about the societal level is that from my perspective society isn't a system. It's a mix of many systems in interaction with each other. Health then would be the degree to which that interaction has a clear purpose or identity, knows where it's going, and has organized its subsystems through some kind of governance process, the governance being the brain, has organized the subsystems to be in optimal competition and collaboration with each other. You could say what's wrong with a lot of societies, maybe particularly the U.S. society, is we've given way too much weight to the power of competition. We have the political parties, government, and business. We have all these institutions more or less at war with each other, and we don't have a system of saying, "Here's where we should have collaboration." In that sense, I would say probably modern capitalist society is unhealthy because it's not integrated.

THE ROLE OF LEADERSHIP

Kathryn Goldman Schuyler: What's the role of leadership in this context? What's its role in creating and sustaining this kind of health, whether at the organizational or societal level?

Ed Schein: Leadership and leaders really are crucial in defining the sense of identity. Leaders create cultures. When those cultures get very embedded, they limit what leaders can do but again, it would be the leader who would say, "We have become dysfunctional, and we have to do something different to correct the situation," what I guess Franklin Delano Roosevelt did when the country was getting too out of whack with too many unemployed or what maybe Theodore Roosevelt did *vis-à-vis* the environment that we were despoiling it too much. Leaders first create a sense of who we are and the values, and then they use whatever power they have to make it happen. That's, to me, the two essentially unique forms of leadership, to create the values and then to ensure that they get implemented.

Kathryn Goldman Schuyler: Where do you see this being done effectively, or well, or do you?

Ed Schein: I think it's probably something that is much more visible at the micro-level than at the organizational level. People always want me to point to some healthy organizations, and I always say, "I don't know of any, but I can think of subunits of organizations that will look healthy."

At one point in its history, Digital Equipment Corporation was a very healthy organization when they were young and growing, but as they got large and old, they became very unhealthy because the subsystems no longer collaborated, and the values of innovation were no longer relevant to the environment. The environment wanted turnkey computers. They didn't want fancy new stuff, and Digital was still producing fancy new stuff. You could see during its age, a healthy company becoming dysfunctional and disappearing. That happens to a lot of organizations; being healthy at one stage doesn't mean you stay healthy.

Kathryn Goldman Schuyler: Do you see examples of organizations reinventing themselves so that they find the ability to learn from the environment in a different level of integration or do they, like us, sort of go downhill?

Ed Schein: I think the only recent case I can think of like that would be IBM, which was really getting unhealthy and then they brought in a leader, Gerstner, who fixed them. He wrote in his book that this primarily meant getting the culture back on track. He understood that it was not some particular act but getting IBM to remember who they were and what they were good at. Other cases like HP don't stay healthy as a single unit but fragment into new organizations. You have Agilent, which broke off many years ago, and HP is going to subdivide again into the computer business and maybe the printer business. Maybe those subunits will be healthy organizations, but HP as a total organization will have disappeared.

IDENTITY, PURPOSE, AND CHANGE

Kathryn Goldman Schuyler: This relationship between an organization and its identity or purpose and the changing environment is really very critical, isn't it, in today's fast changing world?

Ed Schein: More critical today than ever, but it's always been critical. The organisms' systems don't exist in a vacuum. They're always part of a larger system, which has its subsystems. I think you have to allow for random but unanticipated consequences. You can be healthy, and the environment changes, and you're suddenly not healthy anymore.

Kathryn Goldman Schuyler: How do you see that playing out globally? More and more countries came into being over the last 15 years or 20 years. We have this huge number of countries; before that, there were less of them. Parts of nations split off like you were saying that parts of the big corporations are splitting off.

Ed Schein: Because of information technology connecting everybody, and because of technology being more complex and spread around, I think the national cultures are being forced into interaction with each other. How cultures blend, and learn to work together, and maybe become super units that are above national culture, which we may see already in some global corporations, will be the way that it will go. There won't be the same old set of countries and the same old set of routines. There will be new organizations that will blend different national cultures, and different technologies, and work up new kinds of systems, new kinds of organisms. I think it's inevitable that we're going to see new forms.

I think we're going to need to find really new inventions. I see components. I think sensitivity training groups was a new invention. I think Bill Isaacs' Bohm-type dialogues was a new invention. I think intergroup networks are a new invention and in some ways, it's all going to come together around new ideas around mindfulness. I think the most important part of mindfulness will be getting in touch with our own culture's limitations: the most coercive limiting force that you and I have to deal with is our own cultural learning since we know all the right answers as to how to be and what to be, based on our histories — and those are all constraints. If we don't get acquainted with what these constraints are, we are limiting our own creative intelligence.

ELLEN LANGER AND MINDFULNESS

Kathryn Goldman Schuyler: That's interesting—using mindfulness in that context. Mostly people speak of mindfulness in the sense of individuals being present to themselves physically. Some people have written about sociological or societal mindfulness; being really aware of what's going on in the society. I don't think I've heard people using mindfulness in relation to cultural limitations.

Ed Schein: It's my expansion of Ellen Langer's concept. She taught me a lesson that was just mind-blowing. When our granddaughter was two years old, while we were caring for her on the Cape (Cape Cod, Massachusetts) she got a bad cut. We had to drive an hour to Hyannis Hospital where we were waiting for an hour for a doctor and then an hour back to where we were in Truro. The next day, Mary and I are on the tennis courts where Ellen Langer is also playing, and between sets we're chatting, and Ellen says, "How are things?" Mary and I tell her about this horrible night we had, and she, instead of being sympathetic, looks and says, "Well, what else was happening all this time?" Mary and I are still looking blank. She says, "If I understand it, you spent over three hours in the car with this two-year-old. What was happening all this time?"

The fog lifted. Stephanie had been an absolutely charming, entertaining two-year-old the entire time, and all we chose to experience was that it was a horrible ride. I'll never forget what an insight that was. Why did we choose to report the bad instead of saying, "Well, we actually had a very interesting three hours with our granddaughter"? We wiped it all out, and Ellen's point is we do this all the time. We take the immediate experience and say, "That's it!" and we don't notice what else was happening. And my final point is that the choice of reporting the "ain't it awful" stuff was taught to us by our cultural upbringing, not by some innate psychological force.

Another one of her lovely ideas is when someone is complaining about their arthritic pain, for example, she says, "Well, does it hurt all the time?" "Well, no." "Well, what's happening when it isn't hurting? What's happening then? Focus on those times. Why are you always focused on when it's hurting?" She's really got a twist on it that, to me, is far more powerful than mantras or meditation. She says, "Get acquainted with your own judgmental processes and how you wipe out three-quarters of what's happening to you because you don't treat it as relevant."

Kathryn Goldman Schuyler: It sounds to me like you're saying that one of the real key things for having a healthy world is people being able to wake up out of what Jean Houston describes as our *cultural trance*.

Ed Schein: I think that would be a very fair inference, yes. Remember, one of the criteria for health is the ability to learn and adapt. You could argue the healthy person, when they go to China, will not start out by saying, "They're doing it wrong," but will recognize that, "That's the world I'm now in. I've got to learn what they do and why they do what they do. That will also give me a good mirror on myself. I will discover more about my own limitations. Why am in a hurry always? They want to have dinner, and I want to get on with the business. At first, I want to say no, let's not have dinner, but I realize they really want to." I begin to say, "Well, maybe there's some other part of consciousness that I'm not noticing; what is it that goes on at dinner?" It brings us back to this mindfulness thing and discovering that at dinner is where we're doing some of the negotiating and building trust, so the next day when we have the meeting, we can do it in half the time because we've already done some work informally.

Kathryn Goldman Schuyler: If we go back to the notion of a cultural trance and the earlier ones that you were talking about, about defining identities, seeing the environment, learning from what you see, and then internal integration, what would that imply for leadership education? What do you think is needed in leadership education and leadership development in this context?

"GET OUTSIDE YOUR OWN CULTURE"

Ed Schein: I was asked that question once a long time ago and had a glib answer, but I'm not sure it's the wrong answer. The answer is get outside your own culture. We had a student who was curious about what leaders read. He discovered that there were some leaders who only read what their own company literature produces, the accounting stuff, and their own marketing stuff. There are other leaders who do read *The New Yorker* and various things that clearly are outside. He thought he discovered that the ones who were focused on the outside were in fact doing much better than the ones who were encapsulated in their own little company. The implication was if you're an OD person, and you've got one of these executives, and you think you want to improve their health, arrange for them to travel to interesting places, make sure they get to the theater, and see movies, put interesting novels on their desk, externalize them. The biggest trap for business or organizational leaders is to become completely enveloped in their own organizational culture and forget that they are a part of a wider system. Force exposure to things other than your internal stuff and travel to foreign lands is probably the best way to do that. We should by now have a lot of good leaders in this country by this criterion, people who did start working in China and Japan and rather than rejecting it have become bicultural and understand.

Kathryn Goldman Schuyler: Some of the best leaders that I've worked with in companies that were U.S. companies were people who preferred living outside the United States. They had gone to universities where they had to master at least a second language. Speaking languages besides English, they really enjoyed being in other countries. They felt a little bit uncomfortable when they were put back at headquarters and happy when they could go back into the field. I really noticed that they were different than the norm that I was seeing among executives.

Ed Schein: In a way, it starts with the other language. I think if we really got serious about this, we would make it a requirement for a leader to be multilingual, at least two.

Kathryn Goldman Schuyler: I know people who travel, and it doesn't have the effect that we're talking about. I think one would have to set up the travel so that it caused people to experience other people in other settings. I think that one to one contact is something we haven't touched on that has a lot to do with help.

Ed Schein: All right, that takes us to the *Humble Inquiry* book. I believe that a leader who recognizes his or her own dependency on the subordinates will be better off because he or she will form relationships with the subordinates that will allow better communication and, therefore, better problem solving. That's an effectiveness criterion. Do we want to translate it into a health criterion? I haven't thought about that, but I supposed you could easily argue that a leader who cannot form relationships and doesn't believe that others are important is not going to be very healthy.

Kathryn Goldman Schuyler: That gets down to the small group level, doesn't it?

Ed Schein: Yes, I think the health criterion would be the capacity to learn, but what you learn can vary all over the map or what you have to learn. It's seeing the difference that is the key and then the agility, the personal agility to do something different.

It's a very living process. I think all kinds of things are going to happen in the next 50 years we aren't even yet conscious of ... that's what I mean that we need new inventions.

Robert E. Quinn: Becoming an Initiator of Change

Kathryn Goldman Schuyler: What do you see as a healthy organization? How do you define it?

Robert E. Quinn: I see a healthy organization as being very similar to what I call a positive organization. The simplest definition is that it's an organization in which people flourish and exceed expectations. Note that there are two dimensions. One, the people are growing, progressing, feeling good about themselves, and two, they're exceeding expectations. They, themselves, are moving toward positive deviance. Both of these are core to my views.

Kathryn Goldman Schuyler: When you see such flourishing and exceeding expectations, where do you see it? What is happening?

Robert E. Quinn: We see it everywhere. For example, you go into a hospital that's quite conventional, and there are 62 nursing units and they're all quite conventional, but there's one unit that is different from all the others. The turnover rate is almost zero. The others get as high as 70%. The scores on all the hard measures in terms of costs, in terms of patient recovery, they're number one in everything. You have this bright spot in the hospital that's not at all unlike a school teacher who is a bright spot in the school district, but no one sees it. The same thing happens in the hospital, or the bank, or the corporation, or wherever you go: There are always units and sometimes entire companies that are bright spots. But most people don't stop to ask "How can we be like them?" because we believe that we can't. We make that assumption. Yet you find these everywhere. I have always been fascinated about what goes on, on the edge of the system, in these places that exceed everyone's expectations.

CONTRASTING BELIEFS CREATE CONTRASTING REALITIES

Kathryn Goldman Schuyler: What do you see causing this blindness to learning from success?

Robert E. Quinn: Imagine that there are two lists. Here's the first list: People make assumptions. They act with self-interest. They engage in conflict. They become alienated. They fail to learn. They react to constraints. They comply with demands. They prefer the status quo. They fail to see opportunities, and they compete for limited resources.

When you put that list up, that's a very gloomy picture, but what is that list? That list conveys the fundamental assumptions of many social scientists: (1) People are self-interested; (2) Resources are scarce; (3) Conflict is natural. When many social scientists look at the world, whether it's an organization, a group, a team or society, this is what they find, and these become the fundamental assumptions of sociology, psychology, political science, and so on.

Here's the huge question. If you accept this description of reality, if you make these assumptions, which vast numbers of people are trained to do, not only formally in school, but from the time they're three years old, if you make these assumptions and you act on them as a manager, what does that produce? The answer is it reproduces itself. You have self-interested people competing for scarce resources and so on. This is a huge point! Vast armies of people share assumptions and then act according to them and produce organizations that we study. We confirm what's going on. Feed that back into our scholarly disciplines, and we train people that life is transactional. We train people to believe that life is this way.

Now here's a second, very different list. People sacrifice for the common good. They show compassion and respect. They make spontaneous contributions. They build social networks. They live in high-quality connections. They experiment, get feedback, and express voice. They extend the roles across their jobs. They take charge. They express voice. They become generative. They envision possibilities. They expand the resources. This is the exact opposite list. As you look at this picture, it's quite attractive. If these described two organizations, in which one of them are we going to want to work? The answer is pretty clear. You want to work in the second one. When we put that list up during workshops, executives say, "That's Pollyanna," meaning that's not realistic, but our response is, "Actually, this is realistic. This happens all the time. It just happens far less frequently than the first list."

REAL LEADERS TRANSFORM SYSTEMS

Kathryn Goldman Schuyler: And how do you see the role of leaders in this context?

Robert E. Quinn: That is what my work focuses on. There is a certain kind of work that transforms a system, and that work is called leadership. What do real leaders do? They transform the first kind of organization (the conventional organization) into the second kind of organization (the positive organization). They surface and transform existing conflicts, turning them into creative collaboration. Most executives do not know how to do this, but this is what is at the heart of creating a positive, or — to use your terms — healthy, organization: transforming conflict into collaboration. How they do this is through introducing purpose.

I did a series of interviews with CEOs some years ago and found that when they first became CEOs, they did not perceive the role of purpose in organizations. They didn't understand the nature of organizational culture. They didn't see or appreciate the human dynamics of a positive organization. They learned all of this only through crisis. Of course, many don't ever learn it. The astounding thing is that we train people in economics and in the hard sciences, we make them engineers, and they work their way up the entire system — yet they can do so and reach the highest levels with an absolutely emasculated view of the world. They don't have the cognitive complexity to see through the technical problem-solving world into the human dynamics that exist in the system.

I can give an example of how this kind of transformational role works in another setting by describing what I saw among teachers. I published a book with my colleagues entitled, *The Best Teacher in You*, a study of the top 1% of public school teachers in the state of Ohio, as determined by hard measures (Quinn, Heynoski, Thomas, & Spreitzer, 2014). They were selected based on scores that assessed how much they actually moved children's grades.

They were workers of magic. Imagine: you send your little girl to the 4th grade. She comes home doing 7th and 8th grade work, and so are all her peers in that class. How is this possible? The teacher can't work three times harder than the other teachers because there's not enough time in the day to do that. What explains such an outcome? The answer is that these teachers in the top 1% are purpose-driven. They are not there to put information into children: They're there to inspire lifelong learning, to empower the children so that the children can go anywhere they want in life and no longer be trapped by their circumstances. This aspiration is so driving that these teachers go to great lengths to accomplish it. The teacher on the classroom on the left and the classroom on the right are standing and complaining about the district, about the principal, about the kids, about the parents. The 1% whom we studied all have the same constraints, but for some mysterious reason, they are pushing through the constraints and delivering these life outcomes. That's a very powerful message.

In one of the interviews, a teacher said, "I've been doing this for 30 years. This is the way I teach, and for all of those 30 years, no member of the administration has ever walked into my classroom and asked the question, 'How is it you're getting these spectacular outcomes?'" This does seem baffling. In a place where there are so many problems, if someone's succeeding, why aren't we paying greater attention and learning from her? The answer is that administrator lives in a world of problems, and he or she has a full day, every day, of problems, and the whole purpose of life becomes checking things off the checklist and solving problems. It never occurs to them to go look at the successful person. In fact, they often see the successful person as a problem because it's a deviance from the system. The ability to learn from success is almost non-existent in personal life, in family life, in organizations, and in society. We are naturally drawn to the problems of life and using the conventional logic (based on that first list of assumptions) to solve them.

These school teachers would never describe themselves as leaders, but that's what they are. Every September, they get all these strangers. They take these strangers into a room, and they create an organization, a learning organization. Nine of the teachers create a conventional learning organization. One of the teachers creates a positive organization. The students' learning accelerates, growth accelerates. People flourish and exceed expectations. The same thing holds true for the hospital, the bank, the corporation. Somehow some people find their way to this alternative view of reality.

BEING A CHANGE LEADER

So, leadership is about influence, and most managers don't know how to wield influence. They're primitive, clumsy, and self-defeating. I teach a number of courses in the executive MBA program with people flying in for the weekend, with many of them coming from high-level positions. Their first reaction is, "Why do I have to take this core course? I am a leader. I am a change leader. I've had great change projects, and I've managed them." Well, what they are is change managers. They're not change leaders, and that's very offensive to them at first, but then I give them some exercises that they have to do, and it gets very humbling, and they recognize they don't have the slightest idea how to transform human perception. There's an enormous tension between the conventional assumption that leadership is the same as authority or position and the assumption that leadership requires human influence that moves an organization in a direction where people are flourishing and exceeding expectations. That's a very different kind of organization from most workplaces. You can't get people to flourish and exceed expectation by doing things that the managers do.

Kathryn Goldman Schuyler: What happens instead?

Robert E. Quinn: People are trained from the beginning to identify and solve technical problems. At the end of the day, if you solve a technical problem, you can go to your checklist and check it off. There's task closure. That drives people who are in a very busy world. So, people know how to do that. Now, the truth is that the organization is a technical system, it's a legal system, it's a physical system, but it's also a social system and a moral system. It's a complex, adaptive system.

This means that technical problems are not enough. You have to move from the reality of constraints to the reality of possibility. These words are very carefully constructed. The reality of possibility. That's what we are really talking about: bringing the reality of possibility into the world. But people who are doing technical problem solving all day are not orienting to the emerging future and bringing it into the world. They're locked into technical logic. What is the outcome of training so-called leaders in this way? Seventy percent of the people in the United States are unengaged at work. The numbers are even higher across the globe.

Kathryn Goldman Schuyler: If that is the current state of organizations, how do you work to shift it?

Robert E. Quinn: In the positive organization book, we have case after case describing CEOs who are failing and because of their failure, they began to discover the human system and to go through a conversion wherein they became aware of the power of purpose, integrity, empathy, and learning. That is when the organization transforms. The people come to life. They get empowered. They bring in their discretionary energy to work. The organization makes more money.

This seems to violate the economic assumptions: You should be focusing on shareholder value and nothing else. The CEOs who went through traumatic, life-changing experiences and learned their way into positive organizing, almost every one of them said, "I became bilingual." They used different words for it, but bilingual is the term we have adopted. By going through that conversion, they can still do technical problem solving, and they can still go down and sit with 20 engineers and talk to them in their language, and they know that if they speak the language of positive organizing to those 20 young engineers, the engineers won't have the slightest idea what they're talking about. So, they become deeply sensitive to how to move those engineers forward, giving them what they can digest at the time. Such CEOs learned how to elevate their organizations and lead them into high-level functioning, how to have a healthy organization, if you will, and make more money as well.

It is normal for me (and everyone) to be in a state where I am comfort-centered, externally directed, self-focused, and internally closed. In the first case, I do not want to engage new challenges, in the second I respond to norms and expectations, in the third I worry about myself, and in the fourth, I am closed to authentic feedback and limited in my ability to learn and co-create with others. In this state, my consciousness and my influence operate at a normal level.

Yet, I am always free to create a change in this state. I can ask myself four transformational questions: What result do I want to create? Am I internally directed? Am I other focused? Am I externally open? When I specify authentic answers to these four questions, I immediately see new possibilities and new strategic alternatives. I tend to pursue them with purpose, integrity, empathy, and openness. In this state my influence skyrockets, because I have become a source of positive variation. People must pay attention and decide to support or reject me. I become an initiator of change.

Kathryn Goldman Schuyler: This sounds somewhat like a heroic view of leaders. You seem to place a lot of power in the individual, as distinct from the relationships and sets of interdependencies – but perhaps that is what you emphasize in focusing on positive deviance?

TRANSFORMATIONAL LEADERSHIP

Robert E. Quinn: The whole field of transformational leadership is about when one individual chooses to see the world differently and then enacts that vision into reality and draws other people into that new reality. The vast majority of the time, most people totally ignore the exception; they not only ignore it, they don't believe in it because the pattern is so dominant and frequently seen that they can't even see the exception. They don't believe in the exception, and they become naturally disempowered. So it's a very powerful message to be looking for the transformational leader or the positive deviant or the empowered employee, or whatever it might be, and learning from those positive exceptions because most learning today is about learning from failure. We know very little about learning from success. To an amazing degree, it doesn't happen, even when it's obvious that it should happen.

Kathryn Goldman Schuyler: How have you seen this function in the corporate arena?

Robert E. Quinn: I'll give you a specific example. Gerry Anderson, at DTE Energy, which is the Detroit energy company, was trained in hard sciences, then trained in finance. Then, he went to McKinsey. Then he went to DTE, and he solved technical problems, but he just kept moving up. He would get the climate scores, comparing DTE to other companies. They were always on the bottom quartile. He would take the report and throw it in the trash. He didn't care about the whole.

Then he became president and was responsible for the whole. To improve engagement he held people accountable for their engagement scores. At first this technical approach seemed to work. Costs went down. Then he noticed that his managers were angry and it became clear that his approach was not sustainable. This was 2008, and a few weeks later, the recession hit and he was in Detroit, Michigan, which was the epicenter of the recession. Within a couple of weeks, they were $127 million behind. The only logical option was to downsize. Yet if he did, he knew he would lose their commitment forever.

Instead he turned to the people and admitted that there could be no solution from the top. The only possibility was for them to lead from the bottom. They had to initiate the changes that would save the company. They did, and he was transformed by the experience. He began to realize the power of purpose and how it brings forth human potential.

People throughout the company began to ask how they could help surrounding communities that were suffering from the recession, not just their own company. He said, "These people did amazing things. They brought their discretionary energy to work and they not only succeeded, they were thrilled that they were succeeding. Then, they started coming to me and saying, 'You know, General Motors just went bankrupt and this community over here is collapsing. What can we do to help them?' I'm listening to people in a utility company coming to me saying, 'How can we help people?' Again, that was an enormous, stunning learning experience. I went home, and I started to contemplate our purpose. Together we developed a purpose statement about being the best possible energy company because we touch every company in every community and reach into those communities."

"We started doing things we never dreamed we would do. We continued to increase in profit, and we continued to increase the scores on the engagement assessments. Pretty soon, we were above 90 percentile. We were in the bottom quartile, and now we're above 90 and then, we won a Best Place to Work award. A utility company doesn't win a Best Place to Work award. I was totally transformed by the experience." I've heard many, many other stories, but in his story you can find most of the other stories where people are locked into a single language, the language of economics, or conventional assumptions which lead to conventional outcomes, and suddenly discover the exact opposite set of assumptions, which are not about what is. They are about what can be, and they begin to pursue those. All of a sudden, there are great gains.

Kathryn Goldman Schuyler: How would you like to close, Bob? What haven't we addressed in enough depth?

"WE ARE DESIGNED TO BE PURPOSE-DRIVEN ORGANISMS"

Robert E. Quinn: We should go deeper into the importance of purpose. Higher purpose is outside the system in many ways. It's outside the ego, and the moment we start serving a higher purpose, we give more. There's lots of data from the intrinsic motivation world that verifies that. We are designed to be purpose-driven organisms. In fact, one CEO said it very beautifully. He said, "There are two forces in the world. There's inertia and there's purpose." Most people, I would argue, are trapped in inertia. They live in their comfort zones, and it's not until we get outside our comfort zones that we commit to some higher purpose, that we start to really grow because we go the zone of uncertainty, and we stay there until we learn what to do. That's what leadership is.

Purpose really matters and when we pursue it and go into a kind of servant-leadership mode, we start to see completely differently. We start to feel better about ourselves, and when we feel better about ourselves, we feel better about others. We see their potential. We see their humanness. Our fears go away. We find the capacity to love.

Let me give you a wonderful illustration. I was interviewing one of the great teachers that we spoke about early in our conversation. She said, "You know, I went to the school of education, and they taught me how to teach, but then, I went to the first day of class and found 30 strangers looking at me. Every child in that room was unique and different. They all had different needs and interests. If I was going to be a good teacher, I had to learn all those needs and interests, so I did, and I think I became a good teacher." I was quite impressed and I was writing this down and then, she said, "Then, I went to the next level." I said, "What do you mean?" She said, "I went to the next level. I discovered that they were all the same." "What do you mean that they're all the same?" She responded, "Once you come to understand them deeply, you realize that no matter what they say or do, every child wants to be respected, wants to be loved, and wants to succeed. When you discover that, you break the code. You can teach anybody, it doesn't matter whether they are young or old, gifted or in special education. They are all the same ...."

The conclusion I draw is that if you have empathy and love and you see the whole system, you can go to the Middle East or Detroit and you can envision alternatives to what is. You can become an initiator of change.

I'll end with another story. I was grading papers in my leadership course, and in one of the early papers a student said, "I'm a Muslim. The first two weeks, I hated this course and the reason I hated it, it was telling me how to live and I only let Islam do that. But then, I made a breakthrough. I realized that this class is Islam," so I put that paper down and I thought, that's pretty curious. A few papers later, another student said, "I'm a devout Christian. I figured out that this class is about Romans, Chapter 5," and he went on and wrote about that. In another paper, a student said, "I was an Israeli helicopter pilot for 14 years and I rely heavily on the spiritual core of Judaism. This class is Judaism," and in one of the last papers a girl wrote, "I was an active Buddhist, but I went inactive when I started the MBA program. When I took this class, I went back to my temple because this class is Buddhism." I put all of the papers down, and said to myself, "Whoa, what's going on here?" This book that they were referring to is all science, not religion. My friend Mark Kriger has a great paper where he looked at the five largest world religions and asked not how are they different, but how are they same with regard to leadership. Basically what he discerned is that there is a common model of consciousness that arrives at sensing or perceiving a state of oneness. Kriger said that every religion has a different word for it, but when you get past political differences and doctrinal arguments, there's an underlying model of human consciousness that these systems have spent thousands of years honing.

If you look at the positive approaches to social science, they are coming to the same conclusion: that you can be disciplined around human growth. You can increase consciousness, which increases choice and power. It's very striking to me that there is so much overlap: that it's about the expansion of human consciousness. I think the work of science in going into these areas is a huge asset for the human journey.

Kathryn Goldman Schuyler: That's fabulous. What haven't we touched on yet that you think would be important to include?

Robert E. Quinn: I think we've covered a lot of ground.

Kathryn Goldman Schuyler: I do, too, and you can't see me, and we don't really know one another, but I keep tearing up as you're talking, because what you're saying reminds me of things in books that my mother had on the coffee table when I was a child. Sitting here listening as you speak, I go back and forth between listening from a cognitive place and from one that is deeply personal.

Robert E. Quinn: Which I think is exactly the right place to be. That's what leadership needs to do today: to bring those two types of listening and action together.

Peter Senge:
We Need a New Mythos ...

Kathryn Goldman Schuyler: In your view, what is a healthy organization?

Peter Senge: I guess you'd look at it through different lenses. First, just the impact on the people who are members of the organization. Do they grow as people? Do they consider this real work, not just a job? Something that has meaning and purpose to them. Bob [Robert] Kegan has started to use the term *deeply developmental organizations*, organizations that by their nature and their intent, their explicit intent, are really developing human beings. So, that will be one lens. The second would be its impact beyond the members. What's the larger impact on communities, larger systems. For example, take the organizations that comprise the Sustainable Food Lab companies (www.sustainablefoodlab.org). This is about a 50–50 mix of business and NGOs, including many of the world's largest food businesses like Unilever and Mars and global NGOs like Oxfam. There are over 50 organizations learning how to work together to make all together to make sustainable agriculture the mainstream system over the coming decades. As many today now realize, food systems, both locally and globally, are very problematic today. If you are part of these systems, is it part of your organization's intent and practice to make the larger systems of which you're a part more resilient, more capable of nurturing life? Do they contribute to social and biological well-being?

Those are the first two lenses you'd want to look at: the impact on people and the impact on the larger systems of which you are a part. In between those two, there are customers and people immediately in the system, such as vendors and customers. Any organization functions as a result of a network of collaboration with its organizational partners — other organizations, without whom it can't really do what it does. That would be the third lens. Do those people and organizations thrive? Do they become healthier as a result of working together? And fundamentally, you'd also want to have operational definitions of well-being. Is the organization really increasing well-being and how do you assess such improvement?

Kathryn Goldman Schuyler: What do you suggest?

Peter Senge: I think the important thing is what people see for themselves. We started using a term about 15 years ago, when a

division of HP was working very closely with the Chilean biolo-
gist Humberto Maturana. They were developing a discipline of
regularly reflecting on how work gets done and the networks
of collaboration essential for getting work done and the impact of
those networks. They called them "their loving relations" — that
was literally the terms the engineers used. Working with
Humberto, they developed this particular definition of love, *the
act of allowing another to be a legitimate other*. It had real meaning to them that there were these networks of collaboration.
These always exist, by the way. This is not an idealistic or romantic notion! No organization can ever produce any work of any
sort without networks of collaboration: people who need to help
each other to get anything done.

Just by introducing this notion of well-being in the context of
this work, people figured out what it meant to them. It's like Bob
Kegan's notion of deeply developmental organizations. What's
development? Bob and his group have their whole concept of
developmental stages from developmental theory. But what really
matters is how the people in the organization make sense of their
own day-to-day work as being developmental. I think with terms
like well-being and human development, you can have abstract
definitions but the most important definitions are the definitions
the people come up with themselves. Then, you have to help
them define their idea operationally, such that they can come to
their own assessments of progress. For example, at HP they
developed practical methods for mapping their collaborative networks by reflecting on who helped who in solving particular
technical problems, and whether or not the networks were getting stronger by virtue of people giving and receiving more help.

With a little thought, people usually have some notion of
whether they are getting healthier or less healthy. We all go
through ups and downs: that's the nature of a living system. It's
never static. But I always like the Chinese definition or basic sense
of health: Does the system restore balances? Not "Is it in or out of
balance?" but "Does it restore balance?" We get a cold; does the
cold go away naturally in a couple of days? That's usually a sign of
a pretty healthy person. We would call it a healthy immune system.

People can talk about health in a personal level, that's always
an anchor. Do they feel they're in a work environment that's
healthy for them? They can talk about the quality of relationships.
Is there a lot of trust and collaboration? Do people really help each
other voluntarily, and do people take risks on behalf of one
another? There's a relational quality that will always come into

play if you ask people to assess the health of their enterprise. Then, there's always the financial aspect, and whether the organization is innovative. Is it an organization that people admire? And then there's the impact it has on its larger social and ecological systems. I think the important thing is people thinking for themselves about what these different lenses mean and how would they judge.

Kathryn Goldman Schuyler: That's great Peter, very, very helpful. In that context, what's the role of leadership? What is leadership?

WHAT IS LEADERSHIP?

Peter Senge: I start with distinguishing leadership from positions of authority. In the way we have framed the subject in our work, there are at least three types of leadership roles: executive leaders, local line leaders, and internal network leaders. The first two of these have a formal position of authority, whether it's organization-wide or is at the front lines of an organization where the value is actually created in any enterprise. But you also need the people who are building these internal networks of collaboration, because they're boundary crossers and they're connecting people around important, difficult problems or tasks. To me, *leadership* and *organizational learning* are just two different lenses on the same fundamental phenomena. They are inseparable. Leaders are people who build organizational capacities.

My favorite definition of leadership has always been this really simple one: **leadership is the capacity of a human community to shape its future.** I like this definition, partly because it's paradoxical, in the sense that it talks about leadership as a quality of a human community not of individuals. And secondly because I think it gets at what, in my experience, really matters to people regarding this whole business of leadership. When people talk about being in organizations with great leadership, there's always this element of shaping the future, doing something that's really exciting, accomplishing things that really matter, things that many might have even thought impossible. From Ron Heifetz's standpoint, this sense of creating is embedded in the view that, "If you can't deal with your toughest problems, you're not going to be able to really shape your future."

But creating and problem solving are not the same. I prefer what I just said, because I think it's a larger context. Shaping the capacity of an enterprise to create its future would then include dealing with your toughest problems, but it doesn't define leadership just by problem solving, which I personally don't like.

I think there's something so fundamentally different about the creative spirit and the creative orientation. It's always been a cornerstone of our work — how you build the capacity of people to create, to shape their future. To me, that's the most fundamental and useful definition of leadership.

Kathryn Goldman Schuyler: That's wonderful. Thank you so much. Where do we see this today?

Peter Senge: You see it all over. There's no shortage of leadership anywhere, you just have to know how to see it. Wherever you see something inspiring (chuckling) being accomplished, people are creating something. That's leadership. Leadership is at work there. I think leadership is a meaningless concept if you separate it from what's being accomplished — then it becomes all about style, which easily slips into how people impress one another, not what they accomplish. The kinds of examples that I am mindful of vary based on areas that I'm working on at one time or another. Today, it's not nearly as much just businesses as it used to be, because I'm not working with businesses so much. In pre-K-12 education, there are wonderful stories of people creating very different types of schools in very difficult settings. It always amazes people what's actually getting accomplished.

Kathryn Goldman Schuyler: And you're working worldwide on that?

Peter Senge: The focus now is to build more of a global network of collaboration because I think the problems with our Industrial Age school model are really global. I don't think it's about any one country's schools. I think it's about the industrial age schools and the mismatch of that model of education with the reality of the world today and the world today's students will live into. It is naïve to think that the types of societal changes needed in the coming decades to deal with our massive social and ecological imbalances will be achieved without this — we must remember that the systems generating these imbalances are shaped by highly educated people — that is, us!

CREATING A HEALTHIER WORLD

Kathryn Goldman Schuyler: Jumping a bit, how is such leadership critical in creating a healthier world? And what is the role of healthy organizations in creating a healthier world?

Peter Senge: Well, these are two questions. So you want to take them both?

Kathryn Goldman Schuyler: Sure.

Peter Senge: To me, it's almost a tautology. In other words, when you ask what is the role of leadership in creating a healthy organization, they're one and the same. There's no point in talking about leadership without talking about the results being achieved. And, the results are always about health and well-being at multiple levels, as we just discussed. At a larger scale, our world works the way it works because of many, many interacting networks of many different types of organizations. Not just organizations individually but industries, business supply chains, interactions across sectors, which either enable or impede working on really tough, systemic issues like climate change or the destruction of critical ecosystems. It's always about organizations in that sense. You or I couldn't destroy a species if we tried. No individual could ever do that. But we do a perfectly good job of achieving just this result as our actions are mediated by the networks of interacting institutions that shape how the world works. It isn't individuals that shape how the world works. It's interacting networks of institutions, of organizations.

Kathryn Goldman Schuyler: Given that, what do you see as the key factors for us together, all of us, creating a healthy world say in 50 years or so?

Peter Senge: First off, the problems we've created are going to take 5 to 15 decades to reverse. People have to understand this. Climate change is an archetypal example. The delays built into the system are many, many decades — delays like replacing long-lived capital like buildings and transportation systems (and their embedded carbon-footprint), delays like reversing the growing concentration of greenhouse gases — which will only start once we have reduced global emissions by 80% or so — and delays like achieving a new thermal equilibrium of the earth's atmosphere once the concentration of greenhouse gasses stops rising. The industrial age has been unfolding for over 200 years, depending exactly what part of the world you're talking about. It's going to take a long time to dig our way out of the holes that we've created. That's important for people to understand.

Taking climate as just one example, this is one of the great frustrations of climate scientists — getting people to understand this. While the governments of the world declare that we must halt rising temperatures before we reach 2 °C above pre-industrial levels, we probably already reached that level a couple of decades ago, given the inertia created by these delays — unless there is a radical U-turn in public understanding and policy. You could make similar arguments about the delays around core social issues like inequity — it is just that the physical issues like climate change are easier to quantify. That's why the more you understand about the depth of such issues, the more you understand how extensive and deep the imbalances are in creating real well-being. It's going to take a long time. That's why many people look at it soberly and throw up their hands and say, "Well, I don't see how this is ever going to change," because the delays are really long.

There is no question that this will take a revolution of will, but whose will? It's got to be a collective will. The reason I don't like the word leadership much — I often just avoid it entirely — is because the prevailing mythos is so individualistic. It's so much about the heroic individual — and usually of course, a masculine image — as opposed to the community and how people collectively can lead, shape the future. It's the capacity of a human community as contrasted with an individual. I think that's really important because problems are absolutely unsolvable from the viewpoint of our mainstream myths of heroic individual leaders and hierarchical power. You could say the sign of our times is the inability of existing hierarchical institutions and their associated images of heroic individual leaders to have any chance whatsoever to deal with the breadth and depth of the problems we face. They just can't do it. As a teacher of mine in China put it, "The problems of collective karma cannot be overcome by heroic individuals."

Another way to say this is we need a new mythos: a new myth of leadership that's more commensurate with the nature of the real problems we face. We need a way of thinking about leadership that's compatible with the systemic nature of the problems, and our predominant myths are not. If you can get away from the heroic individual, then you can really make some progress. I even find the very word leadership problematic. As another (Indian) teacher said years ago, "We don't need more leadership; we need more mothership." I thought that was a really wonderful prod at our conventional mindset.

BEYOND HEROIC LEADERSHIP

If we could take time to get our understanding anchored in collective leadership, distributed leadership, leadership as a quality of human communities, and get away from the heroic individual, then we might really make some progress. For example, community organizing is a wonderful established field where I think a lot of these ideas are deeply embedded. I remember years ago in the famous bible of community organizing, Alinsky's (1946/1989) *Reveille for Radicals*, he said that "The best leader is the one that no one knows." Interestingly, Lao Tzu said the same thing 2,500 years ago: "The wicked leader is the one the people revile. The good leader is the one who the people respect. The great leader is the one who, when all is said and done, the people say 'we did it ourselves.'"

But leadership is also deeply personal — there is a personal journey to developing ourselves as leaders. To try to bridge the individual <u>and</u> collective nature of leadership, we recently came up with a new term *system leaders*, which we defined as individuals who are really adept at catalyzing collective leadership. It's a particular way to walk on both sides of the street. At some levels, it's perfectly appropriate to take an individualistic lens to understand the deep, developmental journey of learning how to listen, of cultivating one's steadfastness of mind and clarity of vision, of sensing into the larger unfolding in any complex situation. The problem is, the agency that's ultimately needed on all these big issues is collective. Somehow, we have to find a way to harmonize our desire to understand these things at the individual level with the simple imperative that what we really need is collective leadership.

Kathryn Goldman Schuyler: What other key factors might there be? How does system leadership develop the capacity of human communities to shape their future? What are the key factors for this to happen in enough different places so that humanity starts turning these things around?

Peter Senge: I think that's where we get to a lot of the key theories and models we all work from. In the traditional "five disciplines model" of organizational learning (see Senge, *The Fifth Discipline*, 1990, 2007), you would say the key factors are a compelling vision and sense of purpose that really means something to people, something they naturally will commit to because it matters that much to them. Then, there is a level of openness and reflection so that people are continually challenging their ways of seeing the world. And through that process, people are continually getting better at seeing the larger systems they're a part of. If you look at it from Scharmer's (2009) *Theory U* perspective, you've got sensing, which has a lot to do with sensing the larger system, redirecting your attention so that you're not just looking outside but you're looking outside and inside; so there's more of a reflective element built in. And then presencing (Scharmer & Kaufer, 2013), where there is a greater opening to the underling source of purpose and vision. You could say both models are illuminating the same core capabilities, both to define effective system leadership and to define effective organizations.

Kathryn Goldman Schuyler: Besides community organizing, what else builds collective capacity?

Peter Senge: I find it useful to distinguish different levels of "collective." First, you've got a team, "a group of people who actually need each other to get something particular done." Then you've got larger networks, because teams come and go around different problems or tasks. Where do they come from and go to? Well, they come from larger networks or larger communities. I always think that the "rubber meets the road" in most practical matters in the challenges of building a strong team. I think that's a traditional view that comes out of the business world.

This sometimes gets lost in the social sector. Educators don't work in teams. Teaching is inherently or traditionally a very individualistic profession. As a result of that, this first level of collaboration is often completely missed: the importance of developing really generative teams. It's not missed in the world of business, but it's often missed in the social sector, where a lot of lip service is paid but there little real know-how as to how to do this. People often make the mistake of thinking that a strong sense of purpose or mission, which you find in many social sector organizations, is enough. It is not. As a consequence, you don't see people working nearly enough on how to build a really effective teams — the discipline, skills, and experience are really lacking. As a result, people miss the first stage in building collective capability. To me that's where it all starts — building learning teams is the natural training ground for fostering collective leadership at larger scales. Nobody misses this point in team sports. You either build a good team or it doesn't matter how talented you are. In the theater, you would probably use a term like "ensemble" rather than "team," but you are building small groups of people with a very high level of trust and mutual understanding who can take risks together, who can really support each other in their own learning. So it's very analogous.

Kathryn Goldman Schuyler: That's great, Peter. By the way, the reason this book is happening at all was because the members of the editorial team on the last book (*Leading with Spirit, Presence, and Authenticity*, 2014) experienced working together as a "dream team."

Peter Senge: (Laughs) Very interesting … when you have that experience, you know how meaningful it is to people. Again, my understanding of this has its roots in the business world, but having been around many extraordinary teams that accomplished things that were just impossible, it's very clear that this experience, from a human development standpoint, is really important. It just has so much meaning to people, and your story is a beautiful example of what it does to be part of really generative teams.

An Overview of the Interviews and Key Themes

These interviews were very rich experientially and in content. I will parse them by looking at four main topics that we discussed:

What is health, fundamentally, in organizations, and in society?

What is the role of leaders with regard to organizational and societal health?

What is the current situation in the world in this regard?

And finally, what is essential in leadership development?

Following this, I will offer some thoughts about how their thinking might offer foundations for a model of organizational and societal health that could be used for consulting and for helping leaders to think about the health of their organizations.

WHAT IS THE ROLE OF LEADERS WITH REGARD TO HEALTH?

Margaret Wheatley linked health to sustainability and spoke of it in terms of what we *know*, what we *do*, and how we are, our *being*. She repeated many times that health relates to what we know: that we know that we and our systems are deeply interconnected, we know when we need time, we know what well-being feels like. When we don't know these things, we aren't healthy. And leaders have an additional thing to know: They know that they host people's potential. She believes that in order to foster health, leaders create an understanding of broader contexts than most people in a given organization typically have. In contrast to being a source of ongoing pressure for those within an organization, which is how she perceives many so-called leaders today, those who lead toward health know the value of such actions and naturally step into them. In addition, they are wholehearted about what they see as their work. To sustain themselves, they have practices that nourish their stability of mind and sense of "peace and possibility." I would sum up her views by saying that such leaders know how to create the conditions for people to come together and feel whole, be thoughtful, and resolve challenges creatively.

Like Wheatley, **Otto Scharmer** also emphasized the connection of health and wholeness, pointing out its common root in the notion of *holy*. He views health as a process of making whole and contextualizes it in relation to his perception of our current world as having three major divides: the ecological divide that separates us from our environment, the social divide that separates us from one another, and the spiritual divide that indicates how we are so much of the time feeling out of touch with our own self. A healthy organization supports people in cultivating the capacity of making whole at all levels: individual, team, unit, and organization wide. For Scharmer, one must ask "Whose health?" Leaders will ideally embody health on the deepest levels, tapping into their sources of creativity and paying attention to those who are marginalized or excluded by others. Real cultivation of oneself is essential for leaders. This means connecting with their own essence, sourcing their own well-being, which then allows them to emanate a quality of attention and well-being that are transformational. By aligning what one pays attention to with what one wants to create in life and work, each person can lead, wherever they may be in an organization or community; leaders are not those who are appointed to specific positions.

Speaking immediately from a systems perspective, **Ed Schein** said that a healthy system needs a sense of identity, an understanding of its purpose, the ability to live in its environment, the capacity to learn, and internal integration of all its component systems and parts, in order to generate optimal levels of competition and collaboration. Looking at people as systems, Schein added connectedness to reference groups as a key element. When he discussed corporations, Schein reflected on what happens to them as they expand and grow older. He sees more health in parts of such large organizations than in large corporations, which he had experienced becoming dysfunctional as they age. From his perspective, at its core health is the capacity to learn and relate, so that a healthy individual, team, or organization can continue to evolve as the environment changes. The role of leaders is to influence the culture by creating and implementing the values, but this too he sees working better at the level of subunits, rather than in whole corporations.

Robert E. Quinn sees a healthy organization as a workplace where people flourish and exceed expectations. These two dimensions are inter-related: as people flourish, they tend to exceed expectations. For concrete examples, he described experiences with teachers and in the corporate world where teachers and executives have created cultures that exceeded everyone's expectations. In the schools, children developed a love of learning, and during the recession in Detroit, one corporation went from losing millions to being profitable, helping others in their community, and winning a Great Place to Work award. He sees the difference between conventional workplaces and these healthy ones (or positive ones — to use his terminology) as being grounded in the different assumptions about life that people bring with them to work. He focuses on the influence of people's assumptions on their actions and in turn on the organization, rather than looking at the web of interdependencies in both direction, being particularly interested in how individuals become *positive deviants* who generate change. He defines leading as system transformation. Leaders are the key to organizational change; they are people who shift out of what he calls the conventional logic (focusing on themselves and their own comfort) and instead focus on purpose, are open to other people and their perspectives, and create collaborative environments.

Peter Senge has a multi-part way of describing organizational health, looking first at three levels of impact and then at well-being as seen from the perspective of the members of the given organization. He suggested that we first consider the impact of the organization on its members. Do they consider what they are doing to be meaningful work? Second, he recommended considering the impact on the larger communities and systems of which it is a part: Does the organization increase their resilience and capacity to nurture life? Third, inquire whether the people and organizations with which it has to interact in getting work done are thriving — for example, do suppliers become healthier? In addition to considering the impact of the organization in these three ways, Senge suggested that it's essential to define well-being from the perspective of those within the system, not from outside or from an abstract point of view. He emphasized that all people have some notion of whether they are becoming healthier or less healthy. He provided an example of a way of thinking that was developed within Hewlett Packard by a group of engineers working with Humberto Maturana about 15 years ago. They felt it was essential to reflect regularly on the networks of collaboration with what they literally called their "loving relations": those people and groups that are necessary for getting any real work done. He sees leaders and the organizations they lead as completely inseparable: two ways to view the same thing — how the organization gets work done. His foundational definition of leadership is "the capacity of a human community to shape its future." This mitigates the exclusive focus on individuals, while broadening beyond problem solving to emphasize the importance of creativity.

Implications for conceptualizing health

These interviews pose several options for conceptualizing organizational health.

(1) It can be understood either as a set of characteristics of a system or by considering the system and its impacts on the sociosphere/biosphere. In other words, one's view can focus solely on the system itself, assessing health with regard to some set of standards (as most of those who look at health as "performance" tend to do), or one can consider its impacts on the world to define whether it is healthy or not. Considering organizations from an open systems perspective, even from what Scharmer regards as a linear or "old mainstream" stage of open systems thinking, as compared with autopoietic systems and self transcending systems, I believe that as a field we have to consider the impact on the world as part of the definition of the health of a system.

(2) Scharmer's question of "whose health?" can be understood in two ways. First, does a system to be healthy have to include in its health all and everything it touches, excluding none? Second, who decides what it is to have a beneficial impact, the members of the system or external judges? This is more complex than it may appear, as it easily slides into the ethical question of relativism, particularly in today's world where members of some systems see it as healthy to consider women to be property, to use one example.

(3) Is health a state to be achieved or an ongoing process? One might almost make it a verb: "At this point in time, our company is really healthing!" — meaning that the company has effective processes for identifying and restoring balances. In this context, it would not be healthy or toxic, but always in motion, and the directionality would be the focus.

THE CURRENT SITUATION IN THE WORLD WITH REGARD TO ORGANIZATIONAL AND SOCIETAL HEALTH?

Margaret Wheatley sees increasing decay and pressure all around the globe, so that many people are almost at a breaking point. She sees the times as destructive of human spirit, with more and more need to work so fast that one cannot pause to think. She sees people as being fearful, exhausted, and even in a state of terror about their individual and collective futures, with the likelihood of outbreaks of barbarism — which we have certainly seen in the genocides of the last 50 years in Africa, Asia, and Eastern Europe. To support this perspective, she mentioned statistics on days lost for mental health and stress-related illness in the United States. She sees people being pushed to do more and more tasks with less and less meaning, leading to demoralization and exhaustion. A strong image she used is that people are "like these very tired little donkeys who are already carrying much too much weight and have no interest in" new projects.

For **Otto Scharmer**, the current situation is one where both presencing and its opposite, absencing, are strong, but the reality of places where absencing dominates is emphasized by the media, so people tend to see it as more dominant than it may actually be. He sees a real opportunity for a major transformation of society, comparable to the Renaissance, lying in the extent to which wholes are falling apart, whether individuals, families, communities, or corporations. His most recent book *Leading from the Emerging Future* (with Katrin Kaufer, 2013) contains many examples of presencing: corporations, government agencies, and communities where individuals have been able to turn around situations where many had previously felt trapped in hopelessness, and the widespread interest in his work in areas as diverse as China, Brazil, and Scotland suggest the possibilities for such transformation. Nonetheless, he acknowledges that all of this is very small, compared with the scale of the challenges that human beings and the planet face at this time. He is aware of the significant material improvements that have occurred for many populations around the globe that have been documented in various ways by the growth of new indicators of real progress, but holds that the inner dimension is still largely unaddressed. It is this dimension of consciousness and connection to source by highly aligned groups of people around the world that Scharmer sees as the potential driver of fundamental changes toward societal health.

Ed Schein suspects that in the United States we have given too much weight to competition, so that systems are "more or less at war with one another," with too little collaboration in North American society. In addition, he focused on how changes in the global environment have been causing contact among cultures and a blending of cultures that are forced into interaction, whether the leaders and members of the culture wish this or not.

He feels that this makes it inevitable that new forms will emerge, forms that we cannot yet predict. He sees mindfulness as key to getting in touch with our own culture's limitations.

Robert E. Quinn mentioned that 70% of people in the United States are not engaged at work and that worldwide the statistics are worse. He sees most people operating out of a set of self-defeating assumptions with a focus on technical problem solving, whereas it is possible to turn this around and instead become aware of the power of purpose, integrity, empathy, and learning. He is optimistic, having seen many major breakthroughs of this nature in all types of organizations, from education to government and corporate.

Peter Senge is convinced that it will take from 5 to 15 decades to reverse the damage that humans have created because of the delays built into system change, as described in *The Fifth Discipline* (1990, 2006) and *The Necessary Revolution* (2007). Climate change is only one example. Such change requires a huge shift of will which is not easy to imagine or create. He is convinced that the depth of change required cannot come from existing hierarchical institutions and individualistic, masculine images and styles of heroic leadership, but only from shifts among human communities to commit to shaping their futures. He believes that we as human beings need a "new mythos" that matches the systemic nature of today's problems: It needs to have a collective quality, like the old sayings from various cultures that when leadership works best, the people say "we did it ourselves."

Implications of their views of the current situation

There was substantial alignment that this is a time of tremendous change, that people experience much in their world as falling apart — countries, families, businesses, traditions. Here it becomes a matter of emphasis from one thought leader to another. Wheatley focuses on the exhaustion people are experiencing, and the need for "warriors of the human spirit" to help humanity through this time, whereas Scharmer focuses on how the forces of both "presencing" and "absencing" are so strong that it creates potential for major change, perhaps comparable to the Renaissance. Both see huge changes, but the tone differs. Schein too sees the inevitability of major new innovations in areas we cannot yet predict, and Quinn emphasizes the role of the individual in becoming an initiator of change through processes of positive deviance. Senge alone mentioned the systems time lag that means it will take many decades, even perhaps life-times, to reverse the damage that has already been caused to the biosphere.

WHAT IS ESSENTIAL IN LEADERSHIP DEVELOPMENT?

The world as **Margaret Wheatley** sees it needs leadership development that helps leaders to develop the inner discipline that will support them in this hosting of potential, regardless of extreme pressures and breakdowns. This means training in steadiness of mind, learning to understand issues at the deepest levels of causation, developing the capacity to use intuition wisely. It means training leaders in practices that sustain them so they can sustain others, among which would be the practice of always making time for reflection.

Given **Otto Scharmer's** views about the nature of leadership and the scale and nature of societal change needed, he focuses on developing people's capacity to create conditions for others to become whole, but starting with oneself. He emphasizes the importance of making taken-for-granted assumptions of our culture visible and conscious, so that leaders can help people cross what he calls the three divides: to face the issues impeding environmental sustainability (the ecological divide of self from the world), to end the exclusion and marginalization of so many groups of people (the social divide of self from others), and to tap into the social field and live nourished by source (the spiritual divide of self from self). I noticed how when he spoke he brought in others' perspectives and not just his own, pointing out how much the others interviewed for this book have contributed to such leadership development — thereby exemplifying his commitment to valuing and caring for others. He has created the U-Lab as a medium for convening tens of thousands of participants in most countries around the world to learn and use such tools to prototype "seeds" of solutions that together may yield a change at the systems level.

Ed Schein emphasizes the importance for leaders of getting outside of one's own culture, whether at the level of a company or a nation. In this context, he mentioned the value of being multilingual as a key skill for leaders in today's world, although this focus seems to be decreasing as a focus in the United States. He suggested that leadership development needs to help leaders become mindful and reinforce their capacity to form relationships. Core to his perspective of what leaders need is the belief that others are important. This may be hard to teach if a person doesn't have it, so Schein has experimented over the years with various experiential practices that cause leaders to see the world through others' eyes. One is called an *empathy walk*: leaders are asked to find someone who is as different from themselves as they can and then spend anywhere from a couple of hours to a day with this person. Simple as this practice may sound, Schein believes it is transformative in its impact — and Scharmer has encouraged its use in his MOOCs.

Robert E. Quinn is interested in developing transformational leadership, which he described as what happens when one "chooses to see the world differently and then enacts that vision into reality and draws other people into that new reality." In place of trying to have people emulate or copy leaders, Quinn seeks to have them get in touch with their own deepest values as a source for leading transformational change. The focus becomes shifting the underlying mindset, so they are clear on their sense of purpose and feel empowered to take action.

Peter Senge focuses on skills that support the development of collective leadership. He has expanded on what was already presented in *The Fifth Discipline* (1990, 2006), developing it further in recent articles on *systems leaders* (Senge, Hamilton, & Kania, 2015). Many of these skills have long been mentioned in leadership development, but of course it is far simpler to espouse them than live them: the ability to build a generative team, to cultivate a compelling shared vision that is meaningful to all involved, and both individual and systemic capacity for reflection. He also mentions other skills emphasized by Scharmer in his work: sensing and presencing. Finally, Senge discussed a contrast he sees between the extent to which businesses understand the importance of team development and what he finds in the social sector, for example, within educational institutions. In these latter areas, he has seen a serious lack of capacity in developing generative teams and even in appreciating the need for them, which undermines practical work in collective capacity building.

Implications of their views on leadership development

Their approaches to developing leaders have different qualities, coming from the differences in language that they use. Just as they differ from one another as individuals, they create different atmospheres for supporting people's movement in a shared direction. This means that there are more distinctions with regard to implementation than in their underlying goals for leaders, organizations, and society. What I believe they have in common is a focus on leaders becoming conscious of their assumptions and transcending any that are limiting. They all see the interdependence of consciousness and action: how where we "come from" colors what we are able to perceive and then turn into action. For each of them, this means that a leader needs to do inner work before and while focusing on the organizational culture, but what this would involve for the leader may differ substantially across the five approaches.

SHARED PERSPECTIVES AND COMMON THEMES

Before articulating what I see as a possible model that emerges from these interviews, I will briefly mention a few common themes on these key areas.

Health

While the five emphasized different aspects, they view health as the capacity to make whole and to recognize the need for wholeness. They look at health systemically and see it as intrinsically impossible without learning and growing.

Healthy organizations

All five agree that healthy organizations nourish their people and those with whom they interact and serve purposes that contribute beyond their boundaries in some way to society. As discussed, each brings nuances that color their own version of healthy organizations.

The leaders' role

None defined leaders as those with positional power. They used their own terminology, but all focused on leaders as people who are able to "host others' well-being" — to create conditions for wholeness and integration — to nourish collective wisdom and action. All spoke about how leaders create environments that nourish people or respect their views and support them in collaborating with others.

Leadership development

To attempt to consolidate their approaches and seek similarities does not seem useful. Although alignment of basic assumptions about organizational and societal health and discussion of this topic across social science fields is very important, it can be helpful for there to be different flavors and colors in developing leaders. Individuals and human cultures are so varied. The tendency to obliterate the rich variety of cultures that have developed in different parts of the world is problematic. This seems comparable to reducing biodiversity: not helpful and even dangerous. It makes life thinner to have less variation. Looking from a systems perspective at how infants learn (Feldenkrais, 1972, 1979; Goldman Schuyler, 2004), experimentation with varied ways of doing anything is an important source of development.

Hence, the rich variety of methods, courses, activities, and contexts available from these thought leaders and others is a great benefit for leadership development. The contrast between Wheatley's call for warriors of the human spirit, Scharmer's MOOC on *Transforming Business, Society, and Self*, and Quinn's keynotes on *The Positive Organization* will speak to different people. Systems thinking refers to a need for *requisite variety*: the richness and complexity of one's responses needs to match that of the problems. In this context, the variety present in approaches to leadership development is not only healthy but essential.

AN EMERGENT MODEL OF SYSTEMIC HEALTH

After reviewing the interviews many times and reflecting on what each said as well as what they had in common, I began to see five main elements that may characterize all healthy systems. Based on these interviews, these themes are: Wholeness, Interdependence/relatedness, Inclusion/inclusivity, Removing toxins/rebalancing, and Emergence. At this point in our thinking, I wonder whether using these in questions about an organization, community, or even society might help action researchers, leaders, and consultants generate shareable data about this process of "healthing" in the world. Are all healthy organizations perhaps characterized by these five elements? Might we formulate a template of questions incorporating these elements that could be useful in many ways to encourage thinking and action related to organizational and societal health?

Wholeness

Healthy comes from the same root as the word *whole*, and, as Wheatley and Scharmer pointed out, is related to the notion of *holy*. It makes little sense to talk of the health of an organization except as a whole — it does little good to have brilliant product creators if no one can produce the product, or to design products for markets that do not exist. Just so for us as individuals — health is about our aliveness and vitality more than about the functioning of our parts; we have all known incredibly alive people in their 80s or 90s who had a lot or problems with various "parts" yet were amazing in their presence and impact on the quality of many others' lives. Appreciating health involves appreciating the systemic, interdependent nature of living systems and helping them "be whole" especially when they seem to be degrading or losing their wholeness. This applies at all levels of systems: individual, teams, departments, whole organizations, communities — whole systems.

Possible questions: How whole do we feel our organization to be? What do we see or feel that leads us to say this?

Interdependence/relatedness

Healthy people and organizations live in active interdependence with others and value this as part of being alive. As Wheatley phrased it during her interview, "Like any living system, our health is predicted by the number and quality of our interconnections. A healthy organization is one that knows it's a complex interconnected system and uses that well." In another way, this can be seen in Scharmer's notion of three divides: the divides impede appreciation of our own wholeness, as well as of our interdependence with others (sociosphere) and the natural world (ecosphere). His description of an emerging shift in consciousness from *ego* to *eco* can be seen also as the restoration of a healthier way of being, one that is realistic about the systemic nature of both individual and community life. As Senge said, love is a particular expression of this "systemness:" in the HP division it was defined by the engineers as the act of "allowing another to be a legitimate other," which was key to developing the networks of collaborations essential for getting work done.

As Senge explained, the engineers at HP used a particular practice to reveal their networks of collaboration: "If you reflect on something you have been part of accomplishing that you are proud of, who was essential to that accomplishment?" They would then list the names of each person and pay attention to how they felt as they listed those names: first they would just notice the immediate emotions (good or bad) and then they would ask themselves, "What would have been the consequences if that person had not been there?" — so they could also see that, regardless of their feelings about that person, their presence mattered, they were a "legitimate other" in their network of collaboration.

Possible questions: Considering each person who has been part of a given effort, what would have happened if they had not been there? In what ways do we depend on one another mutually? What and who do we depend on, as an organization? What and who depends on us? What happens when these inter-dependencies are weakened?

Inclusion/inclusivity

A dynamic living system does not include some of its parts and exclude others: the health of the whole is interdependent with the health of the parts. A healthy society would not exclude some beings because they are poor, or less educated, or their minds or bodies appear to look or function differently from those of the majority, or those that temporarily are the majority. A social system includes all living within it. Many societies have created in-groups and out-groups, defining some people as being "not human" and therefore not needing to be considered in the same way as others. Both Scharmer and Quinn express particular interest in what takes place at the edges of the system, the places that others aren't attending to, as sources of change and innovation. From this perspective, the focus cannot even be limited to human flourishing (see Reason & Bradbury, 2008), as broad as that seems, but has to include all life and the biosphere.

Possible questions: Who lives on the margins in our system? Do we include them in reflecting on health or ignore them? Do we consider them to be "less important"?

Removing toxins/rebalancing

Health is not in stasis: It is an active, ongoing process that involves noticing the need for change and responding to it. It requires sustaining attention to the state of being of the system (oneself, one's organization, one's community) and having ongoing processes for rebalancing, for removing toxins or impediments to the movement of energy. Health is not a state at one end of a continuum; it is an ongoing, living active process, a way of engaging with life, other beings, and the environment.

Possible questions: In what kinds of situations do we lose balance, as an organization? What do we mean by "losing balance"? What creates toxicity in our system? What processes do we have for seeing and removing it? Who pays attention to this? How do we care for those who notice and attend to the toxic aspects of our organization?

Emergence

A healthy organization is evolving and changing, allowing or nourishing the emergence of new forms. This can be seen in Schein's descriptions of the difference between young organizations and what happened when they grew too large and sought stability, in Scharmer's (2009, 2013) including the term "emerging" in both of his book titles, and in Quinn's interest in positive deviance as a source of systems change. How an organization, of whatever size, makes space for the new to emerge seems like a crucial element in health. There isn't only one model for how this happens. Scharmer's (2009) U theory can be viewed as an in-depth analysis of the process people use to catalyze emergence so it can take form in concrete action. Wheatley's emphasis on the leader allowing people to have the time they need to think and the value of retreat in her own life seem related to creating space for emergence, as does Quinn's focus on "elevating oneself" through purpose and Senge's emphasis on reflection and continually challenging one's own way of seeing things, and on the creative process. When Schein says "we need new inventions" — this is another wording for the importance of emergence.

Possible questions: How do we take time to think? And how do we take time to think about our thinking? How do we slow down to sense what is emerging? How do we create such pauses collectively and explore what others see and sense? What do we do with such new kinds of "data"? How do we give it form?

Closing Thoughts and Questions

What are the implications of the views and lives of these five interviewees and of these questions? The points below are addressed in the chapters that follow, in differing ways, and will be returned to by the editorial team as a whole when we discuss the implications of the totality of the book in the closing chapter.

The thought leaders agree that health is about wholeness, and that leaders should aim for wholeness on all levels, beginning with themselves, which in itself conveys a message to the organization. How he or she is speaks louder than what is said — as with parenting. Wholeness is not sameness: a healthy organism is a system with differentiated subsystems, but they need to be integrated, as Schein has emphasized for decades. We in the United States don't seem to have mastered the art of differentiation and integration sufficiently for the issues we face: We seem to be enamored as a culture with watching newscasters and politicians who yell at one another or debate, as contrasted with watching shows where people come together to think and create new possibilities through sharing their thoughts.

The rich differences of language and style that are evident across these thought leaders is valuable in today's world, as it communicates with different groups of people. Seeing how their thinking begins to suggest a model of health, while their styles and action paths differ, is invaluable for today's richly differentiated and interconnected world.

Their writings and actions can inspire those who already self-identify as leaders to do more and can encourage those who do not yet see themselves as leaders. These are not ivory tower academics who only share their thoughts through books or research articles. They *know* through their actions in the world. As Schein said "When my knowledge is helpful to the various practitioners in the field — that is the moment when I know that I know" (quoted in Scharmer, 2009, p. 56). Only such richness and variety is likely to allow social actions to scale up sufficiently to address the largest systemic problem of the planet: the fact that the way humanity is living now, even with hundreds of millions of people living with inadequate water, food, health care, and education, requires 1.5 earths. Unless there are huge changes, how many earths would be required for all to live what is considered "well"? Three? Five? But we only have one earth. So scaling the understandings about healthy organizations and a healthy world is incredibly important — and to that end, speaking different "languages of change" is essential.

What would it take for there to be enough shared will for human beings to self-organize to address our societal and ecological problems without waiting for further and still more urgent crisis-level situations to cry out for attention? Small efforts are being made all over the planet, as readers can see in Part III of the book. Is the accumulation of a great many such small efforts sufficient, or are larger, more coordinated efforts needed? And if they are, how do human beings learn to coordinate while retaining our requisite variety, differentiation, and freedom?

While perhaps the only real way to answer this is through living, the rest of the chapters in the book are here to help us reflect on what kinds of research and change projects we can initiate to contribute to a healthier world. Seeking criteria to help us know when we really know something, Schein said that he knows when he knows something if his knowledge has been helpful to colleagues in the field. Scharmer suggested that Senge's criterion might be valuable: "I know that I know when I develop the capacity to create the results I really care about" (Scharmer, 2009, p. 98). This is close to Senge's definition of leadership: *the capacity of a human community to shape its future*. Perhaps the measure of whether we really do understand leadership is whether we, as human beings and social scientists, are able to create the future we want: a healthy world.

References

Ackoff, R. (1974). *Redesigning the future: A systems approach to societal problems*. NY: Wiley.

Alinsky, S. (1946/1989). *Reveille for radicals*. New York, NY: Vintage.

Baugher, J. E. (2014). Sociological mindfulness and leadership education. In K. Goldman Schuyler, J. E. Baugher, L. L. Falkman, & K. Jironet (Eds.), *Leading with spirit, presence, and authenticity* (pp. 79–89). San Francisco, CA: Jossey-Bass.

Cameron, K. S., Dutton, J. E., & Quinn, R. E. (Eds.). (2003). *Positive organizational scholarship: Foundations of a new discipline*. San Francisco, CA: Berrett-Koehler Publishers Inc.

Eisler, R. (1987). *The chalice and the blade: Our history, our future*. San Francisco, CA: Harper Collins.

Feldenkrais, M. (1972). *Awareness through movement*. New York, NY: Harper and Row.

Feldenkrais, M. (1979). On health. *Dromenon, 2*(2), 25–26.

Frost, P., & Robinson, S. (1999). The toxic handler. *Harvard Business Review, 77*(4), 96–107.

Goldman Schuyler, K. (2004, December). A systems approach to learning and change: Cindy's story. *Somatics, 14*(3), 14–23.

Katz, D., & Kahn, R. L. (1966). *The social psychology of organizations*. New York, NY: Wiley.

Kriger, M. P., & Hanson, B. J. (1999). A value-based paradigm for creating truly healthy organizations. *Journal of Organizational Change Management, 12*(4), 302–317. Retrieved from doi.org/10.1108/09534819910282144

Laszlo, E. (1996). *The systems view of the world: A holistic vision for our time*. New York, NY: Hampton Press.

Quinn, R. E. (1996). *Deep change*. San Francisco, CA: Jossey-Bass.

Quinn, R. E. (2015). *The positive organization: Breaking free from conventional cultures, constraints, and beliefs*. Oakland, CA: Berrett-Koehler.

Quinn, R. E., Heynoski, K., Thomas, M., & Spreitzer, G. (2014). *The best teacher in you: How to accelerate learning and save lives*. San Francisco, CA: Berrett-Koehler.

Reason, P., & Bradbury, H. (Eds.). (2008). *The Sage handbook of action research: Participative inquiry and practice*. Los Angeles, CA: Sage.

Scharmer, O. (2009). *Theory U*. San Francisco, CA: Berrett-Koehler.

Scharmer, O., & Kaufer, K. (2013). *Leading from the emerging future*. San Francisco, CA: Berrett-Koehler.

Scharmer, O., Saxena, S., & Goldman Schuyler, K. (2014). Connecting inner transformation as a leader to corporate and societal change. In K. Goldman Schuyler, J. E. Baugher, K. Jironet, & L. Lid-Falkman (Eds.), *Leading with spirit, presence, and authenticity* (pp. 13–37). San Francisco, CA: Jossey-Bass/Wiley.

Schein, E. H. (1985/2004). *Organizational culture and leadership*. San Francisco, CA: Jossey-Bass.

Schein, E. H. (1988). *Process consultation: Its role in organization development*. Menlo Park, CA: Addison-Wesley.

Schein, E. H. (1999). *Process consultation revisited: Building the helping relationship*. Menlo Park, CA: Addison-Wesley.

Schein, E. H. (2000). The next frontier: Edgar Schein on organizational therapy. *The Academy of Management Executive*, *14*(1), 31–48.

Schein, E. H. (2009/2011). *Helping: How to offer, give, and receive help*. San Francisco, CA: Berrett-Koehler.

Schein, E. H. (2013). *Humble inquiry: The gentle art of asking instead of telling*. San Francisco, CA: Berrett-Koehler.

Seligman, M. E. P. (1999). The president's address. *American Psychologist*, Retrieved from http://www.ppc.sas.upenn.edu/aparep98.htm

Seligman, M. E. P., & Csikszentmihalyi, M. (2000). Positive psychology: An introduction. *American Psychologist*, *55*(1), 5–14. doi:10.1037//0003-066X.55.1.5

Senge, P. (1990, 2006). *The fifth discipline: The art and practice of the learning organization*. New York, NY: Doubleday.

Senge, P. (2012). Leaders should be people who are deeply involved in their own realization of being a human being. In K. Goldman Schuyler (Ed.), *Inner peace—Global impact: Tibetan Buddhism, leadership, and work* (pp. 317–328). Charlotte, NC: Information Age Publishing.

Senge, P., Hamilton, H., & Kania, J. (2015, Winter). The dawn of system leadership. *Stanford Social Innovation Review*, *13*(1), 26–33.

Senge, P., Smith, B., Kruschwitz, N., Laur, J., & Schley, S. (2007). *The necessary revolution*. New York, NY: Doubleday.

Singer, P. (2015). *The most good you can do: How effective altruism is changing ideas about living ethically*. New Haven, CT: Yale University Press.

The World Commission on Environment and Development. (1987). *Our common future (The Brundtland report)*. Retrieved from www.un-documents.net/our-common-future.pdf

von Bertalanffy, L. (1968). *General systems theory*. New York, NY: Braziller.

Wheatley, M. (1992). *Leadership and the new science.* San Francisco, CA: Berrett-Koehler.

Wheatley, M. (2012). Ancient wisdom, social science, and the vastness of the human spirit. In K. Goldman Schuyler (Ed.), *Inner peace—Global impact: Tibetan Buddhism, leadership, and work* (pp. 329–341). Charlotte, NC: Information Age Publishing.

Wheatley, M. (2014). *How does Raven know: Entering sacred world — A meditative memoir.* Provo, UT: Margaret J. Wheatley.

Wheatley, M., & Kellner-Rogers, M. (1996). *A simpler way.* San Francisco, CA: Berrett-Koehler.

Air and Water: What Flows Lives

Susan Amber Gordon. *From Afar*. 2015. Acrylic and polymer pigments on canvas, 24″×24″. Collection of the artist

Air and Water: What Flows Lives

Karin Jironet and John Eric Baugher

The thunder, lightning, and rain in Italy is something in its own right. First, a roaring sound rolling close, then silence. Suddenly, lightning, striking close to the tip of the nose, blinding, illuminating the entire sky, and then crushing amounts of water falling, stopping at nothing, yet not falling, but hammering. The next morning, almost apologetically, the sea waves gently, soft as a peach in the sun.

It is shocking. The forces of air and water seem merciless. Yet they sustain life. And reawaken consciousness. An electric thunderstorm on the coast South of Rome could, it seems, wake up the dead.

In the moment of torrent, life is brought into the immediate now. The lightening cuts open old structures and allows for renewal, clarity, and a stillness that is fresh rather than dull. The thinking mind needs this experience to awaken from its ingrained structures, depart from safety-laden constructs and jump into risk, and to see anew the potential of universal openness and the value of life.

The hermeneutics of leadership requires continuous interrogation into its deepest prevailing assumptions. Once taken-for-granted images of leaders and followers are shaken up and, as the storm settles, replaced by others. Contemporary notions of leadership are destined to hold more in the equation: greater diversity, multiple stakeholders, composite perspectives, and simultaneous acknowledgment of material and spiritual realities. In effect, this reconceptualization entails an orientation away from "self-other" dichotomies toward a broad base awareness of "us" as participants in a united humanity living on one and the same planet. Leaders are called to wake up and contribute to the global leadership discourse according to this fundamental and ethical principle.

We live moment by moment, and every instance holds the power of conscious choice. This section takes "awareness" as its venture point for exploring health. These quite diverse chapters formulate a clear consensus — leadership for a healthy world urgently needs to define a clear course forward grounded in awareness. The contributing authors share a vision of what healthy notions of "leadership" look like. This view entails a radical reconceptualization of foundational notions including development, well-being, responsibility, and equality.

In her chapter "Reframing Organizational and Social Change: From Domination to Partnership," Riane Eisler, President of the Center for Partnership Studies, examines conceptual change from cultural and societal perspectives. She articulates how social configurations shift from a domination system to a partnership system through changing views about effective leadership and organizations in their larger social context. Eisler emphasizes that changes in definitions of leadership are directly related to changes in gender roles and relations. She proposes that only a more inclusive view of society and leadership, one that considers the way gender- and parent-child relations are culturally constructed, can meet today's economic, social, and environmental challenges. Although the remaining chapters in this section do not discuss patriarchy as such, each chapter affirms the centrality of a collaborative or partnership consciousness for the well-being of humans and the planet.

Drawing on her multidisciplinary, cross-cultural analysis of social systems over nearly four decades, Eisler describes in her chapter two underlying social configurations that transcend conventional categories such as capitalism versus socialism, right versus left, religious versus secular, and Eastern versus Western: the partnership system and the domination system. She documents challenges to traditions of domination in all areas of life as well as resistance and periodic regression to the domination side of the partnership/domination continuum — and how leadership can support the cultural shift to the partnership side. Eisler concludes with pragmatic leadership interventions that may support the shift to a partnership model, by providing building blocks for creating a healthier, more caring, and sustainable society and economy.

In "Use It or Lose It: About Leadership Ethics in the United Nations," Karin Jironet examines how ethics, revisited and ameliorated, is formative of the United Nation's global leadership role. Through original interviews with UN Deputy Secretary-General, Jan Eliasson, and former Under-Secretary-General,

Inga-Britt Ahlenius, the importance of very personal choices, commitment, and action for the highest good comes alive in its present-day context. Taking a psychospiritual approach, the author discusses the relation between ethics and balance; choice and passion in the development of significant leadership. Jironet, a psychoanalyst and theologian, draws on comparative theory and method while inquiring into the fundamental questions of the role, the ethical obligation, and the personal, moral imperative required of an individual leader within the United Nations. She proposes that psychospiritual development is a prerequisite for sound ethical leadership and that the individual's personal leadership development informs his or her leadership acumen.

Jironet contends that the purpose of the United Nations — peace and development for a healthy world — can only be realized when every leader at the United Nations shares common concepts about the organization's ethics and is engaged in continuous dialogue in defining and redefining these notions to meet with whatever conditions present. She concludes that it is at the interface between the individual's and the organization's ethical choice and passion that the UN today faces its greatest potential for growth.

Two chapters in this section highlight how a deeper form of awareness that allows for wisdom is crucial to leadership for sustainability. In "Ecological Consciousness, Moral Imagination, and the Framework for Strategic Sustainable Development," professor of sociology John Eric Baugher and his coauthors, neuropsychiatrist Walter Osika, and Karl Henrik Robèrt, MD and founder of The Natural Step (Robèrt, 2002), begin by sketching dimensions of the current ecological crisis as outlined in the UN's Millennium Ecosystem Assessment (2005), including the decline of global fish stocks, threatened water supplies, and massive species extinction. The UN report, like The Framework for Strategic Sustainable Development (FSSD), which grew out of Robèrt's work on The Natural Step in Sweden, is grounded in systems thinking and based on collaboration among a network of climate change scientists and other experts worldwide. In these respects, both the framework presented in this chapter and the UN's millennium report embody the dialogic and cooperative dimensions of the partnership model outlined by Eisler.

Baugher, Osika, and Robèrt illustrate the power of the FSSD for coordinating action among diverse constituents through the case of the resort municipality of Whistler, Canada, where more than 60 community stakeholders and businesses have collaboratively created and implemented short-, medium-, and long-term plans for moving the community toward sustainability in 18 key areas, including energy use, waste reduction, watershed management, land use, and public transportation. In this way, this chapter points to a powerful resource for supporting communities, businesses, and other organizations in realizing their intentions of working and living in line with the foundational principles for sustainability. Baugher and his colleagues suggest, however, that the current age of market fundamentalism and consumerism promotes an impoverished notion of individual freedom in opposition to the common good. In such a context, the paradigm shift to sustainability requires an ecological consciousness and moral imagination to think of one's self-interest in broader terms beyond short-term economic gain or consumer satisfaction and with an awareness of the interconnectedness and embeddedness of life and living systems on the planet. Drawing on the work of cognitive scientist George Lakoff (2006), the authors point to the need for a higher rationality, the freedom that comes from seeing our seeing, opening possibilities that we might develop an enlightened understanding of self-interest and freedom that supports the health and flourishing of all.

Samuel G. Wilson's chapter, "Leadership For The Greater Good: Developing Indicators of Societal and Environmental Health," furthers the continuity of the section in several key respects. In line with the broader focus of this section on reawakening awareness and interrogating prevailing cultural assumptions, Wilson articulates how the choices scholars and practitioners make with respect to measuring the health of a society reflect and reinforce an underlying mindset. What is measured in itself constructs value and structures what can be understood and open to collective reflection. There is a wider recognition today that Gross Domestic Product (GDP), which for decades has been taken as virtually synonymous with the "health" of a nation, is silent about the actual well-being of individuals, families, and communities as well as the health of ecosystems that support life on the planet. In recent years, alternative measures have been created, such as the Genuine Progress Indicator, which offers a more nuanced estimate of the overall economic, environmental, and social health of a nation (see also Eisler in this volume). Focusing on the Anglo-American context, Wilson situates the emergence of such measures in historical context and presents a framework for understanding the links between the different elements of these measures.

Like other chapters in this section, Wilson's contribution is largely conceptual, clarifying how existing indicators and information systems of societal and environmental health are unfit for contemporary leadership, as their limited focus and technical sophistication overshadow the social value they may produce. Wilson's central point is that although we now have available to us a variety of complex measures and indicators of societal health, such information is more the purview of management, not leadership. The distinction Wilson makes here is between information and wisdom, between expert problem solving and collaborative inquiry, between technical orientation and adaptive leadership. What we need, according to Wilson, are not ever more complex measures of health that orient us to the past in "highly abstract and decontextualized" ways, but prospective indicators that can help us navigate toward a desired future.

Wilson's focus on creatively imagining "discrepancies between the world as it is, and the world as it might be" resonates with the FSSD approach outlined by Baugher and his coauthors that involves envisioning a sustainable future and then "backcasting" from that vision to create a path for moving toward sustainability in the short, medium, and long-term. A focus on wisdom and moral imagination likewise connects the narratives of these two chapters on sustainability with Jironet's chapter on the UN. Just as the "wicked" problems of global climate change and resource depletion require systems thinking and a deep awareness of our fundamental interconnectedness, what defines outstanding leaders, according to Jironet, is the capacity to embody and impart a set of ethics that inspire individuals and constituent partners "to passionately seek morally grounded choices in the service of the world as a whole."

In the final chapter in this section, "Developing Relational Leadership in Africa," Charles J. Palus, Steadman Harrison III, and Joshua J. Prasad bring us full circle by articulating how a relational view and practice of leadership is crucial for skillful action in an increasingly interdependent world. Approaching organizational health as stemming from stakeholders' adaptive ability, the authors propose a model for how leadership can contribute to healthier organizations and societies. The authors draw on the Action Logic theory and methodology developed by William Torbert to conceptualize the shift away from more individualist and "heroic" approaches to leadership toward a more relational ontology that holds greater power for reframing complex problems in new ways, generating personal and organizational transformations, and integrating material, spiritual, and societal transformations.

The relational model presented in this chapter is grounded in a case study of the author's own organization, the Center for Creative Leadership (CCL), and in particular, CCL's collaborative work with World Vision Ethiopia. Central to the work of CCL are the practices of design thinking and collaborative inquiry, dialogic processes that are crucial in developing more process-oriented forms of leadership and mission-based leadership strategies attuned to the cultural and structural realities of local contexts. The focus at CCL on the social processes of directing and aligning wise action resonates with the distinction Wilson draws between a hierarchical, expert management orientation and collaborative and cocreative leadership for the greater good. Likewise, the relational ontology outlined by Palus and his coauthors resonates with the underlying ethic and practices of the partnership model developed by Eisler.

The authors contributing to this section share common views on the fundamental conditions necessary for individual, organizational, societal, and ecological health and what it means to be a cultivator of such health as a leader. And as we write this book, the shocks that start a new time and a new outlook, following on the collapse of multiple structures, and the chance of broadening the horizon of leadership, present as a real opportunity. Love, wisdom, compassion, hope, care, kindness — these powerful human sentiments and capacities are not always "on," but often dormant and only awakened when called for. When aware and conscious, such virtues may flow spontaneously in all relationships, and in doing so, sustain health through their inherent genuineness, aliveness, and alertness.

3

Reframing Organizational and Social Change: From Domination to Partnership

Riane Eisler

Over the last decades, there has been much talk about moving to a healthier, more equitable, and sustainable society. At the same time, a new view of effective leadership has been emerging. The old view equates effective leadership with giving orders that are obeyed. The new view equates effective leadership with inspiring, guiding, and facilitating — in other words, with empowering rather than disempowering others.

This sea change in ideas about leadership and power can best be understood from the perspective of two underlying social configurations: the partnership system and the domination system (Eisler, 1987, 1995, 2000, 2007, 2014). New concepts of leadership and power reflect attempts to leave behind entrenched traditions of domination in all areas of life — from the family and education to the workplace, economics, and politics. These changes in definitions of leadership are related to attempts to shift to a more partnership-oriented way of structuring relations — from intimate to international.

This shift toward partnership, in turn, is related to changes in gender roles and relations. This explains why raising women's status and bringing traits and activities stereotypically associated with femininity into workplaces and society at large is so fiercely resisted by those who believe that top-down rankings of domination are natural and moral.

The discussion that follows looks at the tension between the current movement toward partnership on both the social and organizational levels and the resistance to it. It then outlines key interventions that leaders can use to accelerate the shift from domination to partnership — and with this, to a healthier, more equitable, and caring world.

The Social Context of Leadership

We are not used to thinking that gender roles and relations are integral to how we structure social institutions and beliefs. These "women's issues" are at best treated as secondary. Similarly, if the female half of humanity is considered at all in texts on leadership, it is ghettoized in a chapter on women.

However, once we look at leadership from a more inclusive perspective, a different picture comes into view. We see that the occasional women leaders in our history books usually stepped into their positions as widows, daughters, or mothers of men. We also see that, because leadership was an exclusive male preserve, not surprisingly, the definition of leadership we inherited has been practically synonymous with characteristics stereotypically considered masculine such as toughness, aggressiveness, and control.

This definition of leadership was appropriate for a social organization of rigid top-down rankings — be it man over man, man over woman, race over race, religion over religion, nation over nation, or man over nature. In this social structure, women in leadership roles were at best an anomaly. At the same time, anything associated with the "soft" or stereotypically feminine, such as caring, caregiving, and nonviolence, was, along with women, relegated to a subordinate place.

This kind of social organization cuts across familiar social categories such as ancient versus modern, right versus left, religious versus secular, Eastern versus Western, or industrial versus pre- or postindustrial. These conventional categories only focus on a particular aspect of a society such as its ideology, economic organization, and location, rather than on the structure of its family, educational, religious, political, and economic institutions and its guiding system of values. None of them pay attention to how the roles and relations of the two halves of humanity — male and female — are socially constructed, much less to how this impacts values and institutions.

Moreover, societies in all these conventional categories have been repressive, aggressive, and unjust. So if we are to better understand what kind of social configuration can support healthier, more equitable, and sustainable relations, we must go beyond our familiar classifications of society.

In addressing this critical issue of what kinds of social configurations support equitable or inequitable relations, I conducted a multidisciplinary study analyzing how key components of a society relate to one another to maintain the larger whole (see, e.g., Eisler, 1987, 1995, 1997, 2003, 2007, 2014). This method of analysis, called the study of relational dynamics, examines data from a wide range of times and places. It draws from many fields, including cross-cultural anthropological surveys (e.g., Coltrane, 1988; Murdock, 1969; Sanday, 1981; Textor, 1969); anthropological and sociological studies of individual societies (e.g., Abu-Lughod,1986; Benedict, 1946; Giddens, 1984; Min, 1995); as well as writings by historians, analyses of laws, moral codes, art, literature (including fiction, biographies, and autobiographies), scholarship from psychology, economics, education, political science, philosophy, religious studies (including the study of "mystery cults" around the Mediterranean from before the rise of Christianity), archeological studies (primarily of western prehistory because of greater availability of materials, but also some of Indian and Chinese prehistory), the study of both western and eastern myths and legends; and data from more recently developed fields such as primatology, neuroscience, chaos theory, systems self-organizing theory, nonlinear dynamics, gender studies, women's studies, and men's studies (for citations of sources, see, e.g., Eisler, 1987, 1995, 1997, 2000, 2003, 2007, 2013, 2014; Eisler & Levine, 2002).

This systemic approach made it possible to see social patterns or configurations that are not visible using the customary unidisciplinary approach. It revealed that underneath the great surface diversity of human societies — transcending such differences as time, place, technological development, ethnic origin, and religious orientation — are two underlying configurations: the *domination* system and the *partnership* system (Eisler, 1987, 1995, 2000, 2007, 2014).

To briefly illustrate, societies that on the surface seem totally different, such as ISIS (the so-called Islamic Caliphate), Hitler's Germany, Stalin's U.S.S.R., Samurai Japan, and the Masai of nineteenth- and early-twentieth century Africa, all conform

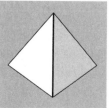

Authoritarian and inequitable social and economic structure

Subordination of women and "femininity" to men and "masculinity"

High degree of abuse and violence

Beliefs and stories that justify and idealize domination and violence

Figure 1. The Domination System. *Source:* Reprinted with permission from Eisler, R. (2007). *The real wealth of nations: Creating a caring economics,* San Francisco: Berrett-Koehler.

closely to the core configuration of the domination system. They are characterized by (1) authoritarian top-down rule in *both* the family and the state or tribe — and all institutions in between, (2) rigid male dominance, (3) a high degree of institutionalized, socially accepted violence, from child and wife beating to pogroms, terrorism, and/or chronic warfare, and (4) beliefs and stories that justify and even idealize domination and violence.

A notable characteristic of these societies is that, along with the ranking of male over female, comes a gendered system of values. So-called masculine values, such as toughness, strength, conquest, and domination are given high social and economic priority, as in the emphasis on weapons and wars. Conversely, so-called feminine values, such as caring, compassion, empathy, and nonviolence are relegated to a secondary, subservient sphere, cut off from the "real world" of politics and economics (Figure 1).

Another notable characteristic of societies orienting to the domination side of the *partnership-domination continuum* — and this is always a matter of degree — is their in-group versus out-group perspective for relationships. That is, difference — beginning with the most fundamental difference in our species between women and men — is equated with superiority or inferiority, dominating or being dominated, being served or serving.

I will presently describe the core configuration of partnership systems. But first, I want to illustrate how using these new social categories makes it possible to see patterns in what otherwise seems random and disconnected.

Challenging Traditions of Domination

If we look at modern history with the configuration of the domination system in mind, we see that underneath its many complex currents and crosscurrents lies a powerful movement challenging entrenched patterns of domination — albeit against fierce resistance and periodic regressions. We see that all the modern progressive movements have challenged different forms of domination backed by fear and force.

This is the common thread in the eighteenth- and nineteenth-century rights of man, antislavery, antimonarchist, socialist, pacifist, and feminist movements. Each of them challenged traditions of domination — from the "divinely ordained right" of kings to rule their "subjects" and the "divinely ordained right" of men to rule the women and children in the "castles" of their homes to the "divinely ordained right" of a "superior" race, religion, or nation to rule "inferior" ones. In the same way, the twentieth-century anticolonialist, participatory democracy, women's rights, antiwar, anti-family violence, and economic justice movements are not isolated phenomena. They are all part of a much larger movement: the movement to create a world in which — be it in our global family of nations, in our organizations, or in our individual families — principles of partnership rather than domination and submission are primary (see, e.g., Eisler, 1987, 1995, 2014).

If we next look at today's organizational development and leadership literature from this perspective, we see this same challenge to traditions of domination. It was once believed — and still is believed by some — that a fear-based, institutionally insensitive, and all too often abusive and dehumanizing leadership and management style is a requisite for both social order and economic productivity. But increasingly this leadership and management style is recognized as an impediment rather than a spur to social order and economic productivity (Eisler, 1991).

A growing body of literature proposes that, particularly in the postindustrial knowledge age, a new leadership and management style based on respect, accountability, and empowerment rather than disempowerment is needed. Concepts such as "servant leadership," "creative leadership," "primal leadership," and "partnership leadership" describe effective leaders and managers as people who facilitate, inspire, and elicit from others their highest productivity and creativity (Cooperrider & Srivastva, 1987; Eisler, 1991, 2007; Goleman, Boyatzis, & McKee, 2002). This is a "softer" leadership and management style, based more on caring than coercion — as in the ideal of how good mothers use power to nurture and empower their children.

Here again we see the weakening of domination gender stereotypes along with the elevation of more "feminine" traits and activities. We also see something else: that the greater valuing of "soft" leadership and management styles did not happen in a vacuum. It came with the rising status of women — and thus of qualities and behaviors associated with femininity, such as nurturance and empathy (Eisler, 1991, 2007).

This is not to say that women are necessarily empathic and caring. Indeed, if women operate in domination structures, they are under tremendous external and internal pressure to prove every inch of the way that they are not "soft." In such situations, women — particularly as middle managers, but sometimes even when they reach the top — have to "step into the shoes of men." This was the case in more domination-oriented times, and we still see it in women such as Sarah Palin or Margaret Thatcher, who was sometimes called "the best man in England" (Eisler, 1991).

On the other hand, because of women's socialization, there is evidence that in situations where they have a strong voice in shaping the system's rewards and incentives, the culture and structure of organizations are fundamentally altered. In a pioneering work in this area, *The Female Advantage: Women's Ways of Leadership*, Sally Helgesen (1990) described the innovative organizational structures and strategies of a number of successful women managers who, through more empathic and relational leadership styles, created more effective organizations.

Other current books on organizational development have introduced concepts such as "learning organizations," with studies showing that these more fluid and participatory structures actually lead to greater business profitability than rigid top-down structures (Senge, 1990; Wheatley, 2002). At the same time, there is a growing body of works on the need for diversity in organizations, with studies again indicating that this makes for greater effectiveness and profitability (Burud & Tumolo, 2004).

Of particular interest are studies showing that companies where there is more gender balance in leadership, as reflected in more women on boards of directors and management, have higher profits. For instance, a 2014 study by Credit Suisse Research of over 3,000 companies confirmed that women in boards and management is empirically associated with higher returns on equity, higher price/book valuations, and superior stock price performance (Dawson, Kersley, & Natella, 2014).

Nonetheless, this information remains largely unused. Indeed, if we look at the on-the-ground reality — be it in organizations or in society at large — much still orients to the domination system.

The Partnership Alternative

The problem is that while there is no shortage of critiques of various aspects of the domination system, far less attention has been given to what is required to build its alternative: a partnership system. The first step in this direction is an understanding of the core configuration of this system. This configuration consists of the following four interconnected, mutually reinforcing components: (1) a more democratic and egalitarian structure in *both* the family and the state — and all institutions in between; (2) equal partnership between women and men; (3) far less institutionalized, socially accepted violence, since it is not needed to maintain rigid rankings of domination; and (4) beliefs that, though recognizing that insensitivity, violence, and destructiveness are human possibilities, highlight the value of empathy, caring, and creativity.

In this type of social organization, whether in the family, the workplace, or society at large, so-called feminine qualities and behaviors are incorporated into the operational guidance systems. In other words, traits and activities such as caring, caregiving, and nonviolence are valued in both women and men, as well as in government and business policies (Figure 2).

The partnership configuration also transcends differences in time, place, and level of technological development. It can be found in tribal societies, such as the Teduray of the Philippines studied by the University of California anthropologist Stuart Schlegel (Schlegel, 1998), and agrarian societies such as the Minangkabau of East Sumatra studied by the University of Pennsylvania anthropologist Peggy Reeves Sanday (2002).

Technologically advanced societies such as Sweden, Norway, and Finland also orient to the partnership side of the continuum

Democratic and economically equitable structure

Equal valuing of males and females and high regard for stereotypical feminine values

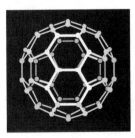

Mutual respect and trust with low degree of violence

Beliefs and stories that give high value to empathic and caring relations

Figure 2.   The Partnership System. *Source:* Reprinted with permission from Eisler, R. (2007). *The real wealth of nations: Creating a caring economics,* San Francisco: Berrett-Koehler.

(Eisler, 2007; Schwab et al., 2014). Here attempts to create a more equitable economic system resulted not, as they did in the U.S.S.R., in a domination form of communism ruled from the top, but rather in a democratic society with a mix of "free enterprise" and "welfare state." In these societies, we also see a strong interest in nonviolent conflict resolution, as well as the first laws against physical discipline of children in families and a strong men's movement to disentangle "masculinity" from its association with domination and violence. At the same time, we see much more equal partnership between women and men in both the family and the state; in other words, attempts to create a more gender-balanced society — one where women, along with stereotypically feminine values, are more highly valued.

We will return to this crucial matter, but first let us take a closer look at what partnership-oriented systems look like in practice. To begin with, as mentioned earlier, no society is a pure partnership or domination system. We are not talking about utopias or ideal societies, but of the degree to which a society falls on the partnership-domination continuum.

Moreover, partnership-oriented systems are *not* completely flat organizations. The difference between the partnership and domination systems is *not* that the domination system is hierarchical and the partnership system is hierarchy-free. The difference is the distinction between *hierarchies of domination* and *hierarchies of actualization* (Eisler, 1995, 2007).

Every society needs parents, teachers, and leaders. So both partnership and domination-oriented structures have hierarchies. But actualization hierarchies are more flexible, allowing many people to be leaders in different contexts.

Hierarchies of domination are held in place by the kind of power that is idealized as "masculine" in cultures that orient primarily to the domination system — the power to dominate. In contrast, hierarchies of actualization are not based on power *over*, but on power *to* — creative power, the power to help and to nurture that is stereotypically considered feminine — as well as power *with* — the collective power to accomplish goals together, as in teamwork.

Another key difference between these two types of hierarchies is that in hierarchies of domination, accountability and respect flow only from the bottom up, while in hierarchies of actualization, they flow both ways. Actualization hierarchies utilize everyone's knowledge and input and promote relational practices that result in greater organizational capacity through open lines of communication, rather than just one-way orders from above as in hierarchies of domination.

But here again we must avoid simplistic thinking. Despite the often-heard notion that all would be well if people would only cooperate, the difference between the partnership system and the domination system is *not* that people only cooperate in the former. We only have to look around us to see that people cooperate all the time in monopolies, criminal cartels, and terrorist organizations — all domination systems.

Neither is the difference that there is no competition in partnership systems. However, rather than the "dog-eat-dog" competition of domination systems, here competition is driven largely by the striving for excellence that is often spurred by seeing others excel. Nor is the difference that there is no conflict in partnership systems. Conflict is inevitable in human relations. But in domination systems it is typically suppressed through fear or force, so it explodes in destructiveness or even violence. In partnership systems, conflict is viewed as an opportunity for creative problem solving, for trying to find ways to improve people's relationships and lives.

Humanizing Organizations — and Society

As we have seen, how gender roles and relations are structured is a key element in both domination and partnership systems. It is also a major factor in the shift toward partnership in organizations and society at large.

Once we look at social and organizational change taking gender into account, we can see that the increasing entry of women into the paid labor market has been a major driving force behind flextime, day-care and elderly care programs, parental leave and other workplace policies that, as Patricia Aburdene and John Naisbitt wrote in *Megatrends for Women* (1992), are forcing a humanization of the workplace. It is also not coincidental that as women began entering the workforce *en masse*, employee training and management consulting increasingly focused on better work relationships. The socialization of girls and women emphasizes building and maintaining relationships. In fact, this once went as far as defining women's life roles only in terms of their relationships as wives, mothers, or daughters — as is still the case in more rigid domination cultures.

This socialization to focus on relationships is one of the reasons women leaders can make a special contribution to the creation of a more humane workplace. Of course, men also have a very important role to play, as it will require women and men working in full and equal partnership to move forward.

That a growing number of men (even CEOs of major corporations) are rejecting old stereotypes of masculinity is part of the movement toward partnership. But if more men are finding it possible to adopt "feminine" values and behaviors, it is because the status of women is changing and, with it, men's attitudes toward what is feminine and what is masculine. This is because only when women rise in status do men seem to leave behind the old notion that, at all costs, they must never be like women — as we vividly see in the current trend toward men redefining fathering to include nurturing behaviors stereotypically associated with mothering.

However, here too we must beware of simplistic thinking. Some traits defined as masculine in domination systems, such as conquest, domination, and the suppression of empathy and caring, along with "effeminate" aesthetic sensibility, have stunted men's full human potential. But other qualities that are also stereotypically considered masculine, such as decisiveness, assertiveness, and risk taking, are valuable. And this is so not only in men but also in women, who are still often told that when they exhibit these traits they are not properly feminine.

As Susan G. Butruille writes in "Corporate Caretaking" (1990), women and men are increasingly concerned about workplace policies and practices that support balancing life and work. But since this ethos of corporate caretaking in essence stems from what in domination societies is considered a feminine ethos, this transformation cannot take root unless there are also fundamental redefinitions of stereotypical gender roles, both masculine and feminine.

Moving Forward or Back

That the contemporary movement toward gender equity is an integral part of a larger partnership movement should not surprise us. The domination of one half of humanity by the other half is a basic model for all forms of domination — whether based on racial, ethnic, or other differences. Conversely, the equal valuing of the two halves of humanity teaches children from early on to value diversity, rather than seeing it as grounds for ranking "superiors" over "inferiors."

It is not coincidental that those parts of our world where the movement to raise the status of women has been most successful are also more generally democratic (Inglehart, Norris, & Welzel, 2002). Neither is it coincidental that women are being pushed back to their "traditional" or subordinate place in places where we see regressions to a more rigid and brutal domination system (see, e.g., Eisler, 1987, 2007, 2013) (Table 1).

Yet, ironically, many people who think of themselves as progressives still view the status of women as "just a women's issue." If nothing else, they need to look at the mounting body of empirical evidence demonstrating that what is good for women is good for everyone, and what is bad for women is bad for everyone.

A pioneering study showing this, "Women, Men, and the General Quality of Life," was conducted by the Center for Partnership Studies (CPS), based on two bundles of statistical

Table 1. Partnership and Domination Systems.

Component	Domination System	Partnership System
1. Structure	Authoritarian and inequitable social and economic structure of rigid hierarchies of domination.	Democratic and economically equitable structure of linking and hierarchies of actualization.
2. Relations	High degree of fear, abuse, and violence, from child and wife beating to abuse by "superiors" in families, workplaces, and society.	Mutual respect and trust with low degree of fear and violence, since they are not required to maintain rigid rankings of domination.
3. Gender	Ranking of male half of humanity over female half, as well as of traits and activities viewed as "masculine" over those viewed as "feminine," such as caring and caregiving.	Equal valuing of male and female halves of humanity, as well as high valuing of empathy, caring, caregiving, and nonviolence in women, men, and social and economic policy.
4. Beliefs	Beliefs and stories justify and idealize domination and violence, which are presented as inevitable, moral, and desirable.	Beliefs and stories give high value to empathic, mutually beneficial, and caring relations, which are considered moral and desirable.

Source: Reprinted with permission from Eisler, R. (2007). *The real wealth of nations: Creating a caring economics*, San Francisco: Berrett-Koehler.

data from 89 nations (Eisler, Loye, & Norgaard, 1995) (see appendix). One bundle consisted of measures of a nation's general quality of life, all the way from infant mortality rates and access to potable water to human rights and environmental ratings. The second bundle consisted of measures of the status of women from these 89 nations. It found that the status of women can be a powerful predictor of general quality of life (Eisler et al., 1995).

This study was published in 1995, in time for the UN Women's conference in Beijing. Since then, its findings have been verified by other studies, including the World Economic Forum's Gender Gap Reports, which show that nations with the lowest gender gaps are regularly in the highest ranks of the World Economic Forum's Global Competitiveness Reports (Schwab et al., 2014). So not only does the status of women correlate strongly with general quality of life but also with national economic success.

One reason for these findings is the simple fact that women are half the population. But there are also the additional dynamics we have been examining: that when women are devalued so also are those traits and activities stereotypically associated with women — caregiving, nonviolence, empathy — the very traits and activities needed to build a healthier future.

Tools for Creative Leadership

This takes us to a matter that requires particular attention: the need for thinking outside the box of the old economic models, whether capitalist or socialist. Of course, we should retain the best elements of both markets and government planning. But meeting today's unprecedented economic, environmental, and social challenges requires new economic models, as well as widespread assimilation of mental categories that foster feminine values (Jironet, 2010). It requires economic measurements, policies, and practices that give visibility and real value to the most important human work: the work of caring for people, starting in early childhood, and caring for our natural environment (Eisler, 2007, 2012).

Consider that we are now well into the shift from the industrial to the postindustrial knowledge/service era — a time when economists never tire of telling us that the most important capital is what they like to call "high quality human capital": flexible, innovative people, who can work in teams and not just take orders from above, who can solve problems creatively. We know from neuroscience, not just psychology, that whether or not people develop these capacities heavily hinges on the quality of care and education children receive early on when their very brains are being formed. So we have an unprecedented opportunity to use a purely economic benefit argument for changing the gendered system of values we inherited from more rigid domination times that devalues the "women's work" of caregiving and early childhood education (Eisler, 2007).

The first step is changing how we measure productivity. Our conventional measure, Gross Domestic Product or GDP, includes activities that take life and destroy our natural habitat. Coal burning and cleaning the environmental damage it causes, selling cigarettes and the medical and funeral costs of the health damage they cause, these are on the positive side of GDP. But not only do these measures put negatives on the positive side; they do *not* include the unpaid caregiving work primarily performed by women, be it in their homes, or in their communities as volunteers — even though these services contribute so much to everyone's well-being.

To provide a more accurate way of measuring what is, and is not, productive, the Center for Partnership Studies (CPS) developed Social Wealth Economic Indicators (SWEIs) (De Leon, 2012; De Leon & Boris, 2010; Ghosh, 2014a, 2014b). These new metrics show how quality of life and economic health and competitiveness interrelate to ensure human capacity development — the main ingredient for personal, business, and national success in our new knowledge-service technological era. They bring together data demonstrating the financial and social return on investment in the work of care primarily performed by women for low wages in the market and no remuneration in families — a devaluation that largely accounts for women's disproportionate poverty worldwide.

For example, SWEIs provide data valuing the care work in homes at between 30 and 50 percent of reported GDP. SWEIs also show the ROI from supporting healthy family/employment balance by substantiating the benefits of paid sick leave, paid parental leave, flextime, high quality childcare, and early childhood education (Ghosh, 2014a).

SWEIs were developed as part of CPS's Caring Economy Campaign (www.caringeconomy.org), which also offers online trainings for women and men who want to show how caring policies and practices benefit us all, not only in human terms but also in purely financial terms. These leaderships trainings draw not only from SWEI data but from many other sources; for example, from studies showing that companies that regularly appear on the *Working Mothers* and *Fortune 500* lists of the best companies to work for have a substantially higher return to investors (Burud & Tumolo, 2004; Eisler, 2007).

CPS's leadership and learning programs (http://caringecon-omy.org/onlineclasses/) also provide data showing that nations benefit from investing in more caring policies. To illustrate, let us briefly turn again to nations such as Sweden, Norway, Finland that at the beginning of the twentieth century were so poor that there were famines but that today have low poverty rates and a generally high quality of life for all (Pietila, 2001). Participants in the CPS leadership trainings learn how a major factor in this shift was that these nations instituted caring policies: universal health care, stipends to help families care for children, elder care with dignity, high quality early childhood education, generous paid parental leave for both mothers and fathers.

Here I again want to note that these caring policies did not spring up in vacuum; they came with a cultural shift from the con-figuration of a domination system to the configuration of a part-nership system. And part of this configuration, as we already saw, is a more equal partnership between women and men in *both* the family and the state. So women are 40–50 percent of national legislatures in Sweden, Norway, and Finland. But is not only that women as a bloc tend to vote for more caring policies; as we have seen, when the status of women rises, men no longer feel so threa-tened in their status to also embrace more stereotypically feminine values and priorities such as caring, caregiving, and nonviolence.

Conclusion

I want to close with six levers for systemic change:

1. Use the lens of the partnership-domination continuum to reexamine and re-create organizational and social structures.
2. Bring "women's issues" to where they belong: from the back to the front of the political and economic agenda.
3. Envision and help create a partnership economics that no longer devalues women and stereotypically feminine traits and activities, such as caregiving, nonviolence, and empathy.

4. Use new economic measurements such as SWEIs that demonstrate the social and economic benefits of raising the status of women and of policies that support the work of caregiving stereotypically relegated to women.
5. Develop, support, and disseminate partnership economic inventions such as paid parental leave and caregiver tax credits that give visibility and value to caregiving — whether performed by men or women.
6. Expand women's role in policy-making and form leadership alliances of women and men to work together to shift from domination to partnership — locally, nationally, and internationally.

We need creative leaders who have the courage to step out of their old comfort zones. By this I mean leaders at all levels who use the partnership-domination continuum as the frame for changing thinking, policies, practices, and structures. The old story that our only alternatives are either dominating or being dominated is wrong; as I have briefly sketched in this chapter, there is the partnership alternative as the basis for a healthier, more equitable, way of life.

The shift into the postindustrial era offers an unprecedented window of opportunity for transformative change. As automation, robotics, and artificial intelligence become ever more prevalent, and "work" as conventionally defined becomes ever more scarce, we can, and must, revalue what is and is not productive work.

The issue is not one of money; it is one of social and economic priorities — of what is or is not really valued. We must change these priorities — and give adequate value to the most important human work: the work of caring for people, starting in early childhood, and caring for our natural environment.

Social and economic systems are human creations. They can and will change as we shift further into the postindustrial age. Be it as scholars, educators, leaders, or practitioners, each one of us can play a part in ensuring this change is in the caring and effective partnership direction needed for a healthy world.

References

Abu-Lughod, L. (1986). *Veiled sentiments*. Berkeley, CA: University of California Press.

Aburdene, P., & Naisbitt, J. (1992). *Megatrends for women*. New York, NY: Villard Books.

Benedict, R. (1946). *The chrysanthemum and the sword: Patterns of Japanese culture*. Boston, MA: Houghton Mifflin.

Burud, S., & Tumolo, M. (2004). *Leveraging the new human capital*. Mountain View, CA: Davies-Black.

Butruille, S. G. (1990, April). Corporate caretaking. *Training and Development Journal, 44*(4), 48–55.

Coltrane, S. (1988, March). Father-child relationships and the status of women: A cross-cultural study. *American Journal of Sociology, 93*(5), 1060–1095.

Cooperrider, D. L., & Srivastva, S. (1987). Appreciative inquiry in organizational life. *Research in Organizational Change and Development, 1*, 129–169.

Dawson, J., Kersley, R., & Natella, S. (2014). *The credit Swiss gender 3000*. Zurich: Credit Swiss Research.

De Leon, E. (2012). *National indicators and social wealth*. Washington, DC: Urban Institute.

De Leon, E., & Boris, E. (2010). *The state of society: Measuring economic success and human well-being*. Washington, DC: Urban Institute.

Eisler, R. (1987). *The chalice and the blade: Our history, our future*. San Francisco, CA: Harper & Row.

Eisler, R. (1991). Women, men, and management: Redesigning our future. *Futures, 23*(1), 3–18.

Eisler, R. (1995). *Sacred pleasure: Sex, myth, and the politics of the body*. San Francisco, CA: HarperCollins.

Eisler, R. (1997). Cultural transformation theory: A new paradigm for history. In J. Galtung & S. Inayatullah (Eds.), *Macrohistory and macrohistorians*. Westport, CT: Praeger.

Eisler, R. (2000). *Tomorrow's children: A blueprint for partnership education in the 21st century*. Boulder, CO: Westview Press.

Eisler, R. (2003). Culture, technology, and domination/partnership. In D. Loye (Ed.), *The great adventure*. Albany, NY: State University of New York Press.

Eisler, R. (2007). *The real wealth of nations: Creating a caring economics*. San Francisco, CA: Berrett-Koehler.

Eisler, R. (2012). Economics as if caring matters. *Challenge, 55*(2), 58–86.

Eisler, R. (2013). Protecting the majority of humanity: Toward an integrated approach to crimes against present and future generations. In M. Cordonier Segger & S. Jodoin (Eds.), *Sustainable development, international criminal justice, and treaty implementation*. Cambridge: Cambridge University Press.

Eisler, R. (2014). Human possibilities: The interaction of biology and culture. *Interdisciplinary Journal of Partnership Studies, 1*(1), article 3. Retrieved from https://sites.google.com/a/umn.edu/ijps/home/vol1-iss1-art3

Eisler, R., & Levine, D. S. (2002). Nurture, nature, and caring: We are not prisoners of our genes. *Brain and Mind, 3*(1), 9–52.

Eisler, R., Loye, D., & Norgaard, K. (1995). *Women, men, and the global quality of life*. Pacific Grove, CA: Center for Partnership Studies.

Ghosh, I. (2014a). *Social wealth economic indicators: A new system for evaluating economic prosperity*. Pacific Grove, CA: Center for Partnership Studies.

Ghosh, I. (2014b). Social wealth economic indicators for a caring economy. *Interdisciplinary Journal of Partnership Studies*, *1*(1), article 5. Retrieved from http://pubs.lib.umn.edu/ijps/vol1/iss1/5

Giddens, A. (1984). *The constitution of society*. Berkeley, CA: University of California Press.

Goleman, D., Boyatzis, R., & McKee, A. (2002). *Primal leadership: Realizing the power of emotional intelligence*. Cambridge, MA: Harvard Business School Press.

Helgeson, S. (1990). *The female advantage: Women's ways of leadership*. New York, NY: Doubleday Currency.

Inglehart, R. F., Norris, P., & Welzel, C. (2002). Gender equality and democracy. *Comparative Sociology*, *1*(3–4), 321–346.

Jironet, K. (2010). *Female leadership: Management, Jungian psychology, spirituality and the global journey through purgatory*. New York, NY: Routledge.

Min, J. (Ed.) (1995). *The chalice and the blade in Chinese culture*. Beijing: China Social Sciences Publishing House.

Murdock, G. P. (1969). *Ethnographic atlas*. Pittsburgh, PA: University of Pittsburgh.

Pietila, H. (2001). Nordic welfare society – A strategy to eradicate poverty and build up equality: Finland as a case study. *Journal Cooperation South*, *2*, 79–96.

Sanday, P. R. (1981). *Female power and male dominance: On the origins of sexual inequality*. New York, NY: Cambridge University Press.

Sanday, P. R. (2002). *Women at the center*. Ithaca, NY: Cornell University Press.

Schlegel, S. A. (1998). *Wisdom from a rain forest*. Athens, GA: University of Georgia Press.

Schwab, K., EIde, E. B., Zahidi, S., Bekhouche, Y., Padilla Ugarte, P., Camus, J., & Tyson, L. D. (2014). *The global gender gap report 2014*. Geneva: World Economic Forum.

Senge, P. M. (1990). *The fifth discipline*. London: Century Business.

Textor, R. (1969). *Cross cultural summary*. New Haven, CT: Human Relations Area Files.

Wheatley, M. (2002). *Turning to one another: Simple conversations to restore hope to the future*. San Francisco, CA: Berrett-Koehler.

Appendix

The nine measures used in the study *Women, Men, and the Global Quality of Life* (1995) to assess the degree of gender equity were: the number of literate females for every 100 literate males; female life expectancy as a percentage of male life expectancy; the number of women for every 100 men in parliaments and other governing bodies; the number of females in secondary education for every 100 males; maternal mortality; contraceptive prevalence; access to abortion; and based on measures used by the Population Crisis Committee (now Population Action International), social equality for women and economic equality for women. The 13 measures used to assess quality of life were: overall life expectancy; human rights ratings; access to health care; access to clean water; literacy; infant mortality; number of refugees fleeing the country; the percentage of daily caloric requirements consumed; GDP as a measure of wealth; the percentage of GDP distributed to the poorest 40 percent of households; the ratio of GDP going to the wealthiest versus the poorest 20 percent of the population; and as measures of environmental sensitivity, the percentage of forest habitat remaining, and compliance with the Convention on International Trade in Endangered Species. When exploring the relation between the gender equity and quality of life variables with descriptive, correlational, factor, and multiple regression analyses, the study found a strong systemic correlation between these two measures.

These findings were consistent with the hypothesis that increased equity for women is central to a higher quality of life for a country as a whole, and that gender inequity contracts the opportunities and capabilities, not only of women but of the entire population. The link between gender equity and quality of life was confirmed at a very high level of statistical significance for correlational analysis. Sixty-one correlations at the .001 level with 18 additional correlations at the .05 level were found, for a total of 79 significant correlations in the predicted direction. This link was further confirmed by factor analysis. High factor loadings for gender equity and quality of life variables accounted for 87.8 percent of the variance. Regression analysis also yielded significant results. An R-square of .84, with statistical significance at the .0001 level, provided support for the hypothesis that gender equity is a strong indicator of quality of life.

4

Ecological Consciousness, Moral Imagination, and the Framework for Strategic Sustainable Development

John Eric Baugher, Walter Osika, and
Karl-Henrik Robèrt

D ecades of scientific data irrefutably show that ecosystems on our planet are in decline, largely as a result of unprecedented unsustainable industrial production and consumption by humans. The Millennium Ecosystem Assessment (2005), which was called for in 2000 by United Nations Secretary-General Kofi Annan and based on the work of over 1,360 experts worldwide, concluded that human activity has led to the decline of global fish stocks, created climate change and nutrient pollution threatening water supply and other necessities for billions of people, and has "taken the planet to the edge of a massive wave of species extinctions, further threatening our own well-being" (p. 3). Given the depth of this crisis we are facing, there is an urgency to act swiftly and effectively. According to Lester Brown (2003), founder of the World Watch Institute and Earth Policy Institute, "Throughout history, humans have lived on the Earth's sustainable yield — the interest from its natural endowment. But now we are consuming the endowment itself," and what is required today is "an unprecedented degree of international cooperation to stabilize population, climate, water tables, and soils — and at wartime speed. Indeed, in both scale and urgency the effort required is comparable to U.S. mobilization during World War II" (pp. 25, 28). Brown (2003) pointed to the rapid transformation of the automobile and other industries for wartime production in just a matter of months as evidence that "a society and, indeed, the world can restructure its economy quickly if it is convinced of the need to do so" (p. 29).

In the face of the current ecological crisis, there has been a growing interest in leadership for sustainability as evidenced by the many recent books, symposiums, and executive training programs in the field. Yet as leadership scholar Benjamin Redekop (2011) has observed, "although much has already been written on the general requirements and dimensions of sustainability, much less has been written on the particular processes by which leaders can help make it happen" (p. 244). Due to a lack of strategic sustainability competence, politicians, business leaders, and other decision-makers often engage in reactive measures that, while motivated by good intentions, end up addressing one problem while creating or exacerbating others. As long as measures are not planned and modeled in relation to a robust definition of sustainability, the end result is the further narrowing possibility of viable options for a sustainable future.

In this chapter, we present the Framework for Strategic Sustainable Development (FSSD) as a resource for supporting a paradigm shift from unsustainable to sustainable development (see Ny, MacDonald, Broman, Yamamoto, & Robèrt, 2006; Robèrt, 2002; Robèrt, Broman, & Basile, 2013; Robèrt et al., 2002). We begin by considering how political decision-making often leads to investments that may appear "green" and in the short term have positive benefits for constituents, but due to a lack of systems thinking do not move society toward sustainability over the long term. We use the production of biofuel from corn as an illustrative case of this process. We then present the key dimensions of the FSSD followed by an application of the framework, the ecomunicipality in Whistler, Canada, to illustrate how it has been used to coordinate action among diverse constituents for successful long-term sustainable planning. Central to the FSSD is a robust definition of sustainability and a systematic process for supporting organizations and communities in "backcasting" from an imagined sustainable future based on that definition to allow for strategic planning and rational step-wise action.

Whether one is drawn to use the FSSD in the first place, however, is facilitated by an ecological consciousness (O'Sullivan & Taylor, 2004) and moral imagination (Johnson, 1993) that the framework itself does not provide. We use the reality of climate change denial among conservative politicians and associated think tanks in the United States to reflect on the power of moral identities and cultural frames to limit and enable possibilities for transformational learning and skillful action in relation to the ecological crisis we face. While others have proposed useful strategies for exposing the logical fallacies and other errors of reasoning that inform climate change denial (see, e.g., Diethelm and McKee, 2009), we draw on cognitive science to highlight the need to move beyond the rationalist myth that scientific facts alone can be the basis for motivating cultural change toward sustainability (Lakoff, 2006). Science provides methods for understanding the depth and causes of the ecological crisis, and with that understanding, the conditions that must be met to move organizations, communities, and societies away from unsustainable practices and toward sustainable ones. Yet in the postmodern era, what is accepted as scientific "truth" is contested (see Seidman, 2013). As George Lakoff and Mark Johnson, (1980) have articulated, truth is based on understanding, and what can be understood is fundamentally shaped by cultural metaphors that, consciously and unconsciously, structure experience and guide actions.

When we speak of metaphors or metaphoric understanding in this chapter, we are not simply referring to figures of speech, but to deep cognitive structures that shape how one reasons, what one is able to know as true, and in turn, what one sees as reasonable courses of action. Central to our concern is how metaphors of "freedom" construct understandings of the nature of, and relations among, self, society, and environment (see Lakoff, 2006). For climate change deniers in the United States, freedom is premised upon an atomistic, individualistic, and competitive construction of the human, an absolutist faith in the morality of market forces, and a fundamental opposition toward the state, the United Nations, or any other governing body passing environmental regulations that restrict what is perceived as one's "right" to pursue one's economic interests (McCright & Dunlap, 2010). In our view, such an understanding of freedom reflects a failure of moral imagination grounded in metaphoric thinking that does not truthfully represent the conditions necessary for the survival and flourishing of life on the planet. Garrett

Hardin (1968) pointed to "the tragedy of the commons" decades ago, how in the context of an expanding population, individuals pursuing their own short-term economic interests harms all in the long term. In this way, businesses and communities choosing to use the FSSD framework to guide their activities can be thought of as a form of enlightened self-interest.

Political Decision-Making and the Systems Thinking Iceberg

There are no easy solutions to the current ecological crisis. What is clear is that humanity cannot continue on the path of reacting to problems one by one as if the sustainability challenge were simply a collection of isolated issues that could be fixed one after the other. A prime example of the need for systems thinking is the production of biofuel from corn. In the mid-2000s, corn-based ethanol was presented by then president of the United States, George W. Bush and others in industry and government, as a "solution" to oil dependency with predictions that it would "replace gasoline consumption" (Bush, 2006; CBS News, 2006; The Monitor's View, 2006). Consequently, large sums of public funds were invested in the face of intensive lobbying ($5.7 billion in tax credits in the United States in 2006; The Monitor's View, 2006), and little was said about how to produce ethanol without competing with food production or how to make use of the many ethanol-factories once automobiles are switched, for example, to solar-powered electricity.

The problems with corn-based ethanol are many. While biofuel seemed like a move away from fossil fuel use, a systems perspective shows that "the fossil fuel energy used to grow the corn using modern farming methods offsets most of the energy in the fuel, essentially making corn ethanol into another form of fossil fuel" (Stayton, 2015, p. 153). The use of biofuels produced from other food crops such as sugar cane and soybeans may, under certain conditions, emit even more net carbon than using petroleum fuels (Conca, 2014). From whatever source, biofuels also do not address the fundamental issue of the poor efficiency of heat engines (25–35 percent), which requires burning three to four times more fossil fuel energy than the electricity and motive power energy that is produced (Stayton, 2015, p. 240). Biofuels also do not address the inefficiency of the whole fuel sector (sourcing, transport, refineries, gas stations), which can be bypassed when electricity becomes the norm energy for the traffic sector. Perhaps most troubling is the moral issue created by corn-based ethanol production — rising food costs in a world where millions are underfed. From 2003 to 2008, for example, there was a 50 percent increase in the cost of U.S. corn following a large expansion of corn-to-ethanol production in 2003–2004 (Petrou & Pappis, 2009). One recent survey suggested that increased biofuel production accounted for 20–40 percent of food price increases in 2007 and 2008, a time when the price of many crops doubled (Stayton, 2015, p. 153). Additional unintended effects of the turn toward fuel crops has been clear-cutting forests, over-pumping aquifers, increased use of chemical fertilizers, and other destructive farming practices (Conca, 2014).

As the example of biofuels illustrates, moving toward a sustainable future requires breaking through the "functional silo syndrome" (Ensor, 1988) and engaging in systems thinking that takes into consideration the short- and long-term ecological and social consequences of potential courses of action and then finds the most strategic and economic routes to get there. Systems thinking in practice builds on collaborative work that avoids the reactive process of blaming others for discrete events, acknowledges interdependencies, and engages in generative dialogue to apprehend deeper causes behind patterns of behavior (Senge, Smith, Kruschwitz, Laur, & Schley, 2010). Crucial to engaging in generative dialogue is having a shared framework for organizing data into pictures that are relevant for decision-making in different organizational and institutional contexts. Without such a framework, debilitating power struggles and decision paralysis are likely, or what Peter Senge (2006) calls "political decision making," referring to "situations where factors other than the intrinsic merits of alternative courses of action weigh in making decisions" (p. 60). The Iowa Renewable Fuels Association, for example, seeks to "educate" political candidates about the benefits of biofuels, enlisting farmers to help "keep the pressure" on candidates eager to win electoral votes in Iowa, the first state to hold U.S. presidential primary elections every four years (Lucht, 2015; Notaras, 2011). The message the group promotes focuses largely on the short-term economic benefits to Iowans of investment in crop fuel production, although materials on their website also claim that biofuels are crucial to solving the country's "dependence on foreign oil" and are "one of the easiest options to protect student health."[1] The sorrows of the discourse around biofuels are not that all science is lacking; the tailpipes of school buses burning biodiesel do emit less carbon monoxide and other harmful emissions than buses burning petroleum diesel. But a lack of systems thinking allows biofuel investment to be presented as the "green" choice in a binary manner in contrast with the interests of "Big Oil" (Page, 2015), rather than introducing biofuels as a step toward sustainably produced energy for transportation (see Stayton, 2015).

Systems thinking allows us to understand how the most obvious "solutions" to problems, which may seem to have positive consequences in the short term, often reinforce underlying system dynamics that in the long run make those problems more intractable (Meadows, 2008; Senge, 2006). Drawing on the metaphor of a "systems thinking iceberg," Senge and his colleagues (2010) point to the increased leveraging for transformational change that comes from moving beyond surface explanations of discrete events to understand the trends, systemic structures, and cultural assumptions underlying the ecological crisis (p. 174). From this perspective, current efforts to "save" or "protect" the environment are akin to "bailing out the *Titanic* with teaspoons" (Hawkins, 1993, p 5) to the extent that they involve responding to this or that issue without addressing the deeper, interconnected causes of the crisis.

The Framework for Strategic Sustainable Development

The FSSD builds a bridge between science and decision-makers in business, government, and other sectors by offering (a) a robust definition of sustainability that provides a clear objective to head toward and (b) a systematic process for "backcasting" from that imagined future to allow for strategic planning and rational step-wise action and collaboration across organizations and institutions. The FSSD has been developed over a 25-year period through a rigorous scientific consensus process including numerous consultations and iterations amongst top scientists,

---

[1]See the various press releases and other promotional materials of the IRFA at http://www.iowarfa.org/index.php

thinkers, and business executives from across the world. This consensus process elaborated four basic socio-ecological principles or boundary conditions for social and ecological sustainability as follows:

In a sustainable society, nature is not subject to systematically increasing

1. concentrations of substances extracted from the earth's crust (such as heavy metals and fossil CO_2 from fuel fumes),
2. concentrations of substances produced by society (such as PCBs and dioxins), or
3. degradation by physical means (such as overharvesting or irrigation causing declining water tables).
   Likewise, in a sustainable society,
4. People's trust is not systematically eroded by structural obstacles to health, influence, competence, impartiality, and meaning-making.

The first three of these principles are derived from the natural sciences, whereas the fourth is grounded in social science and is explored by studying overriding mechanisms for erosion of trust — the glue of the social web (see Missimer, 2015). The intention behind the framework is not to proscribe a particular moral order; whether we want the civilization to go on or not cannot be determined scientifically. But if an *ecological consciousness* that acknowledges humanity's fundamental embeddedness in nested social contexts and natural ecosystems, from which our well-being and life itself are inseparable, leads us to make this choice (see O'Sullivan & Taylor, 2004), we can ask science to tell about the conditions that must be met for this value-based intention to be realized. In this way, science can offer a useful resource for members of organizations, communities, and other social groupings to realize their own intentions to live and work sustainably.

A systematic process to help people jointly apply the above principles has been developed and utilized in many business, corporate, municipal, urban, and academic contexts (see Ny et al., 2006; Robèrt, 2002; Robèrt et al., 2013). This process is referred to in the literature as the ABCD process and includes (A) discussing with participants the *basic principles* of sustainability, and what they imply as boundary conditions for any vision or joint venture they may dream of; (B) assessing current challenges and strengths of one's organization in relation to the desired objective of sustainability; (C) brainstorming possible *steps and solutions* that would comply with the sustainability objective and its underlying principles; and (D) setting in motion *concrete actions* as part of a step-wise transition plan, where early actions and investments are prioritized to strike a balance between short-term interests (e.g., income) and pace toward the objective. To make the most of any particular tool, its use should be put in the context of the above outlined strategy. This means laying on the table the gap between how an organization looks today and how it will look in a sustainable society, designing the overall strategic plan to bridge that gap, and only then selecting and designing the tools that will be needed (Robèrt et al., 2002). Finally, it is when the basic principles of sustainability are understood that value-based polarities can be inspirational and further creativity and collaboration regarding the design of sustainability goals and the choice of transition paths to move toward such ends.

To illustrate the importance of distinguishing among these steps in the process of strategic sustainable development, consider again the example of biofuel production. Renewable energy is often inaccurately described as a principle of sustainability. Switching to renewable energy may be aligned with sustainability principles and something an organization or society might opt to do. But if done incorrectly, for example, through widespread deforestation by excessive biofuel production (Conca, 2014), or through utilizing corn as biofuel such that food prices increase (Petrou & Pappis, 2009), there would be conflicts with the third and fourth sustainability principles outlined above. What tangibly occurs in practice must not be conflated with the strategies of how to arrive at the objectives. Again, without such systems thinking, we risk trying to solve one problem while creating another.

Whistler, Canada: An Early Role Model for Sustainable Communities

By 2000, the Canadian Resort Municipality of Whistler had made significant progress in committing to sustainable development and had begun building community partnerships, but in 2000, municipal leaders began looking for a clearer way of planning and communicating this new priority with the broader community and, in particular, with local businesses. As with most communities, there were so many interests, so many diverging wants and needs that it was hard to develop a common approach for sustainability.

The municipality joined with key stakeholders and businesses, and together they learned about the FSSD and applied the framework to engage the broader community and deepen awareness of the challenges and opportunities presented by sustainability. In 2005, the community then developed Whistler 2020 (RMOW, 2005), a long-term community sustainability plan that represented a mid-way point on its vision to become a sustainable community by 2060. Whistler 2020 is not a municipal plan; it is a community-wide sustainability plan, representing a partnership between the municipality and over 60 stakeholders in the community. This plan has won numerous awards, including the Federation of Canadian Municipalities national award for sustainable community planning and the UNEP LivCom award for best long range planning. The Whistler 2020 website (www.whistler2020.ca) also won an innovation award from the Canadian Association of Municipal Administrators.

Whistler developed a vision of success in a sustainable future, framed by the four FSSD sustainability principles. It chose 18 issues to include in its holistic sustainability plan and developed task forces for each issue area, which included affordable housing, energy, water, education, recreation, and transportation. After training in the FSSD, each task force asked themselves the following questions: Where are we today relative to those four sustainability principles? What does success mean for energy, water, etc. in a sustainable society informed by the four principles? What actions could take us toward our description of success in the short-, medium-, and long-term?

Whistler's approach to energy planning exemplifies how a set of principles and a robust decision-making framework can improve how decisions are made for sustainability. Faced with increasing energy needs, extreme pressures on the existing infrastructure, and the need to prepare for the 2010 Olympics, Whistler asked its energy supplier Terasen Gas Inc. to propose a solution. Terasen proposed building a 6-inch high-pressure natural gas pipeline with the ability to supply up to 20,000 GJ/day to Whistler, which would replace its propane system and cost $43 million, amortized over 50 years. At first glance, it seemed like a good investment: Natural gas has less carbon per energy unit than propane, so greenhouse gas emissions would go down. Whistler, nonetheless, turned down the proposal, because its vision of energy success implied being free of fossil fuels by 2060. Investing in the proposed natural gas pipeline would require increasing usage to make it affordable, putting demands on more investments at the user's side of energy delivery, which, in turn, would tie up capital for inherently unsustainable practices for 50 years. Using the FSSD framework, Whistler realized that the natural gas pipeline, while attractive in the short term, was not a flexible platform for future improvements and ultimately would not lead the municipality toward its vision of success. This breakthrough in thinking led Terasen to propose a smaller natural gas pipeline to serve as an intermediate solution as well as creating a locally owned utility to develop capacity for geothermal district heating, along with other renewable solutions that would meet Whistler's description of energy success. Whistler won the Olympic bid, according to Mayor Ken Melamed, largely because of their clear and sophisticated view on sustainability. Whistler has taken numerous similar actions, including significant achievements in waste reduction, watershed management and land-use planning, green building, affordable housing, and public transportation.

Following Whistler's lead, other communities in North America are using the FSSD to develop community sustainability plans and to engage stakeholders to develop a shared vision of sustainability and a shared way of moving step by step in the right direction.[2] Canadian examples include the District of North Vancouver, the town of Canmore, the towns of Olds, Aidrie, Pincher Creek, Thorhild, Chauvin and Clairesholm, Alberta, the city of Halifax, and the town of Wolfville, NS. In the United States, a number of cities and towns have become "eco-municipalities" that aspire to develop an ecologically, economically, and socially healthy community for the long term, using the FSSD as a guide, and a democratic, highly participative

---

[2]Similar developments are taking place in Europe. In Sweden, for example, where the FSSD has its roots, there are currently 100 municipalities and cities gathered in an eco-municipality association (SEKOM), where the FSSD is acknowledged as the overriding and unifying framework for sustainable development. Another example is how the corporation Philips, using the FSSD for sustainable development as well as innovation, has asked the city of Eindhoven to join the network of FSSD-informed cities and municipalities. Eindhoven, where Philips has its head office, is applying the FSSD for cross-sector community building towards sustainability.

development process as the method (see James and Lahti, 2004). These municipalities include the cities of Madison, Ashland, Washburn, Bayfield, Marshfield, LaCrosse, Jefferson County and Johnson Creek, Wisconsin, Vandergrift and Pittsburg, Pennsylvania, Lawrence Township, New Jersey, Portsmouth, New Hampshire, Duluth, Minnesota, and Corvalis, Oregon.

In 2000, the American Planning Association, an independent not-for-profit educational organization in the United States whose mission is to "provide leadership in the planning of vital communities," adopted the four sustainability principles of FSSD as the foundational objectives for their Policy Guide on Planning for Sustainability.[3] While this is a promising development, we notice that among the current eco-municipalities in the United States none is located in southern states raising sociological questions regarding the potential barriers to widespread strategic sustainable development.

Moral Imagination, Climate Change Denial, and the "American Way of Life"

A formidable barrier to sustainable development in the United States has been the concerted effort by industry groups, conservative Republican politicians, and associated "think tanks" to deny the scientific consensus on the human impact on climate change (Dunlap and Jacques, 2013; Freudenburg, Gramling, & Davidson, 2008; McCright & Dunlap, 2003, 2010; Oreskes & Conway, 2010).[4] Such "denialism," or the "employment of rhetorical arguments to give the appearance of legitimate debate where there is none" (Diethelm and McKee, 2009, p. 2; see also Schroyer, 2006), has been motivated largely by the perceived threat climate research poses to the "free market" prerogatives of corporations to pursue profits without regard for environmental impacts. The Heartland Institute, for example, a think tank whose stated mission is "to discover, develop, and promote free-market solutions to social and

---

[3]See https://www.planning.org/policy/guides/pdf/sustainability.pdf

[4]Here, we use climate change denial as an example of a barrier to sustainable development, although one should keep in mind that the FSSD view of unsustainability is not limited to human-induced climate change, nor do we take a stance here on whether this or that impact from inherently unsustainable actions is already a fact or will occur only later.

economic problems," seeks to "educate" politicians and the general public that "There is no need to reduce carbon dioxide emissions and no point in attempting to do so," since, as the group claims, "carbon dioxide is [not] a pollutant."[5] On the organization's website is a list of endorsements including 20 politicians, all republicans, including Jim DeMint, U.S. Senator from South Carolina, who praises the organization for promoting free market capitalism, "a priceless, God-given right," in the face of "the socialist agenda threatening America." Another endorser is James Inhofe, Senator from Oklahoma, who claims that "man-made global warming is the greatest hoax ever perpetuated on the American people" (McCright & Dunlap, 2010, p. 122). For Inhofe, it is an article of faith that "man can't change the climate" and that it is "arrogant" to think otherwise. In January 2015, he and other members of the Republican-controlled U.S. Senate voted down a bill acknowledging that climate change is real and significantly affected by human activity (Cockerham, 2015).

Climate change deniers among U.S. political leaders and in the general population more widely are predominately conservative white males (McCright & Dunlap, 2011). Some have ties to the fossil fuels industry, although what drives the reactionary denial and disregard of the boundary conditions for sustainability is not primarily economic interest, but a *self-identity* based on short-term and non-systems thinking. Just as the attacks of 9/11 challenged the "First Worldism" of the United States, "the loss of the prerogative, only and always, to be the one who transgresses the sovereign boundaries of other states, but never to be in the position of having one's own boundaries transgressed" (Butler, 2003, p. 27), so too does climate impact science challenge the ontological security of those with an unreflexive faith in technology, material abundance, unilateralism, and free market capitalism. In both cases, the response has been a reactionary attempt to shore up the certitude and rightness of one's identity and realize a "fantasy of mastery" that with enough force and will power one can create reality as one pleases and without regard for ecological or social boundary conditions (Butler, 2003, p. 18; McCright & Dunlap, 2010, p. 105, 127). Epitomizing this rigid, unreflexive stance is the statement made to the Earth Summit in 1992 by then-president of the United States, George H.W. Bush,

---

[5]https://www.heartland.org/policy-documents/global-warming-crisis-over

that "the American way of life is not up for negotiation" (Schroyer, 2009, p. 39).

The concept of *moral imagination* can illuminate what makes the paradigm shift to an ecological consciousness possible for some and seemingly beyond the pale for others who cling ever more strongly to denial and other habitual tendencies of narrow self-protection. Our capacities for reflection, awareness, and moral reasoning are central to our nature as humans, and as cognitive science makes clear, we engage such capacities first and foremost through narrative understanding (Lakoff, 2006). Moral reasoning involves imagining different possibilities in our present situation playing out and choosing among them based on how well they allow us to live out a narrative of a meaningful and significant life (Johnson, 1993). This focus on the narrative dimension of moral reasoning resonates with the work of Ronald Heifetz and his colleagues' (2009, p. 20) view that challenges are 'adaptive' *when they threaten an important part of the story we tell about ourselves*. What is it about the "American way of life" that is so resistant to change in the face of increasingly dire consequences global climate change will have for human civilization including massive forced migrations and an increasing number of people killed, made homeless, or otherwise affected by floods, droughts, and other hydrometeorological disasters (see Roberts & Parks, 2007; WHO, 2014)? And most important from the perspective of adaptive change, what cultural resources are precious and worth preserving and extending into the future (see Heifetz, Grashow, & Linsky, 2009, p. 23) as ways of thinking inherited from the past become increasingly out of sync with new social, economic, and ecological realities (see Scharmer & Kaufer, 2013)?

The American way of life as understood by climate change deniers centers on particular notions of freedom and individual responsibility linked to an absolute faith in the unregulated market as an inherently moral institution (Lakoff, 2006). Freedom from this perspective is constructed negatively as a freedom from constraint, namely, the constraint of government-imposed environmental regulations that restrict one's "right" to pursue one's economic interests without regard for the impact of one's actions on ecosystems, other species, or others humans, including those yet to be born. Individual responsibility from this perspective is one's obligation to take care of oneself, or at most, one's nuclear family, which one does through seeking one's own economic interest in competition with others. Competition implies that there are winners and losers, but since unregulated market processes are seen as inherently moral, whether one wins or loses in the market is seen as a moral outcome. For those who hold a faith in the (God-given) rightness of the market, it is difficult to see the impact of one's "freedom" on other humans, other species, or the ecosystems that support life on the planet.

Crucial to overcoming the immunity to change unsustainable ways of living is cultivating the capacity to "see our seeing" (Senge, Scharmer, Jaworski & Flowers, 2004), to "look at" not just "look through" our metaphoric ways of knowing (Kegan & Lahey, 2009, p. 50). As Lakoff (2006) writes, we need a "higher rationality" that does not reduce the "American way of life" and the foundational commitment to "freedom" to a singular political ideology, but instead gives us the "deepest form of freedom — the freedom that comes from knowing your own mind" (p. 15). As he explained,

> If you are unaware of your own deep frames and metaphors, then you are unaware of the basis for your moral and political choices. Moreover, your deep frames and metaphors define the range within which your "free will" operates. You can't will something that is outside your capacity to imagine (pp. 15–16).

Freedom is precious not only to Americans, but to all of humanity, including generations who have not yet been born. As we discuss below, both the modern West and indigenous cultures offer resources for knowing our own minds and for imagining freedom in ways that support human flourishing and planetary well-being.

Discussion and Conclusions

In this chapter, we have stressed the need for systems thinking in the face of the ecological crisis on the planet. The FSSD offers a definition of sustainable development and a decision-making process for addressing the scientifically derived basic and universal challenges of shifting organizations, communities, and societies away from destructive processes of production and consumption toward environmentally sustainable ones. That process involves envisioning how one's organization, community, or society would look in a sustainable future, and then backcasting from that vision to create a path to move toward that vision in the short-, medium-, and long-term. Yet the paradigm shift from unsustainable to sustainable development is fundamentally an "adaptive" challenge requiring changes in "norms, beliefs, habits, and loyalties" (Heifetz et al., 2009, p. 19). As the reality of climate change denial among political elites in the United States reveals, the value of the FSSD is contingent upon whether those with decision-making authority respect the validity of scientific knowledge, cultivate the capacity to remain open and flexible (rather than closing down and becoming defensive in the face of perceived threats to their self-identities), and commit to refuse to do harm to the social and ecological conditions that sustain life on the planet (see Baugher, 2014; pp. 84–85, Fröding & Osika, 2015, Gelles, 2015).

The scientific facts regarding anthropogenic climate change and other harmful consequences of unsustainable production and consumption do not speak for themselves. Rather, the capacity of individuals and social groupings to see, much less respond skillfully to, the dire consequences of unsustainable ways of living is shaped by the cognitive frames offered by one's culture, the power of which resides largely in them being taken-for-granted (Lakoff, 2006). A central barrier to sustainable development in the United States is a particular construction of "freedom" premised upon an atomistic, individualistic, and competitive construction of the human and an absolutist faith in the morality of market forces (McCright & Dunlap, 2010). Such fundamentalism notwithstanding, we see no inherent contradiction between acknowledging the value of market principles and living into the sustainability principles outlined above, and in fact, many have argued the "business-case" of improving environmental performance (see, e.g., Finster & Hernke, 2014). From this perspective, and in contrast to the short-term and non-systems thinking view of self-interest, cooperation across value chains and with other stakeholder groups to arrive at dignified goals for the common good could be described as "enlightened self-interest." Such a focus on the common good may serve an ecological consciousness that allows us to apprehend that the "benefits" to our well-being of healthy, vibrant forests, oceans, air, soil, and the like are more fundamental than can be expressed by current market principles.

A recent volume on sustainability leadership concluded that "one of the great unsolved questions of the new millennium is really one of the oldest: how to reconcile individual rights and freedoms with the needs and requirements of 'the group' and by extension its shared resources and habitat" (Redekop, 2011,

p. 215). In our view, such oppositions between individual and society, self-interest and the environment, reflect a failure of moral imagination grounded in metaphoric thinking that does not truthfully represent the conditions necessary for human flourishing and planetary well-being. Both the modern West and indigenous cultures offer resources for reconciling self-interest and environmental necessity. Drawing on Buddhist and other indigenous sources, Arne Naess, Joanna Macy, and other deep ecologists conceive of the self as inseparable from the wider environment (e.g., the forests are our lungs, they are just outside of our body), such that environmental protection is no more altruistic than is caring for one's own body (see Wenz, 2001, pp. 222–225; Macy & Johnstone, 2012). Deep ecologists offer an alternative narrative of the self to the modern view of the atomistic individual only responsible to himself. Modern Western liberalism likewise offers resources for ecological thinking, if only we can remember these sources. As political scientist Thomas Spragens (1995) explains, it is anachronistic to reduce the notion of freedom to the right to pursue one's interest in the market, since liberal thinkers prior to the 19th century understood the prerogative to pursue individual economic interest "within the context of a commitment to 'the common good', for which societies are instituted" (p. 44). The individual, as conceived by John Locke, John Stuart Mill, Adam Smith, and other modern liberal thinkers, "enjoyed his or her freedom only within the context of complementary obligations, deriving from communal attachments and obligations, from the restraints of a valid moral order, and from the force of human sympathy" (Spragens, 1995, p. 43).

It is beyond the scope of this chapter to compare and contrast the power of an environmental stewardship ethic versus other frameworks for reconceiving relationships among self, society, and environment (see Larson, 2011; Ostrom, 1990; Schroyer, 2009; Wenz, 2001). What cognitive and social sciences make clear, however, is that cultural frames structure experience and shape how one reasons and attributes meaning to different courses of action. Our freedom to make wise choices, then, depends on our capacity for reflexivity, the ability to see what is implicit in our seeing, and to consider the merits of other ways of seeing. We make two further points in this regard. First, the capacity for reflexivity is not only a meta-cognitive skill, but an emotionally embodied capacity since disruptions in previous ways of looking at the world can produce anxiety and other uncomfortable emotions. A central component of sustainability leadership, then, involves attuning to the existential dimension of transformative change and the capacity to create contemplative spaces that support people through the painful process of apprehending the disjuncture between "the illusions we live by in contrast to the realities we live in" (see McGrane, 1994, p. 63). Individual contemplative practices may therefore be crucial for sustainability leadership. Recent findings from neuroscience show that it is possible to change both the structure and function of the brain (Ricard, Lutz, & Davidson, 2014; Woollett & Maguire, 2011) and that such changes can be accompanied by increased cognitive flexibility, resilience, self-awareness, compassion toward one self and others, and sensitivity to context (see Fröding & Osika, 2015; Gelles, 2015, Jankowski & Holas, 2014), capacities that may be crucial in developing moral imagination and ecological consciousness.

Second, we would like to turn a reflexive lens back on the foundational metaphor of the FSSD: sustainable development. Some scholars suggest that the metaphor of "development" is suspect because it invokes a productive mode of being that is a central cause of the ecological crisis (see, e.g., Larson, 2011, p. 49). We are sensitive to this concern, yet we distinguish sustainable *development* from the expansion of material outputs. Growth without limits premised on the fear of scarcity is the "the mythical condition under which the modern western way of life was formed" and is now being globalized (Schroyer, 2009, p. 39), whereas all complex systems, including human society within the biosphere, are subject to boundary conditions that place limits on physical growth. In contrast, development focusing on expansion of real value that improves the human condition in terms of health, education, human connectedness and the like is unlimited. This understanding of sustainable development resonates with the post-materialist shift beyond the limited focus on Gross Domestic Product toward qualitative growth of such dimensions as community vitality, democratic engagement, and ecological diversity and resilience (see Samuel G. Wilson, in this volume). We presented the case of the ecomunicipality of Whistler in the chapter precisely to show this qualitative dimension of development as well as to illustrate a practical application of creative, collaborative systems thinking.

We recognize that violations of the sustainability principles outlined in the FSSD are the unintended consequences of the sum of actions and practices from many nested actors of society. Organizations seeking to move toward sustainability using the

FSSD, therefore, cannot only look at their respective internal activities, and whether those violate the sustainability principles. Instead, what is needed in terms of leadership are the analytic skills and capacities to draw conclusions regarding sustainability-related challenges, opportunities, and desirable transition paths within organizations and across value chains and other stakeholder groups. How, for example, could a business truly be sustainable if, by necessity, all of its goods were shipped through current unsustainable means of transportation? As illustrated by the Whistler case, the FSSD is most powerful as a resource for widespread societal change when it serves as a shared mental model for community building among diverse stakeholder groups. Without such a shared framework, individual organizations using the FSSD often find themselves not moving as fast as wanted, sub-optimizing their own pace toward sustainability, because others are sub-optimizing theirs. Among other examples, the Green Charge project in the south of Sweden, likewise, illustrates how the FSSD is being used for multi-stakeholder community building, including not only business but also municipalities, cities, and politicians (see Borén, Nurhadi, & Ny, 2013; Robèrt, Borén, Ny, & Broman, 2015).

The problems of sustainability in the current global capitalist system result from interrelated patterns of unsustainable *production* and *consumption*. One way this reality of interconnectedness is being addressed in industry is in terms of "product service systems" (PSS), a business model that offers a mix of products and services to meet the needs of customers without necessarily selling a tangible product (e.g., providing heat for a building without selling a radiator). Crucial to the eco-efficiency of PSS are innovative interactions among multiple stakeholders that allow greater needs to be met through lower resource utilization (see Vezzoli, Kohtalo & Srinivasan, 2014).[6] PSS were first introduced in industrial settings, although creative applications exist today in relation to retail consumers, such as the Local Food Van Link in Skye, Scotland, through which a van shared by 40 farmers links producers, caterers, retailers, and consumers in delivering organically and sustainably grown food in a sustainable way (Vezzoli et al., 2014, p. 75). As this example illustrates, how a product is transported is interconnected with what that product

---

[6]The FSSD lends itself well, as a shared mental model, when PSS is used to arrive at sustainable services (see Thompson, 2012).

is and how it is produced. The Food Van Link is able to work on the island of Skye precisely because the people of the island have a taste for fresh, locally grown, seasonal vegetables. And as the case of food more widely illustrates, the sustainability of any PSS initiative depends on what consumers desire and how much they desire. Such desires are not formed in a vacuum.

Corporations are arguably the most powerful institution in late modern industrial societies such as the United States (Derber, 1998), and much of their power to shape dominate cultural frames is the many billions of dollars spent on advertising (Schor, 2004). This dynamic can be seen in the fast food industry where massive advertising campaigns totaling more than $4.6 billion in 2012, including direct advertising to children (Yale Rudd Center, 2013), create desires for portions of meat and other products with addictive salt-sugar-fat combinations that are harmful to the health of individuals, communities, and the planet. The rhetoric of the food industry suggests that children and other consumers simply need to make wiser choices (see, e.g., Achbar, Abbot, & Bakan, 2003), yet such a surface view of events does not acknowledge the systems thinking iceberg; namely the deeper trends, systemic structures, and cultural assumptions underlying the related ecological and public health crises we face (see Schor, 2004; Senge et al., 2010). The FSSD can be helpful in moving us beyond such an impasse.

As we outlined above and illustrated with the Whistler case, the FSSD does not view development in terms of the expansions of material outputs, but instead as the expansion of real value. Most precious among all human values is health, including the health of individuals and the health of ecosystems that support life on the planet. We have used the reality of climate change denial in the United States to highlight how the shift toward a sustainability mindset requires the capacity to critique dominate cultural frames and the moral imagination and courage to allow unsustainable practices and ways of being, however cherished, to die. One set of such practices is the massive, strategic, and persistent corporate marketing activities that contribute to destructive overconsumption and the creation of "artificial value" through "projecting pleasurable images onto the products they sell" (see Payutto, 2002, p. 77). The industrial production and marketing of sickening foods threatens the health of humanity across the globe with 600 million humans obese in 2014 and with obesity now linked with more deaths per year than being underweight (see WHO, 2015). Most of the excess calories humanity now consumes compared to a few decades ago come from one, highly government subsidized, source — corn. Systems thinking allows us to see the sorrows of the production of biofuels from corn. The massive consumption of corn syrup is likewise out of sync with the boundary conditions for a healthy humanity and a healthy planet. And it is no irony that the same individualistic notion of freedom and lack of moral imagination which undergirds climate change denial likewise defends direct marketing of sickening products to children. May we develop an enlightened understanding of self-interest and freedom that supports the health and flourishing of all children, including those yet to be born.

References

Achbar, M., Abbot, J., & Bakan, J. (2003). *The corporation*. Zeitgeist Films.

Baugher, J. E. (2014). Sociological mindfulness and leadership education. In K. Goldman Schuyler, J. E. Baugher, K. Jironet, & L. Lid-Falkman (Eds.), *Leading with spirit, presence, and authenticity* (pp. 79–89). San Francisco, CA: Jossey Bass.

Borén, S., Nurhadi, L., & Ny, H. (2013, August). How can fossil fuel based public bus transport systems become a sustainable solution for Swedish medium-sized cities? *Poster session presented at LCM 2013: 6th international conference on life cycle management in Gothenburg, Sweden*. Retrieved from http://green-charge.se/wp-content/uploads/2014/06/Bus-study-poster-LCM-2013.pdf

Brown, L. R. (2003). Rescuing a planet under stress: Rising to the challenge. *The Futurist*, 37(6), 25–29.

Bush, G. W. (2006). Bush delivers speech on renewable fuel resources. *Congressional Quarterly Transcriptions*. April 25. Retrieved from http://www.washingtonpost.com/wp-dyn/content/article/2006/04/25/AR2006042500762.html. Accessed on June 29, 2015.

Butler, J. (2003). Violence, mourning, politics. *Studies in Gender and Sexuality*, 4(1), 9–37.

CBS News. (2006). The ethanol solution: Could corn-based fuel help end America's dependence on imported oil? *60 Minutes*, May 4. Retrieved from http://www.cbsnews.com/news/the-ethanol-solution/. Accessed on June 27, 2015.

Cockerham, S. (2015). In 50-49 vote, US senate says climate change is not caused by humans. *Bangor Daily News*, January 22. Retrieved from http://bangordailynews.com/2015/01/22/politics/senate-not-ready-to-tie-climate-change-to-mankind/. Accessed on July 17, 2015.

Conca, J. (2014, April 20). It's final — Corn ethanol is of no use. *Forbes*, 2014. Retrieved from http://www.forbes.com/sites/jamesconca/2014/04/20/its-final-corn-ethanol-is-of-no-use/. Accessed on June 27, 2015.

Derber, C. (1998). *Corporation nation: How corporations are taking over our lives and what we can do about it*. New York, NY: St. Martin's Press.

Diethelm, P., & McKee, M. (2009). Denialism: What it is and how scientists should respond. *European Journal of Public Health, 19*(1), 2−4.

Dunlap, R. E., & Jacques., P. J. (2013). Climate change denial books and conservative think tanks: Exploring the connection. *American Behavioral Scientist, 57*(6), 699−731.

Ensor, P. (1988). The functional silo syndrome. AME Target, p. 16.

Finster, M. P., & Hernke, M. T. (2014). Benefits organizations pursue when seeking competitive advantage by improving environmental performance. *Journal of Industrial Ecology, 18*(5), 652−662. doi:10.1111/jiec.12106

Freudenburg, W. R., Gramling, R., & Davidson, D. J. (2008). Scientific certainty argumentation methods (SCAMs). *Sociological Inquiry, 78,* 2−38.

Fröding, B., & Osika, W. (2015). *Neuroenhancement: How mental training and meditation can promote epistemic virtue.* New York, NY: Springer International Publishing.

Gelles, D. (2015). *Mindful work: How meditation is changing business from the inside out.* Boston, MA: Houghton Mifflin Harcourt.

Hardin, G. (1968). The tragedy of the commons. *Science, 162,* 1243−1248.

Hawkins, P. (1993). *The ecology of commerce: A declaration of sustainability.* New York, NY: HarperCollins Publishers.

Heifetz, R., Grashow, A., & Linsky, M. (2009). *The practice of adaptive leadership: Tools and tactics for changing your organization and the world.* Boston, MA: Harvard Business Press.

James, S., & Lahti., T. (2004). *The natural step for communities: How cities and towns can change to sustainable practices.* Gabriola Island, BC: New Society Publishers.

Jankowski, T., & Holas, P. (2014). Metacognitive model of mindfulness. *Conscious Cognition, 2014*(28), 64−80.

Johnson, M. (1993). *Moral imagination: Implications of cognitive science for ethics.* Chicago, IL: University of Chicago Press.

Kegan, R., & Lahey, L. L. (2009). *Immunity to change: How to overcome it and unlock potential in yourself and your organization.* Boston, MA: Harvard Business Press.

Lakoff, G. (2006). *Whose freedom? The battle over America's most important idea.* New York, NY: Farrar, Straus and Giroux.

Lakoff, G., & Johnson, M. (1980). *Metaphors we live by.* Chicago, IL: University of Chicago Press.

Larson, B. (2011). *Metaphors for environmental sustainability: Redefining our relationship with nature.* New Haven, CT: Yale University Press.

Lucht, G. (2015). Biofuels supporters look to 2016 elections. *Iowa Farmer Today,* February 5. Retrieved from http://www.iowafarmertoday.com/news/crop/biofuels-supporters-look-to-elections/article_237261d6-aca4-11e4-a84e-f7efd9b17935.html. Accessed on June 30, 2015.

Macy, J., & Johnstone, C. (2012). *Active hope: How to face the mess we're in without going crazy.* Novato, CA: New World Library.

McCright, A., & Dunlap, R. E. (2003). Defeating Kyoto: The conservative movement's impact on U.S. climate change policy. *Social Problems, 50*(3), 348–373.

McCright, A., & Dunlap, R. E. (2010). Anti-reflexivity. *Theory, Culture, and Society, 27*(2–3), 100–133.

McCright, A., & Dunlap, R. E. (2011). Cool dudes: The denial of climate change among conservative white males in the United States. *Global Environmental Change, 21*(4), 1163–1172.

McGrane, B. (1994). *The un-TV and the 10 MPH car: Experiments in personal freedom and everyday life.* Fort Bragg, CA: The Small Press.

Meadows, D. H. (2008). *Thinking in systems: A primer.* White River Junction, VT: Chelsea Green Publishing Company.

Millennium Ecosystem Assessment. (2005). *Living beyond our means: Natural assets and human well-being, statement of the board.* Retrieved from http://www.millenniumassessment.org/documents/document.429.aspx.pdf. Accessed on June 27, 2015.

Missimer, M. (2015). *Social sustainability within the framework for strategic sustainable development.* Doctoral dissertation, Blekinge Institute of Technology, Karlskrona. Sweden.

Notaras, M. (2011). All biofuels are political. *Our World,* February 18. Retrieved from http://ourworld.unu.edu/en/all-biofuel-policies-are-political. Accessed on June 30, 2015.

Ny, H., MacDonald, J. P., Broman, G., Yamamoto, R., & Robèrt, K. H. (2006). Sustainability constraints as system boundaries: An approach to making life-cycle management strategic. *Journal of Industrial Ecology, 10*(1–2), 61–77.

O'Sullivan, E., & Taylor, M. (2004). *Learning toward an ecological conscious-ness: Selected transformative practices.* New York, NY: Palgrave Macmillan.

Oreskes, N., & Conway, E. M. (2010). *Merchants of doubt.* New York, NY: Bloomsbury Press.

Ostrom, E. (1990). *Governing the commons: The evolution of institutions for collective action.* Cambridge: Cambridge University press.

Page, T. J. (2015). Consumers take back seat to big oil in White House RFS pro-posal. Iowa Renewable Fuels Association, Press Release, May 29. Retrieved from http://www.iowarfa.org/IRFAStatementonRFSProposal.php. Accessed on June 30, 2015.

Payutto, Ven P. A. (2002). Buddhist perspectives on economic concepts. In A. H. Badiner (Ed.), *Mindfulness in the marketplace: Compassionate responses to con-sumerism* (pp. 77–92). Berkeley, CA: Parallax Press.

Petrou, E. C., & Pappis, C. P. (2009). Biofuels: A survey on pros and cons. *Energy Fuels, 23,* 1055–1066.

Redekop, B. (2011). Conclusion: Towards a new general theory of leadership. In B. Redekop (Ed.), *Leadership for environmental sustainability* (pp. 243–248). New York, NY: Routledge.

Redekop, C. W. (2011). Religion, leadership, and the natural environment: The case of American evangelicals. In B. Redekop (Ed.), *Leadership for environmen-tal sustainability* (pp. 201–217). New York, NY: Routledge.

Ricard, M., Lutz, A., & Davidson, R. J. (2014). Mind of the meditator. *Scientific American, 311(5)*, 38–45.

RMOW. (2005). Whistler 2020: Moving toward a sustainable future. *Resort Municipality of Whistler.*

Robèrt, K.-H. (2002). *The natural step story: Seeding a quiet revolution.* Gabriola Island, BC: New Catalyst Books.

Robèrt, K.-H., Borén, S. G., Ny, H., & Broman, G. (2015). *A strategic approach to sustainable transport system development – Part 1: Attempting a generic community planning process model.* Manuscript submitted for publication.

Robèrt, K.-H., Broman, G., & Basile, G. (2013). Analyzing the concept of planetary boundaries from a strategic sustainability perspective: How does humanity avoid tipping the planet? *Ecology and Society, 18(2)*, 5.

Robèrt, K.-H., Schmidt-Bleek, B., De Larderel, J. A., Basile, G., Jansen, J. L., Kuehr, R., ... Wackernagel, M. (2002). Strategic sustainable development — selection, design and synergies of applied tools. *Journal of Cleaner production, 10(3)*, 197–214.

Roberts, J. T., & Parks, B. C. (2007). *Climate of injustice: Global inequality, North-South politics, and climate policy.* Cambridge, MA: MIT Press.

Scharmer, O., & Kaufer, K. (2013). *Leading from the emerging future: From ego-system to eco-system economics.* San Francisco, CA: BK Currents.

Schor, J. (2004). *Born to buy: The commercialized child and the new consumer culture.* New York, NY: Scribner.

Schroyer, T. (2006). Exposing the hidden realities of corporate domination. In T. Schroyer & T. Golodik (Eds.), *Creating a sustainable world: Past experiences, Future struggles* (pp. 89–98). New York, NY: The Apex Press..

Schroyer, T. (2009). *Beyond Western economics: Remembering other economic cultures.* New York, NY: Routledge.

Seidman, S. (2013). *Contested knowledge* (5th ed.). Malden, MA: Blackwell Publishers.

Senge, P. (2006). *The fifth discipline: The art & practice of the learning organization, revised edition.* New York, NY: Doubleday.

Senge, P., Scharmer, O., Jaworski, J., & Flowers, B. S. (2004). Awakening faith in an alternative future. *Reflections: The SOL Journal on Knowledge, Learning, and Change, 5(7)*, 1–16.

Senge, P., Smith, B., Kruschwitz, N., Laur, J., & Schley, S. (2010). *The necessary revolution: Working together to create a sustainable world.* New York, NY: Broadway Books.

Spragens, T. A., Jr. (1995). Communitarian liberalism. In A. Etzioni (Ed.), *New communitarian thinking: Persons, virtues, institutions, and communities* (pp. 37–51). Charlottesville, VA: University of Virginia Press.

Stayton, R. A. (2015). *Power shift: From fossil energy to dynamic solar power.* Santa Cruz, CA: Sandstone Publishing.

The Monitor's View. (2006). Corn lobby's tall tale of a gas substitute. *The Christian Science Monitor*, May 12. Retrieved from http://www.csmonitor.com/2006/0512/p08s01-comv.html. Accessed on June 27, 2015.

Thompson, A. (2012). *Integrating a strategic sustainable development perspective in product-service system innovation.* Doctoral dissertation, Blekinge Institute of Technology, Karlskrona, Sweden.

Vezzoli, C., Kohtalo, C., & Srinivasan, A. (2014). *Product-service systems design for sustainability.* Sheffield, UK: Greenleaf Publishing Limited.

Wenz, P. S. (2001). *Environmental ethics today.* New York, NY: Oxford University Press.

WHO. (2014). Climate change and health. *World Health Organization, Fact Sheet No. 266,* Retrieved from http://www.who.int/mediacentre/factsheets/fs266/en/. Accessed on June 30, 2015.

WHO. (2015). Obesity and overweight. *World Health Organization, Fact Sheet No. 311,* Retrieved from http://www.who.int/mediacentre/factsheets/fs311/en/. Accessed on August 30, 2015.

Woollett, K., & Maguire, E. A. (2011). Acquiring "the knowledge" of London's layout drives structural brain changes. *Current Biology, 21*(24), 2109–2114.

Yale Rudd Center. (2013). *Fast food marketing research ranking tables, 2012-2013.* Retrieved from http://www.fastfoodmarketing.org/media/FastFoodFACTS_MarketingRankings.pdf. Accessed on August 26.

5

Use it or Lose it: About Leadership Ethics in the United Nations

Karin Jironet

L eadership in complex organizations and in a global society in flux requires a balanced approach. The individual leader brings harmony into chaos by acting in accordance with values held and endorsed by the organization and the society it serves. To inspire peers to act in accordance with such values, the individual leader must personally embody, exemplify, and make decisions on an underlying ethics based on universal comprehension of wholesome life. Such leaders speak to the heart of mankind.

In my work as a psychoanalyst and executive guide, I experience this reality as well as its flipside: An individual knows what the moral choice is, but does not decide, act, or communicate correspondingly, although well aware that this will cause dissonance and unbalance among peers. It is difficult to lead a moral life and impossible to lead others into ethical conduct if the hurdles on the path to personal realization of its values have not been passed. Moral leadership needs daily practice. If not nourished and cultivated through continuous application, leadership ethics will, no doubt, get dispersed and lost.

However difficult, the global community demands of top leaders that they serve, honor the cause of their office, respect and inspire coworkers, and most of all, give lower priority to selfish interests that undermine the greater good. The threat to human life and to Earth posed by migration and death of huge populations, epidemics, climate change and environmental disasters, wars and mass destruction, and other well-known forces can only be met with deeply felt and expressed moral sanity. A healthy world now depends on ethical leadership.

In this chapter, I will discuss the notion of leadership ethics or morals from a psychospiritual perspective. My interest is in exploring the relation between ethics and balance; choice and passion in the development of significant leadership. The United Nations forms the organizational context. What is the role, the ethical obligation, and the personal, moral imperative required of an individual leader within this international organization? How is it acquired? Through interviews with UN Deputy Secretary-General Jan Eliasson and former Under-Secretary-General Inga-Britt Ahlenius, the importance of very personal choices, commitment, and action for the highest good comes alive in its present-day context.

The United Nations — An Organization and an Idea Based on Universal Ethics

The United Nations has been called the world's most universal and multidimensional organization (Rivlin, 2005, p. 5). Its purpose is to enforce values that assist humanity in flourishing and to take measures when these values are endangered. As current Deputy Secretary-General Eliasson has said, "The purpose of the UN is to make the world healthy, in a wide sense, a more secure, advanced, peaceful, wealthy, stable and tolerant world. In this, the UN is not only an organization, it is also an idea."[1]

The UN was formed less than six months after the end of WWII to maintain peace and security, implement global equal rights, and achieve international cooperation in the solution of

[1]Personal communication, May 23, 2015. All quotes in this text are from personal interviews, which the author conducted in May 2015 unless otherwise indicated.

issues relating to peace and human rights.[2] In 1945, UNESCO (the United Nations Educational, Scientific, and Cultural Organization) held its organizing conference in London. The poet, Librarian of Congress, and government official Archibald MacLeish, the first American member of UNESCO's governing board, wrote the preamble to its 1945 Charter. The opening lines captured the spirit of its founders: "Since wars begin in the minds of men, it is in the minds of men that the defenses of peace must be constructed." MacLeish believed that educating people about each other, through UNESCO, would "root out the prejudice and ignorance which have separated them in the past" (Meisler, 1995, pp. 222–223).

Today the Secretariat of the United Nations has an international staff of about 9,000 individuals from 170 countries and 15 peacekeeping operations employing 100,000 soldiers, all headed by the Secretary-General. The Member States contribute to the annual budget of $120 million, and each such state is bound to respect the exclusively international character of the responsibilities of the Secretary-General and the Secretariat staff. With

---

[2]The Charter of the United Nations Article 1 states the purposes of the UN as follows:

> To maintain international peace and security, and to that end: to take effective collective measures for the prevention and removal of threats to the peace, and for the suppression of acts of aggression or other breaches of the peace, and to bring about by peaceful means, and in conformity with the principles of justice and international law, adjustment or settlement of international disputes or situations which might lead to a breach of the peace;

> To develop friendly relations among nations based on respect for the principle of equal rights and self-determination of peoples, and to take other appropriate measures to strengthen universal peace;

> To achieve international cooperation in solving international problems of an economic, social, cultural, or humanitarian character, and in promoting and encouraging respect for human rights and for fundamental freedoms for all without distinction as to race, sex, language, or religion; and

> To be a center for harmonizing the actions of nations in the attainment of these common ends.

headquarters in New York, the UN has offices all over the world, with significant presence in Addis Ababa, Bangkok, Beirut, Geneva, Nairobi, Santiago, and Vienna.

To glance at a few of this unique international organization's accomplishments: More than 80 former colonies, inhabited by 750 million people, gained independence thanks to the UN. In 1990, under Javier Perez de Cuellar's leadership, the International Decade for the Eradication of Colonialism was proclaimed. Today, UN relief agencies provide protection to more than 23 million refugees worldwide. The UN aid organization World Food Program ships over 5 million tons of food annually, feeding approximately 113 million people in 80 countries. The United Nations Children's Fund (UNICEF) buys half of the vaccines produced worldwide every year.

In 2015, the UNESCO youth forum theme, "Young Global Citizens for a Sustainable Planet," focused on sustainable development, climate change, and related global debates. Education today addresses the fate of the planet as much as the role of people. The UN Mission for Ebola Emergency Response (UNMEER), the first-ever UN emergency health mission, was established on September 19, 2014 and closed, handed over to the World Health Organization (WHO), on July 31, 2015, having achieved its core objective of scaling up global action to tackle the Ebola breakout in West Africa (Mouat, 2014).

Like any other nongovernmental organization, its leader, the Secretary-General, may be held accountable for the results of its work. However, unlike most other NGOs, there is neither an overarching framework controlling the leaders of the UN nor a regulating body exercising authority over its leaders or member states. Needless to say, such a mandate places extraordinary demands on the various leaders within the complex web of the UN's internal organization.

To illustrate the level of organizational complexity, Ahlenius, former Under-Secretary-General at the United Nations Office of Internal Oversight Services (OIOS), introduced the following metaphor in her book *Mr. Chance*:

> Imagine a housing association. The house consists of 200 separate contracts and all contract holders are on the Board. Sub-groups are formed around interests: all with a balcony to the South are in one, those who have no balcony form another, and the ones who have no drain form a third subgroup, and so on. Imagine the

interpersonal dynamics that is created by the fact that the top floor consists of an enormous apartment owned by one family, responsible for 20% of the corporation's turnover. (Ekdal & Ahlenius, 2011, p. 63)

Imagine yourself chairing this Board. How would you deal with the competing interests of the board members and their differing power influences? How would you go about creating a shared sense of orientation, commonly endorsed emotional stability, an unwavering mind, and a clear focus on what needs to be done at any given point in time? But, first of all, would you accept the reality of the organization's complexity, and would you commit to dealing with it?

Leadership, Moral Choice, Moral Clarity

The precarious and complex field of the UN, along with the depth of issues regarding peace, health, and equality that the organization faces in many regions of the world, form a challenge to the most important leadership role within the organization. The challenge every Secretary-General faces is to strike the right power balance while maintaining personal authenticity and integrity. Leadership authenticity is not simply a matter of "being yourself"; it entails a capacity for relatedness and continuous appreciation of the values and perspectives of others. Authentic leaders are "those who are deeply aware of how they think and behave and are perceived by others as being aware of their own and others' values/moral perspectives, knowledge, and strengths" (Avolio & Gardner, 2005, p. 321).

According to Ahlenius (2010), who served at the top of the UN from 2005 to 2010, authentic, personal, yet unselfish, engagement are character traits that the Secretary-General must both have a talent for and cultivate and practice on a daily basis. As she explains in her *End of Assignment Report*, the Secretary-General must strike a balance between strength and vulnerability in all his communications.

> A Secretary-General that is seen as "too strong" will certainly receive signals by Member States that will bring him back to "balance." A situation with a weak Secretary-General is more difficult, more subtle. It will take time to see that the balance is lost. There will probably be no early signals from Member States who

might not see any "problem," but rather see the situation as comfortable, the Secretary-General being seen as "harmless," pragmatically accommodating and therefore seen as convenient to Member States. (p. 4)

A Secretary-General who is not perceived as managing the balance damages the reputation and effectiveness of the United Nations and its pursuit of its clearly delineated purpose and goals. Those who do strike the right balance, on the other hand, will show themselves to be as effective in this role as such predecessors as Dag Hammarskjöld, Boutros Boutros-Ghali, and Kofi Annan. Between strong and weak leadership, there is wise leadership.

Before addressing the demands for personal development that the Secretary-General must address, let us for a moment look at that very psychic and moral activity that precedes choice making, clarity, and authenticity. How to understand the nature of choice?

German philosopher Immanuel Kant has contributed immensely to Western understanding of this conundrum. According to Kant, as reasonable beings, we perceive the world as enmeshed in necessities. But our faculty of reason means that we are not completely chained to these necessities, that we are capable of perceiving the opportunity to free ourselves from the order of necessity. It is exactly because humans cannot be reduced to experience, background or the context in which we find ourselves that we have the opportunity to make a moral choice. This freeing from necessity is what our reason demands from us.

In his *Critique of the Pure Reason* (1788/1956), Kant shows that to act morally the individual must act in accordance with rules that can be seen as constituting a universal principle. This excludes acting based on whims, personal interests, or personal idiosyncrasies. Kant postulates that acting without a personal agenda is what makes an individual free.

In order to understand this, we have to ask not only what is the right thing to do but also whether it is actually feasible to take this course of action. It is not uncommon for a leader to justify that certain choices are impossible: the costs are too high, the risks too many, or the moment is not right. To this, Kant responds with a moral imperative. When asked if making a moral choice is really possible, Kant responds: "We can, because we must." In other words, we are *always* capable of doing the right thing. Circumstances, whatever they may be, will never completely erase that possibility.

The radicalness of Kant's position ought not to be misunderstood. It would be naïve to think that leaders in very complex organizations on the interface of even more complex societies should, or even could, ignore the susceptibility to criticism and fallibility of their decisions. If leaders made right choices and only those choices all the time, there would be no issue, no dilemma, no debate, or need to analyze the decision making process of our leaders. This is evidently not the case. But, Kant offers a purely ethical perspective on any given situation, which enables us to measure when and to what extent leaders fall short of moral leadership. When analyzing the ethics of leadership, Kant provides us with a compass by which we may ascertain moral clarity independently of subjective interest and external factors. The independence of such choice is what each UN Secretary-General must stand for.

Inspired by Kant, American moral philosopher Susan Neiman (2009) offers in her book *Moral Clarity* a frame of reference for taking responsible action in response to today's urgent political and social questions. Neiman utilizes a number of classically espoused virtues — happiness, reason, reverence, and hope; virtues held dear by many Enlightenment thinkers and writers. According to Neiman, our current-day commitment to values such as tolerance and fairness is not sufficient to shape and reshape our world — certainly, one might add, to reshape it into a healthy one. We need values that incite passion and are defended with passion. For Neiman, reason and passion are not mutually exclusive but interdependent.

One of the greatest misunderstandings about the Enlightenment is that it promotes only reason to the exclusion of passion, Neiman argues. Such a reputation contributed to the notion that reason turns itself away from real life — that it is cold and calculating, a theory rather than applicable in practice. However, reason was not positioned as contrary to passion and feelings, but opposed unquestionable authority, prejudice, and superstition. Reason is important because it shatters all arguments that ultimately justify actions as being based on a tradition and habit. Thinkers such as Voltaire and Diderot understood very well that reason alone cannot change the world. To rise against injustice, to dare make different choices — they were fully aware that this demands passion as well.

Neiman criticizes the idea that acting responsibly means giving up one's ideals and "becoming realistic." This is not even true realism, but an appeal directed toward downsizing expectations.

Such a strategy does not lead to a full life, personal or collective. It is merely a euphemism for moral resignation. Against such false realism, Neiman argues for the virtue of hope. Hope is not equitable to any level of certainty of a better future, but instead constitutes a capacity to open ourselves to the possibility that the future can be both different and better. Hope gives a sense of calm and trust which are vital to good decision making in challenging circumstances. It requires little explanation to sense just how valuable this capacity is in times of great uncertainty.

Another important virtue, according to Neiman, is reverence. Reverence is not bound to a specific religion, but is rather a more general experience of gratitude and happiness. Gratitude for the world as it is given to us, which inspires us to give something in return. And happiness, because we realize that doing something for the world brings deeper fulfillment than career and material wealth. A life without reverence is truly poor, Neiman writes.

Columbia University professor Sheena Iyengar arrives at the same conclusion in *The Art of Choosing* (2010), in which she speaks about hope and reverence as a matter of faith. In a study she conducted on effects of religious adherence on people's health and happiness, she found that those who had chosen to submit to a certain path experienced greater hope, were more optimistic when faced with adversity, and were less likely to be depressed than their counterparts. Indeed, she found that the people most susceptible to pessimism and depression were those who were atheists (Iyengar, 2010, p. 28). Her findings are much in line with Kant's: Once a categorical choice is made for a moral attitude and orientation in life, when all other choices are abolished, the individual experiences freedom, independence, control, happiness, and reverence for creation.

With this perspective in mind, Ahlenius's statement that the UN Secretary-General represents an idea and a choice for peace and human rights seems only the more significant. Quoting Hammarskjöld, "Never for the sake of peace and quiet deny your own experience or convictions," she recounts her own experience and conviction, namely that it is the Secretary-General's job to strive for peace and human rights at all times, come what may.

Mental clarity, moral choice, and personal passion: How to understand the process of making such moral choices, what the individual's personal development process toward clarity entails, and, how passion is balanced with wisdom? In the following, I explore important components of psychospiritual development that leads to such balanced, authentic ethos: neither universal nor personal — or both.

Personal Character, Ethics, and Purgatory

In the industrial era, the private life of a leader was generally distinguished from his or her public, externally measured performance. And although such differentiation is still used in literature on the topic of leadership, today, in the postmodern paradigm, a holistic view considering multiple, interrelated factors including the leader's lifestyle, cognitive approach, moral compass, work ethos, courage, generosity, humility, and other qualities (or lack thereof) are also held up for scrutiny (Lid-Andersson, 2009). Christopher Peterson and Martin Seligman's groundbreaking handbook *Character Strengths and Virtues* (2004) marked a shift in orientation toward a focus on healthy moral character, established to varying degrees by a person's strengths including authenticity, gratitude, hope, humor, kindness, and persistence.

The proximity rather than distance between character and performance — who you are as person and what you do (and especially what you do not do) as a result of your character — forms an important point of academic focus in leadership development. Fred Kiel (2015), for one, who himself in midlife went through a crisis formed by moral and spiritual emptiness, conducted a study on how moral leadership is reflected in return on assets. His findings show that leaders frequently engaged in behaviors that reveal strong character, including standing up for what is right, expressing concern for the common good, letting go of mistakes and showing empathy, earn five times more return on assets than those executives perceived as self-focused by their subordinates.

Interestingly, Kiel's findings indicate that those most in need of a "moral shape-up" are also the ones least interested in pursuing such development. When asked how such leaders might move past their denial and overcome their character deficits, Kiel offers clear advice: seek guidance from a trusted person and follow it.

Alighieri in his *Divine Comedy* goes through *Inferno*, *Purgatory* and enters *Heaven* in pursuit of self-realization and self-betterment. Driven by a desire to know himself, Alighieri seeks to understand why it matters what choices he makes and how his life is molded in effect of these; why humility, kindness, generosity, and other virtues bring him forward toward the goal. Alighieri does not travel alone though. His guide Virgil leads him along the dangerous path, marked by peril, temptation, uncertainty and … no hope.

Nel mezzo del cammin di nostra vita

mi ritrovai per una selva oscura,

ché la diritta via era smarrita.[3]

Alighieri's *Divine Comedy* is an exemplary study of the ordeals one may expect, once that path has been entered upon. My interest and research has primarily been focused on the second part, *Purgatory*, due to its contemporary relevance for leadership development (Karin Jironet, 2010). When you find yourself in *Purgatory*, you cannot help but move on. Unlike the eternity of *Inferno* or *Paradise*, in *Purgatory*, there is time, night and day — duality — and, hence, development.

Personal development takes place through seven states of human condition. Alighieri distinguishes these states as sins and virtues. The seven sins in Alighieri's definition are caused by a denial, indifference, or excess of love. Denial of love is experienced as pride, envy, and anger. Too much love manifests as avarice, gluttony, and lust. Right in the middle of *Purgatory* on the forth terrace of sloth, the indolent hang around lazily, or run around aimlessly and procrastinating. To them, nothing seems to matter or demand a proper choice or personal commitment. While exploring sloth and the nature of indifference, Virgil says that love is the "seed" of all human acts, both sinful and virtuous (Purgatory canto 17 verse 103–105).

The virtues corresponding to each sin are attitudes that can remedy the sin. They are formed by the qualities that oppose the sin and superseding the forces that cause the sin to occur. The virtue is the antidote, as it were, to sin, but does not erase it. Thus, a sin can quickly become a virtue and the other way around. The way through *Purgatory* teaches a person to deal with these fundamental opposites and ambiguities. This learning process ultimately leads to balance. One who has passed the journey knows how to live and work with duality consciously. He or

---

[3]Alighieri, *Divine Comedy*, Cantica I, *Inferno*. Halfway on the path of our life, I found myself in a dark wood, because the right road was lost. Author's translation.

she has acquired a state of awareness that there are consequences that flow as a result of one's decisions and how one leads one's life. To put it more succinctly, one is cognizant of choices and that one makes these oneself. It is only after passing through "purgatory" and overcoming the grip of duality with its ensuing emotions, however, that a person can claim to choose freely. Until such personal development is acquired, it is really the play of emotions and context that make the choices. The seven sins and virtues are expressions of the fundamental impulses to such choices. It is not any specific behavior or deed that forms a sin, but the attitude with which life is led. How do you function and deal in relation to others, how do you value others in relation to yourself, what do you take and what do you give? UN Secretary-General Hammarskjöld fully realized the essential requirement for self-development.

> Our work for peace must begin within the private world of each one of us. To build for man a world without fear, we must be without fear. To build a world of justice, we must be just. And how can we fight for liberty if we are not free in our own minds? How can we ask others to sacrifice if we are not ready to do so? (Hammarskjöld, 1953, S/G 360)

Every moment of our lives we have the opportunity to pay attention to how we approach the circumstances in which we find ourselves. How we make those choices is not simply a matter of blindly following a set of rules or paying lip service. The human potential for such choice is not a given, although its norm is well embedded and recognized by most, even children. Moral choice is not self-evident, because — it is a choice deeply rooted in conscience and without such it cannot be made convincingly. Jungian psychoanalyst Adolph Guggenbühl-Craig (1980) argues that a psychopath is capable not only of speaking about morality but also defending, even advocating it, while at the same time attaching no personal significance to it. The point being that healthy moral leadership means to live with personal attachment to a set of values and to be passionately committed to those.

According to Deputy Secretary-General Eliasson, deeply held personal values together with maturity, passion, and clear vision are critical to successful leadership. He remarks on role model and colleague, Olof Palme, with whom he collaborated in the diplomatic efforts to resolve the Iran–Iraq conflict: "His political skills were outstanding, but most of all his political energy, his passion, this was really what made the difference for his great accomplishments on the international political scene." Turning to his own experience:

> Growing and maturing as a diplomat and bringing about change through international action — it's all driven by the values I have cultivated and the actions these yielded over time. So, on the one hand, most of the things I do, I do instinctively, on the other hand instinct is very much grounded in a pragmatic and well engrained value system. I try to look at the world and see it as it is, not through rose-colored glasses, and, at the same time look for what can be better and try and diminish that gap.

The virtue lies herein: what you do is the result of choices made. This defines you as a person — you are what you do and how you do it.

The Unique Case of Leadership Within the United Nations

A leader's primary duty to those they lead and society at large is to allow the opportunity to flourish and grow, and to promote core values of trust, service, and the collective good (Moss Kanter, 2011; World Economic Forum, 2013). Although most would agree that leaders ought to serve others rather than pursue their own personal agenda, altruism, or guiding others with the ultimate goal of improving their wellness (Batson, 1991), it is for various leaders an idealistic rather than a realistic concept (Ciulla, 2004). Senior management and top leaders in all fields frequently find themselves occupied by the challenge of simply maintaining their own function. These challenges manifest in the form of politics, conflicting interests, internal power struggles, policy and efficiency agendas, among others and are often so time consuming that little opportunity remains to address the primary purpose of their leadership role — the flourishing and wellbeing of those they lead and society as a whole (Vriesendorp & Jironet, 2006). The current absence of altruist leadership may be one of the reasons that so many feel the world lacks "real" leadership. Despite a prevailing distrust in governments, politicians, and corporate leaders among members of public sectors,[4] the Secretary-General of the UN is still expected to serve the organization and the world it was designed to stabilize. This expectation is neither naive nor idealistic; it is justified and indeed necessary given that the United Nations is itself a value driven and value generating organization. Research in leadership ethics suggests that "prototypicality," the leader's representativeness of group identity and trust, is the mechanism through which a leader's behavior may be identified as ethical (Kalshoven & Den Hartog, 2009, p. 103). A clearly defined ethos enables a leader to serve even in complex contexts, and in doing so earn the trust of the organization. The Secretary-General thus has a dual task: to carry out the UN Charter's objective and to embody its underlying ideal.

To this day Hammarskjöld, UN Secretary-General from 1953 to 1961, remains an influential figure regarding leadership within the United Nations. "The value of life is its content — for others," he wrote in his diary *Markings* on July 29, 1958, embodying the notion that human relationship is central to leadership. Deputy Secretary-General Eliasson observes that "(Hammarskjöld's) diary is an extremely important book and it has grown in importance for me ... It's actually a mystic's account of what it means to be fully human. To me he lives on as a role model of unparalleled capacity."

As Alighieri's journey through Purgatory symbolizes, personal development and maturity entails making choices that help the individual transcend the grip of dualities and move freely between opposing interests. Likewise, the relation between the individual leader's highest personal moral and balance in communication and action can be defined as choice — how else could a leader lead others?

It is the responsibility, not only of the Secretary-General, but of every individual leader within the UN organization to scrutinize personal choices, communicate reasons for standing behind their ethical ground, hold these up against the Charter's designated goals, and reflect on how the personal and collective values are mutually enforcing. Such scrutiny and dialogue serve to ensure that a truly human ethos is endorsed. The positive effect on the organization's health is self-evident.

---

[4]Edelman, *Trust Barometer* in 2012 showed the greatest decline in government trust across the globe since the survey's inception in 1952.

The case of Anders Kompass, director of field operations for the Office of the High Commissioner for Human Rights, disclosed the alleged sexual abuse of children by peacekeeping troops in Africa to the French authorities. His example serves as an illustration of how an individual leader holds the UN responsibility for human rights. Lena Lid-Falkman, UN expert and scholar, commented (personal communication, August 19, 2015),

> The story told through the case of Kompass is a story about passion. In the end it is also a hero's journey and narrative. In July 2014 Kompass, who is Swedish, leaked a report to the French authorities, because he'd established that the UN failed to act quickly to stop the abuse, which it had identified in its own internal report. He told his Director, the deputy high commissioner, that he was going to contact the French. The French wrote back and thanked him. The UN however was not amused. Instead, in May 2015, he was suspended. But Kompass kept up hope that enough evidence, enough voice would be heard to save the children, some as young as nine, from being sexually abused by the peace keeping forces. His courage inspired others to come forward. And they did: a veteran US diplomat, James Wasserstrom, who himself was fired and arrested by UN police because he talked about the corruption by senior officials in Kosovo, came forward and said the case of Kompass revealed how the UN put the blame on whistleblowers and punished them instead of dealing with the mistakes made within the organization. A week later, a judge ordered the UN to lift Kompass's suspension. In June 2015, there was a case brought against the Secretary-General, Ban Ki-moon, because whistleblowers weren't being given any protection or listened to properly. When Kompass was re-installed in his position, it was not only a victory for him, but also for the good values the UN represents, but which are at times resisted inside the organization. This story reminds me of Hammarskjöld saying that the UN is not here to take us to heaven, it is here to save us from hell.

Choice and passion combined form a forceful front against different forms of neglect, provided that such passion and ensuing choice is for the greater good. It is a daily task to maintain and renew this objective. As former Secretary-General Annan states, "The United Nations is an instrument for peace and justice. Use it; respect it; defend it ... Applaud us when we prevail. Correct us when we fail, but, above all, do not let this indispensable, irreplaceable institution whither, languish, or perish as a result of indifference, inattention, or financial starvation" (Crosette, in Mouat, 2014, p. 306).

For the optimal functioning of the organization, its leaders must be outstanding, and it is here where descriptive and normative notions of leadership come together. The individual leaders within the UN are required to possess not only extraordinary leadership skills but above all must embody and impart a set of ethics that inspires fellow staff within the organization, as well as the representatives of its member states, to passionately seek morally grounded choices in the service of the world as a whole.

No One Is an Island

Clearly, orchestrating the UN's numerous initiatives and pursuits is not a one-person job. It is the result of many independent, interdependent, initiatives aligned with and coordinated by the explicit UN ideal and an elaborate administration. It is as well a product of its idea and organization's interface with the rest of the world, which interacts with its pursuits.

It is widely held that an organization with the UN's scope of influence is better at endorsing moral values, as well as in avoiding errors, than the individuals who form the organization. Daniel Kahneman (2011), psychologist and Nobel Prize winner in Economics, explains that intuition and reason complement each other. Individuals tend to make intuitive choices (about morality), whereas organizations, thinking slowly, have the power to impose order and elaborate exercises such as check-lists and *premortems.*[5] Such a balance between instinct and analysis relies on a clear conceptual structure. Kahneman argues that just as a doctor by knowing the name of the disease also knows information related to the disease — symptoms, medication, complication, prognosis — a leader must know the wider scope of bias, such as its causes, its effects, and, what can be done about it.

---

[5]See also Lencioni (2012, p. 173 ff.) on the importance of thorough meeting structures.

This information is available as collective intelligence within the organization. "They (decision makers) will make better choices when they trust their critics to be sophisticated and fair, and when they expect their decisions to be judged by how it was made, not only how it turned out" (2011, p. 418).

It is precisely at the interface between the individual's and the organization's choice and passion that the UN today faces its greatest potential for growth. As Eliasson states, the chief focus of the United Nations at this time must be to manifest the realization of international solutions to global problems. This primary objective, he continues, will entail a conceptual breakthrough. It will demand rigorous re-categorization, promoting expansion of the mind, enabling individual coworkers to transcend the polarization of national and international interests. "Once plain comprehension of our inherent unity, the inevitable necessity of standing by a global formula for peace is evident through human dialogue, supported by an informed conceptual framework, everyone in the entire organization will feel empowered to play their role accordingly," he says. To achieve this, Eliasson emphasizes the need to focus on three distinct organizational areas: (1) *Collaboration*: The UN needs to work more across borders, not only in terms of geographies, but more importantly across functions. Here Eliasson stresses the need for distributed leadership, "We must urgently stop working in silos and top-down manner and instead take a horizontal approach"; (2) *Prevention*: The most important task of the UN today is to prevent destabilization of peace and human rights. In his words, "We cannot wait for the conflict, the atrocities, the deepening of poverty and increasing inequalities"; and (3) *Education*: "Development" is not limited to augmenting material resources, it is equally relevant for ideas, narratives, and community building. As Eliasson points out, "There is no peace without development and no development without peace and none of the above without respect for human rights. It unites us all."

The realization of peace and development for a healthy world can only be achieved when every leader at the United Nations shares common concepts about the organization's ethics and is engaged in continuous dialogue in defining and redefining these notions to meet whatever conditions may be present. The General Secretary is effective once and only when each and every staff member likewise acts with moral integrity, reverence, courage and a balanced, realistic, and hopeful perspective.

References

Ahlenius, I.-B. (2010). *End of assignment report.* New York, NY: United Nations.

Alighieri, D. (1955). *The divine comedy II: Purgatory.* (D. Sayers, Trans.). London: Penguin Classics.

Avolio, B., & Gardner, W. L. (2005). Authentic leadership development: Getting to the root of positive forms of leadership. In *The leadership quarterly* (Vol. 16, pp. 315–338). Amsterdam: Elsevier.

Batson, C. D. (1991). *The altruism question: Towards a social-psychological answer.* Hillsdale, NJ: Lawrence Erlbaum Associates, Publishers.

Burns, J. M. (1978). *Leadership.* New York, NY: Harper & Row.

Ciulla, J. (2004). Ethics and leadership effectiveness. In J. Antonakis, A. Cianciolo, & R. Sternberg (Eds.), *The nature of leadership* (pp. 302–327). Thousand Oaks, CA: Sage.

Ekdal, N., & Ahlenius, I.-B. (2011). *Mr Chance: FN's förfall under Ban-Ki-Moon.* Falun: Brombergs.

Guggenbühl-Craig, A. (1980). *The emptied soul: On the nature of the psychopath.* New York, NY: Spring Publications.

Hammarskjöld, D. (1953). UN Press Release SG/360 (22 December).

Hammarskjöld, D. (2006). *Markings* (L. Sjober & W. H. Auden, Trans.). New York, NY: Vintage Books.

Iyengar, S. (2010). *The art of choosing.* New York, NY: Twelve.

Jironet, K. (2010). *Female leadership: Management, Jungian psychology, spirituality and the global journey through purgatory.* London: Routledge.

Kahneman, D. (2011). *Thinking fast and slow.* New York, NY: Farrar, Straus and Giroux.

Kalshoven, K., & Den Hartog, D. (2009). Ethical leader behavior and leader effectiveness: The role of prototypicality and trust. *International Journal of Leadership Studies, 5*(2), 102–120. Virginia: Regent University School of Business & Leadership.

Kant, I. (1788/1956). *Critique of practical reason.* (L. White Beck, Trans.). Indianapolis, IN: Bobbs-Merrill.

Kiel, F. (2015). Return on character. *Harvard Business Review, 4,* 20–21.

Lencioni, P. (2012). *The advantage: Why organizational health trumps everything else in business.* San Francisco, CA: Jossey-Bass.

Lid-Andersson, L. (2009). *Ledarskapande retorik.* Stockholm: EFI.

Meisler, S. (1995). *United Nations: A history.* New York, NY: Grove Press.

Moss Kanter, R. (2011). How great companies think differently. *Harvard Business Review, 11,* 52–59.

Mouat, L. (2014). *The United Nation's top job: A close look at the work of eight Secretaries-General.* North Charleston, SC: CreateSpace.

Neiman, S. (2009). *Moral clarity. A guide for grown-up idealists.* Princeton, NJ: Princeton University Press.

Peterson, C., & Seligman, M. (2004). *Character strengths and virtues: A handbook and classification* (1st ed.). Oxford: Oxford University Press.

Rivlin, B. (2005). The UN reform conundrum. *American foreign policy interests*, 27(5), 365–384.

Vriesendorp, D., & Jironet, K. (2006). *De rol van het geweten*. Amsterdam: Business Contact.

World Economic Forum. (2013). *The future role of civil society*. Geneva: World Economic Forum. Retrieved from http://www3.weforum.org/docs/WEF_FutureRoleCivilSociety_Report_2013.pdf

CHAPTER

6

Leadership for the Greater Good: Developing Indicators of Societal and Environmental Health

Samuel G. Wilson

Some very serious cracks are beginning to appear in the capacity of our communities and ecosystems to sustain our well-being (Lovelock, 2009). In the context of concerns about the end of a safe operating space for humanity (Rockström et al., 2009; Steffen et al., 2015), there is a growing global view that human societies must drastically change so as to preserve the social and ecological systems that undergird human civilization (Hawken, Lovins, & Lovins, 2000). As humanity's understanding of the value of these interlocking social-ecological systems has increased, indicators and information systems have proliferated to measure and track the state of these systems (AtKisson & Hatcher, 2001).

When we think about measurement, as manifest in indicators and information systems, we are likely to think about management, not leadership. On the face of it, indicators and information systems appear to be more the tools of experts than the instruments of leadership. Yet indicators arise from our values and create our values (Meadows, 1998). This means that our choice of indicators reflects our understanding of what is valuable about ourselves and our world. Indeed, because value judgments are

161

unavoidable (Stiglitz, Sen, & Fitoussi, 2009), our choice of indicators may reveal less about our management of information than it does about our knowledge and wisdom. More broadly, our choices reveal something of our understanding of what human civilization is, or more ambitiously, our vision of what it could or should be.

My purpose in this chapter is to explore the view that creating and implementing indicators of societal and environmental health — the greater good — is central to the work of leadership. Given the importance of the concept of the greater good to the ideas explored in this chapter, I begin with a review of the greater good. Given the elusiveness of the idea, I propose that thinking about the greater good in terms of different types of nonfinancial capital (e.g., social and natural capital) offers a practical, if imperfect, means of rendering abstract ideas about the greater good more concrete and therefore measureable. The measurement of nonfinancial capitals is a distinguishing feature of many of the new indicators and information systems that have emerged in recent years to measure and track the health of nature and society. I argue that although these indicators provide a welcome counterpoint to gross domestic product (GDP) — the singular indicator of the 20th century — they look backwards in time, rather than forward, which means that they provide orientation but not direction. Next, drawing on recent research into future-oriented indicators of the health of the commons, I sketch an approach to developing indicators that can help people navigate into the future. Finally, after an account of the development of these indicators, I proceed to a more general discussion of the qualities of indicators that would bring them more fully into the purview of leadership for the greater good.

Given that the purpose of this chapter is to examine the general relationship between the concept of the greater good, indicators of societal and environmental health, and leadership, I necessarily screen off a number of important issues. First, because I aim to explore the links between the greater good, indicators, and leadership, I do not present a critique of the ideas that comprise these elements but rather present a framework that makes the links between these elements explicit. The absence of critique does not imply uncritical endorsement of the constituent ideas, but a deliberate neutrality. Second, because the worldviews and values that inhere in the ideas explored in this chapter are not universal, it is necessary to situate these ideas historically and culturally. The focus of this chapter is on countries of the Western world, in general, and English-speaking nations (e.g., the United States, the United Kingdom, Australia, New Zealand), in particular. The experience of these English-speaking nations in recent decades is a fascinating context within which to situate an examination of the nexus between the greater good, indicators, and leadership because of the diminution of concern for collective interests and the common good within these nations over the last 40 years (Bauman, 2000, 2007). In these nations, especially in the decades after the Second World War, strong unions, combined with collective bargaining and social welfare provisions, cultivated a period of equality, stability, and order (Judt, 2010; Sennett, 2006). However, as the 1970s drew to a conclusion, the governments of the United States and Britain diverged from the Keynesian consensus that prevailed after the war. Specifically, the Bretton Woods system — the system of regulations and institutions that regulated the international monetary system after the Second World War — collapsed (James, 2008). In contrast to mainland Western European nations where government support was sustained (e.g., Belgium, France, Germany, Italy, Spain, The Netherlands), the governments of Britain and America, coupled with Australia and New Zealand, embraced deregulation and free market ideologies (Albert, 1993; Baumol, Litan, & Schramm, 2007). Considerable research attests to the significant economic and sociocultural changes that have occurred in these nations as a result (Galbraith, 1994; Hacker, 2006; McAuley & Lyons, 2015; Pimpare, 2004; Reich, 2009; Saul, 2009; Sennett, 2006). Specifically, in these countries, many of the institutions and policies that were established to promote equality and stability were dismantled, and with it the ease with which common interests were perceived and valued.

The Greater Good: A Once and Future Idea

Although the term *civilization* has less currency today than it once did (Armstrong, 2009), most people see themselves as living in a civilization (Saul, 2009). As posited by John Ralston Saul, this understanding tends to be centered on a sense of shared destiny. That is, people, as social beings, have shared interests and face a common future, notwithstanding their unique interests and aspirations. The notion of shared destiny is also known as the *greater good* or its synonyms, the *public good, public interest, common wealth,* or *common good.* Currently, especially among people of English-speaking nations whère the authority of the individual is most ascendant, it is unfashionable to think and talk about people as having shared interests or a common future (Bauman, 2000; Giddens, 1991). A corollary of this is that it is unfashionable to think and talk seriously about the greater good (Eliasoph, 1998).

Although the power of the idea of shared interests and collective purpose has subsided in English-speaking nations in recent decades, this has not always been the case and may not remain so for much longer (Salt, 2014). There is, among many people in English-speaking nations, a sense that something is profoundly wrong with the way we live today (Judt, 2010; Schwartz, 2010). There is a pervasive sense that we are in a time of interregnum (Bauman, 2000; Saul, 1995), witnessing the demise of an old pattern and anticipating the emergence of something new (Jironet, 2014; Scharmer & Kaufer, 2013). If there is to be a reawakening of concern for our shared interests and common future, this will require deep reengagement with, and active reimagining of, the idea of the greater good.

The idea of the greater good has a long yet punctuated history, replete with diverging meanings. Plato (1975), for example, imagined an ideal state in which private goods and nuclear families would be relinquished for the sake of the greater good of a harmonious society. Aristotle (1984, 2013) defined it in terms of communally shared happiness, whose key constituents were wisdom, virtue, and pleasure. Moreover, throughout the centuries, Christian theologians such as Augustine (1983) and Aquinas (1981) examined the greater good, as have thinkers from other great faiths (see, e.g., Dwivedi, 2000; Lama, 1988). More sustained engagement with the concept occurred in the 17th century with the rise of social contract theory (Hobbes, 1924; Rousseau, 1913), which held that people ought to forfeit their absolute freedom to live as they wish for the greater good of the security of shared life in a community. Subsequently, 18th- and 19th-centuries' thinkers, such as the utilitarians Jeremy Bentham (1983) and John Stuart Mill (2002), argued that the right course of action is that which creates the greatest "utility" for society. In the 20th century, the greater good received renewed impetus with

John Rawls' (1971) work on justice as fairness. And in the 21st century, intellectuals such as Noam Chomsky (2013) and Slavoj Žižek (2013) are readdressing the concept in affirmative and critical ways, respectively.

Perhaps the most serious limitation of most historical ideas about the greater good is that they are silent on the greater good as it relates to nonhuman species and the natural world. Indeed, terms such as the *public good* and *common good* tacitly restrict the scope of the greater good to humans, the biological status of which is, of course, no guarantee of inclusion in the moral circle, as dehumanization research amply attests (see, e.g., Haslam & Loughnan, 2014). However, growing awareness of the vulnerability of natural systems to human disturbance has heightened concern for those natural systems that ultimately underpin human well-being and human civilization. At minimum, construing these natural resources as the basis upon which all else of value depends (Daly, 1973; Hawken et al., 2000) admits the "commons" into the scope of the greater good.

Of course, the idea of the commons — collective goods to which all group members have free access — is an ancient one. Every society has common-pool resources and public goods that can be used by all of its citizens. Common-pool resources (e.g., potable water, clean air, fisheries) are clearly a vital, if not inevitable (Hardin, 1968), part of the greater good. Public goods, which include tangible (e.g., roads and public utilities) and intangible "goods" (e.g., representative democracy), are another type of collective good. Unlike common-pool resources, however, which begin at full provision, public goods require the members of a community to contribute some form of capital (e.g., time, money, effort) to create and sustain them over time (Parks, Joireman, & Van Lange, 2013).

Although the greater good is neither synonymous with, nor reducible to, collective goods, thinking about the greater good in terms of tangible and intangible collective goods offers a means of rendering abstract ideas about the greater good more concrete and therefore measureable. Moreover, it permits closer inspection of how collective goods are created or acquired; questions that beget further questions about the societal and environmental resources necessary to sustain them, as well as questions about the ideas of justice and intergenerational resource allocation that should inform the distribution of collective goods. Finally, it provides a means of thinking about the social, spatial, and temporal boundaries of the communities within which collective goods are or ought to be shared.

A Capitals Approach to Measuring the Well-Being of the Whole

Imagining the well-being of the whole means little if there is not also some means of accounting for it. Thinking about the whole as a system of interlocking capitals — natural, built, intellectual, organizational, cultural, human, social, and financial — is a practical, if imperfect, means of imagining and accounting for the whole. Although the use of multiple capitals in indicators and information systems is relatively new, and the measurement of nonfinancial capitals relatively undeveloped (Gleeson-White, 2014), construing the well-being of the whole as inhering in a network of interdependent capitals with measureable stocks and flows is a practical step toward the creation of indicators and information systems of the greater good that may be recruited in the service of leadership for the greater good.

Donella Meadows' (1998) report to the Balaton group on indicators and information systems for sustainable development made a signal contribution to the general understanding of how financial and nonfinancial capitals are interconnected and how this system of capitals underpins human well-being. Drawing on Herman Daly's (1973) hierarchical model of the relationship between well-being, society, economy, and nature, Meadows outlined a framework of means and ends that relates natural resources to human well-being through human, social, financial, and built capital. In Meadows' framework, natural capital, which comprises the world's stock of renewable (e.g., forests, fisheries) and nonrenewable resources (e.g., minerals, oil), is theorized as the "ultimate means" upon which human well-being depends. Financial capital (i.e., money) and built capital (i.e., the value of such physical objects as roads and public utilities) are conceptualized as "intermediate means." Human capital (i.e., the value of knowledge and experience, which inheres in individual persons) and social capital (i.e., the value of trust and goodwill, which inheres in the connections between people) are theorized as "intermediate ends." Finally, human well-being and flourishing are conceptualized as the "ultimate ends" of human activity. Notwithstanding the limitations of this framework — its hierarchical structure and anthropocentrism are singled out as especially egregious (AtKisson & Hatcher, 2001; Meadows, 1998) — its heuristic value is clear; human well-being is ultimately contingent on the well-being of the whole.

Four features of Meadows' (1998) framework are particularly noteworthy. First, it highlights the connections among different types of capital. To illustrate, schools (i.e., built capital) enhance personal knowledge (i.e., human capital) and interpersonal trust (i.e., social capital), which ultimately serves the whole economy, as measured by financial capital. Second, it highlights the contingency of capitals on other capitals for their expression. For example, the creation of human capital and social capital in schools requires built capital (e.g., buildings), human capital (e.g., faculty), and intellectual capital (e.g., the school curriculum), which requires financial capital — itself a function of extant capitals. Third, thinking about the whole in terms of capitals brings the dilemmas and trade-offs that attend decision-making about the greater good into sharp focus. Fourth, it raises the prospect that an ethic of sustainability, as expressed through a dynamic network of interlocking capitals, offers a guide to a systemic conception of the structure and well-being of the whole.

Measuring What Matters

The most prominent trade-off relevant to the topic of the well-being of the whole is the long-standing trade-off between the economy, on the one hand, and nature and society, on the other. For generations, economic growth has been synonymous with national welfare; indeed, growth, as measured by GDP, has been the singular indicator of progress in the advanced economies of the Western world (Schroyer, 2009). The problems associated with elevating economic growth to the status of a central organizing idea of society have been well-known for decades. Consider, for example, Jay Forrester's (1971) demonstration that economic growth is a root cause of environmental destruction, resource depletion, poverty, and unemployment. Although Forrester's systems analysis indicated that less growth, not more, was required to address these complex social and environmental challenges, the ideal of growth continues to grip our imaginations so tightly that we seem unable to conceive of alternatives (Judt, 2010; but see Schroyer, 2009).

Forrester's insight can be restated thus: the growth of financial and built capital is a root cause of the depletion of social and natural capital. Although an over-simplification, it highlights an important point; focusing on the growth of a single capital reveals nothing of its effects on other types of capital. More pointedly, the measurement of a single indicator of economic activity — GDP — reveals nothing about the depletion (Hamilton & Saddler, 1997) or accretion (Lancy & Gruen, 2013) of the nonfinancial capitals on which GDP growth depends. This insight about GDP has motivated the new genre of societal and environmental indicators.

There is great diversity among the new genre of indicators and information systems in terms of their purpose. Some indicators and information systems have been specifically created to remedy the limitations of GDP. The most well-known of these is the Genuine Progress Indicator (Cobb, Halstead, & Rowe, 1995; Costanza et al., 2004; Hamilton, 1999; Talberth, Cobb, & Slattery, 2007), which is the successor to Daly and Cobb's (1989) Index of Sustainable Economic Welfare. More recent and less well-known is The Herald/Age-Lateral Economics Index of Australia's Well-being (Gruen & Lancy, 2011). In essence, these information systems adjust GDP for unvalued or erroneously valued elements of economic welfare by including measures of human, social, and natural capital. Yet other information systems such as the United Nation's Human Development Index (UNDP, 2011) combine measures of financial capital with measures of human capital to create entirely new indicators.

Notwithstanding the importance of economic welfare, there is a growing global view that prosperity is not synonymous with a society's economic wealth, especially if a society is failing to meet the basic needs of its citizens to survive, let alone flourish (Jackson, 2009; Porter & Stern, 2015). Consistent with this, a number of information systems have emerged in recent years to measure and track various nonfinancial dimensions of prosperity. Some of these information systems comprise measures of human, social, and natural capital. Examples of such systems include the Canadian Index of Wellbeing (Michalos et al., 2011), Measuring Australia's Progress (ABS, 2013), and the Social Progress Index (Porter & Stern, 2015). Given the relative dearth of indicators of natural capital (but see the WWF Living Planet Report 2014), some information systems focus on indicators of human and social capital. Information systems that are composed principally of indicators of human and social capital include Oxfam Humankind Index (Dunlop & Swales, 2012) and the Gross

National Happiness Index (Bates, 2009; Ura, Alkire, Zangmo, & Wangdi, 2012). Yet other systems are centered on indicators of human capital, such as the Happy Planet Index (Adballah, Michaelson, Shah, Stoll, & Marks, 2012) and the Social Wealth Economic Indicators (De Leon & Boris, 2010; De Leon, 2012; Eisler, 2007; Ghosh, 2014a, 2014b).

These indicators and information systems, which incorporate measures of human, social, and natural capital, represent an important advance on indicators of prosperity that privilege financial information. Moreover, the attempt by some information systems to assess the per capita sufficiency of financial and nonfinancial goods provides a welcome counterpoint to GDP, which is silent on the issue of distribution. A limitation of these information systems is that they look backward, rather than forward, in time. However, this is less a critique and more an obvious statement about how indicators that are constructed with historical data necessarily function. A related limitation is that information systems, including all those reviewed above, quantify stocks and flows of capital but are largely silent on what those stocks and flows should be. Finally, these information systems typically convey information in a highly abstract and decontextualized form, which arguably makes them more the tools of experts than the instruments of leadership.

Developing Indicators of the Greater Good

If direction, not simply orientation, is a desideratum of indicators for leadership for the greater good, what might such indicators and information systems look like? The notion of imaginatively navigating into the future, which is a function of our uniquely human capacity for prospection, provides clues about possible answers to this question. Prospection enables humans to mentally simulate and thus foresee events that have not been experienced (Gilbert & Wilson, 2007). In the context of thinking about the social and natural world, prospection enables people to imagine discrepancies between the world as it is and the world as it should or might ideally be. In the context of thinking about indicators of environmental and social health, prospection enables people to imagine future states of nature and society against which current states of nature and society can be assessed.

The use of prospection to imagine the greater good as it is, relative to what it should be, was central to Samuel G. Wilson and John Fien (2015) Leadership for the Commons index, which was part of a population survey of Australians' beliefs about the state of leadership for the greater good in Australia. Although this index is not proposed as an exemplar of future-oriented indicators of the commons or the greater good, the process of developing this index nevertheless yielded insights that may be useful to researchers interested in the creation of new indicators for a healthy world. Wilson and Fien's index comprises two parts: indicators of stewardship and indicators of stocks of collective goods. I briefly describe the former but focus on the latter because it is most instructive about the challenge of creating indicators and information systems that can inform the practice of leadership for the greater good.

Stewardship is an ethic that embodies the responsible management of resources or capitals. In the context of the greater good, as manifest in a framework of interlocking capitals, the concept of stewardship illuminates what leadership for the commons might look like. Wilson and Fien's (2015) index is an aggregation of four indices that measure beliefs about political leaders' stewardship of collective goods in the domains of nature, economy, society, and governance. These four indices are, in turn, composed of indicators of the stewardship of natural capital (e.g., the quality of the water in waterways), built capital (e.g., the quality of public infrastructure), human capital, as enabled by underlying social and built capitals (e.g., the quality and cost of healthcare), and democratic capital (e.g., citizen engagement with democratic processes, like voting).

Consistent with the indicators and information systems described earlier, the responses to these stewardship questions provide orientation, not direction; that is, they tell us where we are, but not where we should go. To illustrate, when respondents indicate their level of agreement with statements like, "political leaders are doing all they can to preserve the quality and cost of healthcare for future generations," their responses are essentially performance appraisals. Although the answers to questions like these yield information about the perceived performance of political leaders — specifically the quality of their stewardship of collective goods — they are silent on discrepancies between actual and idealized standards of stewardship.

More relevant to the current discussion is the fact that these stewardship questions were preceded by a series of exercises in prospection. Before the stewardship questions were asked, respondents were asked to form a mental picture of the state that specific common-pool resources and public goods should be in so as to enable future generations to flourish. Next, they were asked to evaluate the current state of each collective good relative to the state it should be in for future generations. These exercises in prospection and cross-temporal evaluation, when performed for all indicators, yielded a series of discrepancies between the actual and ideal future condition of these collective goods. Discrepancies between actual and ideal future states are noteworthy because they reveal the goals of a community, and goals are noteworthy because they reveal the future that a community yearns to move toward, all else being equal.

Consider, for example, Wilson and Fien's (2015) finding that 70% percent of Australians believe the current "quality and cost of healthcare" is worse than it should be for future generations. (30% regard the quality and cost of healthcare as "about the same as it should be" for future generations.) In the first instance, this finding reveals that for a large majority of Australians, there is a discrepancy between the current state of healthcare and the desired future state of this public good. More interesting still is what this finding suggests about the collective action that corresponds to this idealized goal state: in order to bequeath to future generations a standard of healthcare that meets their needs, present generations must improve its quality and cost. If future generations of Australians are to experience healthcare as a public good, which it is presently, then remedying the discrepancy between the actual state of healthcare and its desired future state means existing generations must contribute some form of capital (e.g., money, time, effort) in the here and now for the benefit of people who are socially, spatially, and temporally distant; indeed, who do not yet exist.

Although this discussion of the implications of prospection for the development of indicators of the greater good shows how past-oriented indicators can provide orientation (i.e., where are we?) and how future-oriented indicators can imply direction (i.e., where should we go?), these qualities fall short of what is required to bring indicators within the purview of leadership. In order to do so, indicators of the greater good also need to guide navigation (i.e., how do we get there?), which means that they need to illuminate choices about pathways to idealized futures and inform decisions about how to resolve the trade-offs and dilemmas encountered *en route*. Moreover, these pathways and decisions require some criteria against which their virtue can be assessed. This involves asking of a given choice or decision: Is it right? Is it just? Does it impair the ability of future generations to meet their needs? These are questions of practical wisdom, which Barry Schwartz (2010), drawing on Aristotle, defines as the *moral will* to do the right thing and the *moral skill* to figure out what the right thing is. Understood this way, creating indicators that can illuminate desired future states and inform the leadership enacted in their service poses challenges of wisdom equal to the technical challenges of index construction.

Navigating into the Future, Together

In the context of concerns about the end of a safe operating space for humanity, there is an emerging global view that human societies must radically change so as to preserve the natural systems that ultimately undergird human well-being. Despite the existential threats posed by crossing key planetary boundaries (Rockström et al., 2009; Steffen et al., 2015), a salutary effect of these and related challenges is the gradual widening of conceptions of the greater good to include the interests of nonhuman species and the natural world, not simply human interests. In principle, this bodes well for the restoration of concern for the well-being of the whole.

However, these theoretical developments mean little if lay concepts of the greater good are not inclusive of these extra-regarding interests. In the context of English-speaking nations in the late modern age — the focus of this chapter — this concern is amplified because the citizens of these nations are no longer prepared to subjugate their interests in preference to the interests of the broader society (Judt, 2010; Salt, 2104), let alone the interests of the natural world. To the extent that the citizens of English-speaking nations are more concerned with self-regarding than extra-regarding interests, the emergence of widespread concern for the greater human good, to say nothing of the greater planetary good, seems vanishingly unlikely in the near term.

The irony of this situation relates to the tragic or, better, tragicomic, misfit between the existential challenges facing the citizens of English-speaking nations and their widely shared pre-occupation with the pursuit of material self-interest, which may constitute whatever remains of their sense of collective purpose (Judt, 2010). Stated baldly, the irony is this: the approach needed to address these complex challenges is precisely the approach to which the citizens of these nations are currently least receptive. To understand the reasoning that underpins this claim, it is necessary to first understand the relationship that inheres between the ways in which problems are construed and culturally appropriate ways of responding to problems.

As a moment's reflection confirms, problems are not all the same. However, despite obvious differences between problems, problems often have common characteristics that hang together in meaningful patterns. For example, some problems are easy to define and solve, whereas other problems seem intractable, resisting definition, and solution. Forty years ago, Horst W. J. Rittel and Melvin M. Webber (1973) recognized and categorized these patterns in their seminal paper on tame and wicked problems. This was expanded more recently by Keith Grint (2005, 2010) into a typology of critical, tame, and wicked problems, which are associated in the Western world with command, management, and leadership, respectively.

Critical problems are those that arise from a crisis of some sort (e.g., forest fires). These problems are self-evident and must be addressed urgently, allowing little time for decision-making (Grint, 2010). Although the people who are directly affected by a critical problem may not fully understand it or know how to solve it — after all, it is hard to see the forest for the (burning) trees in the middle of a crisis — the expectations of those who are charged with solving critical problems are clear: provide the answer, fix the problem. Because a crisis is not the time to plan strategy (as in management) or build collaboration around values and vision (as in leadership), critical problems are often viewed as warranting a commanding approach to problem solving. Command, however, is not leadership.

Tame or technical problems are familiar or recurrent and can be solved using known decision-making processes and standard operating procedures (Grint, 2010; Heifetz, 1994; Rittel & Webber, 1973). Unilateral acts by experts (e.g., physicians) are often sufficient to solve tame problems. The ability of experts to unilaterally solve tame problems means that problem solving requires minimal involvement of the actors involved in the problem situation. For example, all that a physician needs to successfully fix a broken arm are the right tools. For the most part, she does not need to take into account the peculiar perspectives or beliefs of the person on whom she is operating. Management is, of course, crucial. Management is not, however, leadership.

Wicked or adaptive problems are the antithesis of tame problems. Wicked problems are more than complicated — they are complex, difficult to define, and ever changing (Grint, 2010; Heifetz, 1994; Rittel & Webber, 1973). Whereas experts are often ascribed responsibility for managing technical problems and authorities are often expected to use command and control to fix critical problems, responsibility for addressing wicked problems falls to the actors involved. This means that coordination among those actors cannot be patterned by compliance with experts (as in management) or obedience to authorities (as in command). What is required here is leadership, defined as persuading the people involved in a problem situation to take responsibility for collective challenges and mobilizing them to act collaboratively to address these challenges (Grint, 2010; Heifetz, 1994; Heifetz, Grashow, & Linsky, 2009). What is distinctive about leadership is what it asks of the people involved in a problem situation. It calls on all those who are part of the collective challenge to engage with it and to partly think, partly feel their way toward an understanding of its nature and resolution. Combined with shared imaginings about idealized futures (Carsten & Bligh, 2008), this co-constructed understanding of the problem situation helps all involved to see the forest and the trees (Kahane, 2010, 2012).

It is pertinent, at this point, to return to the earlier assertion that the approach needed to address complex challenges in English-speaking nations is precisely the approach to which the citizens of these nations are least receptive. The reasoning that undergirds this claim may be stated thus: if humanity's toughest social and environmental challenges are properly construed as wicked problems (see, e.g., Lazarus, 2009; Levin, Cashore, Bernstein, & Auld, 2012), and if wicked problems are most appropriately addressed with leadership, which involves persuading the collective to take responsibility for collective problems, then the current tendency of people in these nations to discount the validity of shared interests and collective purpose (Bauman, 2000; Giddens, 1991), combined with their predilection for framing problems as crises that warrant command (Grint, 2010), undermines attempts to address wicked problems adequately.

This insight has profound consequences for leadership for the greater good. If there is to be a reawakening of concern for shared interests and collective purpose among the citizens of English-speaking nations, this will require deep re-engagement with, and active reimagining of, the idea of the greater good.

Crucially, this means that all those who would practice leadership for the greater good must engage, generously, patiently, and wisely, with ordinary citizens who must discover for themselves the hidden connections between the social, economic, and environmental facets of their lives; citizens must discover for themselves that their well-being is ultimately contingent on the well-being of the whole.

Co-creating indicators and information systems of the greater good that are grounded in mutually shared conceptions of the whole is a powerful and nonobvious way to cultivate the sense of collective responsibility necessary for understanding the nature of our toughest social and environmental challenges, the modes of collaboration necessary to address these challenges, and the pathways through which desired futures might be jointly realized. The creation of these instruments of embodied wisdom is thus squarely in the purview of leadership and offers promising new avenues for the practice of leadership for a healthy world.

Acknowledgments

The author gratefully acknowledges John Eric Baugher and Kathryn Goldman Schuyler for their invaluable feedback on earlier drafts of this chapter and Mark Manolopoulos for sharing his insights into the history of the idea of the greater good in philosophy.

References

Adballah, S., Michaelson, J., Shah, S., Stoll, L., & Marks, N. (2012). *The happy planet index: 2012 report: A global index of sustainable well-being*. London: New Economics Foundation. Retrieved from http://www.happyplanetindex.org

Albert, M. (1993). *Capitalism against capitalism* (P. Haviland, Trans.). London: Whurr.

Aquinas. (1981). *Summa theologiae* (Fathers of the English Dominican Province, Trans.). Westminster: Christian Classics.

Aristotle. (1984). *The politics* (C. Lord, Trans.). Chicago, IL: University of Chicago Press.

Aristotle. (2013). *Eudemian ethics* (B. Inwood, Trans.). Cambridge: Cambridge University Press.

Armstrong, J. (2009). *In search of civilization: Remaking a tarnished idea*. London: Allen Lane.

AtKisson, A., & Hatcher, R. L. (2001). The compass index of sustainability: Prototype for a comprehensive sustainability information system. *Journal of Environment Assessment Policy and Management, 3*(4), 509–532. doi:10.1142/S1464333201000820

Augustine. (1983). *City of god* (M. Dods, Trans.). New York, NY: Modern Library.

Australian Bureau of Statistics. (2013). *Measuring Australia's progress 2013: Is life in Australia getting better?* Cat. No. 1370.0. Canberra: Australian Bureau of Statistics. Retrieved from http://www.abs.gov.au/ausstats/abs@.nsf/mf/1370.0

Bates, W. (2009). Gross national happiness. *Asian-Pacific Economic Literature, 23*(2), 1–16. doi:10.1111/j.1467-8411.2009.01235.x

Bauman, Z. (2000). *Liquid modernity*. Cambridge: Polity Press.

Bauman, Z. (2007). *Liquid times: Living in an age of uncertainty*. Cambridge: Polity Press.

Baumol, W., Litan, R., & Schramm, C. (2007). *Good capitalism, bad capitalism, and the economics of growth and prosperity*. New Haven, CT: Yale University Press.

Bentham, J. (1983). Deontology together with a table of the springs and the article on deontology. In A. Goldsworth (Ed.). *The collected works of Jeremy Bentham*. Oxford: Clarendon Press.

Carsten, M. K., & Bligh, M. C. (2008). Lead, follow, and get out of the way: Involving employees in the visioning process. In R. E. Riggio, I. Chaleff, & J. Lipman-Blumen (Eds.), *The art of followership: How great followers create great leaders and organizations* (pp. 277–290). San Francisco, CA: Jossey-Bass.

Chomsky, N. (2013). The Dewey lectures 2013: What kind of creatures are we? Lecture III: What is the common good? *The Journal of Philosophy, 110*(12), 685–700.

Cobb, C., Halstead, T., & Rowe, J. (1995). *The genuine progress indicator: Summary of data and methodology*. San Francisco, CA: Redefining Progress.

Costanza, R., Erickson, J., Fligger, K., Adams, A., Adams, C., Altschuler, B., et al. (2004). Estimates of the genuine progress indicator (GPI) for Vermont, Chittenden county and Burlington, from 1950 to 2000. *Ecological Economics, 51*, 139–155. doi:10.1016/j.ecolecon.2004.04.009

Daly, H. E. (1973). *Towards a steady state economy*. San Francisco, CA: W. H. Freeman and Company.

Daly, H. E., & Cobb, J. (1989). *For the common good: Redirecting the economy towards community, the environment, and a sustainable future*. Boston, MA: Beacon Press.

De Leon, E. (2012). *National indicators and social wealth*. Washington, DC: Urban Institute.

De Leon, E., & Boris, E. (2010). *The state of society: Measuring economic success and human well-being*. Washington, DC: Urban Institute.

Dunlop, S., & Swales, K. (2012). *The Oxfam humankind index for Scotland*. Scotland: Oxfam GB. Retrieved from http://policy-practice.oxfam.org.uk.

Dwivedi, O. P. (2000). Dharmic ecology. In C. K. Chapple & M. E. Tucker (Eds.), *Hinduism and ecology: The intersection of earth, sky, and water* (pp. 3–22). Cambridge, MA: Harvard University Press.

Eisler, R. (2007). *The real wealth of nations: Creating a caring economics*. San Francisco, CA: Berrett-Koehler.

Eliasoph, N. (1998). *Avoiding politics: How Americans produce apathy in everyday life*. Cambridge: Cambridge University Press.

Forrester, J. W. (1971). *World dynamics*. Portland, OR: Productivity Press.

Galbraith, J. K. (1994). *A journey through economic time: A first hand view*. Boston, MA: Houghton Mifflin.

Ghosh, I. (2014a). *Social wealth economic indicators: A new system for evaluating economic prosperity*. Pacific Grove, CA: Center for Partnership Studies.

Ghosh, I. (2014b). Social wealth economic indicators for a caring economy. *Interdisciplinary Journal of Partnership Studies, 1*, article 5. Retrieved from http://pubs.lib.umn.edu/ijps/vol1/iss1/5

Giddens, A. (1991). *Modernity and self-identity: Self and society in the late modern age*. Stanford, CA: Stanford University Press.

Gilbert, D. T., & Wilson, T. D. (2007, September 7). Prospection: Experiencing the future. *Science, 317*, 1351–1354. doi:10.1126/science.1144161

Gleeson-White, J. (2014). *Six capitals: The revolution capitalism has to have— Or can accountants save the planet?* Crows Nest: Allen & Unwin.

Grint, K. (2005). Problems, problems, problems: The social construction of 'leadership'. *Human Relations, 58*, 1467–1494. doi:10.1177/0018726705061314

Grint, K. (2010). The cuckoo clock syndrome: Addicted to command, allergic to leadership. *European Management Journal, 28*, 306–313. doi:10.1016/j.emj.2010.05.002

Gruen, N., & Lancy, A. (2011). *The herald/age-lateral economics index of Australia's well-being*. Retrieved from http://lateraleconomics.com.au/wp-content/uploads/2014/02/Fairfax-Lateral-Economics-Index-of-Australias-Wellbeing-Final-Report.pdf

Hacker, J. S. (2006). *The great risk shift: The assault on American jobs, families, healthcare, and retirement and how you can fight back*. New York, NY: Oxford University Press.

Hamilton, C. (1999). The genuine progress indicator methodological developments and results from Australia. *Ecological Economics, 30*, 13–28. doi:10.1016/S0921-8009(98)00099-8

Hamilton, C., & Saddler, H. (1997). *The genuine progress indicator: A new index of changes in well-being in Australia*. Canberra: The Australia Institute. Retrieved from http://www.tai.org.au/documents/downloads/DP14.pdf

Hardin, G. (1968, December 13). The tragedy of the commons. *Science, 162*, 1243–1248. doi:10.1126/science.162.3859.1243

Haslam, N., & Loughnan, S. (2014). Dehumanization and infrahumanization. *Annual Review of Psychology, 65*, 399–423. doi:10.1146/annurev-psych-010213-115045

Hawken, P., Lovins, A. B., & Lovins, L. H. (2000). *Natural capitalism: The next industrial revolution*. London: Earthscan.

Heifetz, R. A. (1994). *Leadership without easy answers*. Cambridge, MA: The Belknap Press of Harvard University Press.

Heifetz, R., Grashow, A., & Linsky, M. (2009). *The practice of adaptive leadership: Tools and tactics for changing your organization and the world.* Boston, MA: Harvard Business Press.

Hobbes, T. (1924). *Leviathan.* London: Dent.

Jackson, T. (2009). *Prosperity without growth: Economics for a finite planet.* London: Earthscan.

James, O. (2008). *The selfish capitalist: Origins of affluenza.* London: Vermillion.

Jironet, K. (2014). Awareness and beyond: Why moving on means letting go. In K. Goldman Schuyler, J. E. Baugher, K. Jironet, & L. Lid-Falkman (Eds.), *Leading with spirit, presence, & authenticity* (pp. 3–13). San Francisco, CA: Jossey-Bass.

Judt, T. (2010). *Ill fares the land.* London: Penguin Books.

Kahane, A. M. (2010). *Power and love: A theory and practice of social change.* San Francisco, CA: Berrett-Koehler.

Kahane, A. M. (2012). *Transformative scenario planning: Working together to change the future.* San Francisco, CA: Berrett-Koehler.

Lama, D. (1988). *Humanity and ecology.* India: The Office of his Holiness the Dalai Lama.

Lancy, A., & Gruen, N. (2013). Constructing the herald/age-lateral economics index of Australia's wellbeing. *The Australian Economic Review, 46*(1), 92–102. doi:10.1111/j.1467-8462.2013.12000.x

Lazarus, R. J. (2009). Super wicked problems and climate change: Restraining the present to liberate the future. *Cornell Law Review, 94,* 1153–1233. Retrieved from http://www.lawschool.cornell.edu/research/cornell-law-review/upload/Lazarus.pdf

Levin, K., Cashore, B., Bernstein, S., & Auld, G. (2012). Overcoming the tragedy of super wicked problems: Constraining our future selves to ameliorate global climate change. *Policy Sciences, 45,* 123–152. doi:10.1007/s11077-012-9151-0

Lovelock, J. (2009). *The vanishing face of gaia.* Camberwell: Allen Lane.

McAuley, I., & Lyons, M. (2015). *Governomics: Can we afford small government?* Carlton: Melbourne University Press.

Meadows, D. (1998). *Indicators and information systems for sustainable development.* Retrieved from http://www.iisd.org/pdf/s_ind_2.pdf

Michalos, A. C., Smale, B., Labonté, R., Muharjarine, N., Scott, K., Moore, K., et al. (2011). *The Canadian Index of Wellbeing,* Technical Report 1.0., Waterloo: Canadian Index of Wellbeing and University of Waterloo.

Mill, J. S. (2002). What is utilitarianism? In G. Sher (Ed.), *Utilitarianism and the 1868 speech on capital punishment* (2nd ed., pp. 6–26). Indianapolis, IN: Hackett Publishing Company.

Parks, C. D., Joireman, J., & Van Lange, P. A. M. (2013). Cooperation, trust, and antagonism: How public goods are promoted. *Psychological Science in the Public Interest, 14*(3), 119–165. doi:10.1177/1529100612474436

Pimpare, S. (2004). *The new victorians: Poverty, politics and propaganda in two gilded ages.* New York, NY: The New Press.

Plato. (1975). *The republic* (D. Lee, Trans. 2nd ed.). Harmondsworth: Penguin.

Porter, M. E., & Stern, S. (2015). *Social progress index 2015*. Washington, DC: Social Progress Imperative. Retrieved from http://www.socialprogressimperative. org/publications

Rawls, J. (1971). *A theory of justice*. Cambridge, MA: Harvard University Press.

Reich, R. (2009). *Supercapitalism: The battle for democracy in an age of big business*. London: Icon Books.

Rittel, H. W. J., & Webber, M. M. (1973). Dilemmas in a general theory of planning. *Policy Sciences, 4*, 155–169. doi:10.1007/BF01405730

Rockström, J., Steffen, W., Noone, K., Persson, A., Chapin III, S., Lambin, E. F., & Foley, J. A. (2009, September 24). A safe operating space for humanity. *Nature, 461*, 472–475. doi:10.1038/461472a

Rousseau, J.-J. (1913). *The social contract*. (G. D. H., Col, Trans.). London: Dent.

Salt, B. (2014). Collective cheers as age of entitlement nears end. *The Australian*, November 6. Retrieved from http://www.theaustralian.com.au

Saul, J. R. (1995). *The unconscious civilization*. New York, NY: Simon & Schuster.

Saul, J. R. (2009). *The collapse of globalism: And the reinvention of the world*. Camberwell: Penguin.

Scharmer, O., & Kaufer, K. (2013). *Leading from the emerging future: From ego-system to eco-system economies*. San Francisco, CA: Berrett-Koehler.

Schroyer, T. (2009). *Beyond western economics: Remembering other economic cultures*. New York, NY: Routledge.

Schwartz, B. (2010). *Using our practical wisdom*. Retrieved from http:// www.ted.com/talks/barry_schwartz_using_our_practical_wisdom?language=en

Sennett, R. (2006). *The culture of the new capitalism*. New Haven, CT: Yale University Press.

Steffen, W., Richardson, K., Rockström, J., Cornell, S. E., Fetzer, I., Bennett, E. M., et al. (2015, February 13). Planetary boundaries: Guiding human development on a changing planet. *Science, 347*, 736. doi:10.1126/science.1259855

Stiglitz, J., Sen, A., & Fitoussi, J.-P. (2009). *Report of the commission of the measurement of economic and social progress*. Retrieved from http://www. stiglitz-sen-fitoussi.fr/documents/rapport_anglais.pdf

Talberth, J., Cobb, C., & Slattery, N. (2007). *The genuine progress indicator 2006: A tool for sustainable development*. Retrieved from http://rprogress.org/ publications/2007/GPI%202006.pdf

United Nations Development Programme. (2011). *Human development report 2011: Sustainability and equity: A better future for all*. Basingstoke: Palgrave Macmillan.

Ura, K., Alkire, S., Zangmo, T., & Wangdi, K. (2012). *A short guide to the gross national happiness index*. Thimphu: Centre for Bhutan Studies. Retrieved from http://www.grossnationalhappiness.com/wp-content/uploads/2012/04/Short-GNH-Index-edited.pdf

Wilson, S., & Fien, J. (2015). *Swinburne leadership survey 2014: Index of leadership for the greater good.* Hawthorn: Swinburne Leadership Institute. Retrieved from http://www.swinburne.edu.au/leadership-institute

WWF. (2014). In R. McLellan, L. Iyangar, & N. Oerlemans (Eds.), *Living planet report 2014: Species and spaces, people and places.* Gland: WWF. Retrieved from http://www.awassets.panda.org/wwf_lpr2014_low_res_full_report.pdf

Žižek, S. (2013). In Y.-J. Park (Ed.), *Demanding the impossible.* Cambridge: Polity Press.

7 Developing Relational Leadership in Africa

Charles J. Palus, Steadman Harrison III, and Joshua J. Prasad

There has been a profound shift in recent years in theory as well as in practice away from an individualistic and heroic approach to leadership to more collective leadership beliefs and practices with an underlying relational ontology (Day, 2000; Drath, 2001; Drath et al., 2008; McCauley et al., 2008; Ospina & Uhl-Bien, 2012). Individualistic conceptions of leadership sharply distinguish between leaders and followers, whereas a relational ontology reframes leadership as social beliefs and practices for creating shared direction, alignment, and commitment (Drath et al., 2008). An advantage of a relational view of leadership is that it brings into view the complex social processes that create and develop leadership. Even more so, a more relational view of leadership is crucial for addressing complex organizational and societal health challenges in an increasingly interdependent world (Palus, McGuire, & Ernst, 2012).

In this chapter, we examine how a relational view of leadership development can support greater organizational health and societal well-being. We understand organizational health as an adaptive ability to deliberately create and sustain strategic positive organizational change including increasing value for society (Porter & Kramer, 2011). The mode of adaptive leadership versus technical problem solving is key for long-term survival of any organization (Heifetz, 1994). Adaptive leadership requires a cultural shift in how people understand their shared work and how they learn and grow in the face of adaptive challenges (Heifetz, Linsky, & Grashow, 2009). To support such a shift in one's organization, leaders must cultivate their own maturity and moral development by thinking and acting within a series of progressively more relational and complex action logics (Nicolaides & McCallum, 2013).

To illustrate this shift to a more relational perspective on leadership development, this chapter unfolds in three sections. First, we draw on Bill Torbert's (2004) work on adult epistemological development and seven potential stages of leadership transformation. Second, we describe our experiences cocreating leadership development experiences in Eastern Africa, highlighted by the case of World Vision, a nongovernmental organization working on the health needs of children, families, and communities. We conclude with strategic lessons from our work in Eastern Africa regarding innovation in leadership development for organizational health and societal well-being in an increasingly interdependent world.

This is also a case study of our own organization, the Center for Creative Leadership (CCL), and how we had to adapt and develop our own beliefs and practices to collaborate effectively on leadership development in Eastern Africa. CCL is a US-based not-for-profit organization with the mission of advancing the understanding, practice, and development of leadership for the benefit of society worldwide. Around 2004, CCL reviewed its mission in terms of "society worldwide" and emerged with a commitment to reach under-served populations at the base of the economic pyramid. This new vision called for "democratizing leadership development" by helping more people participate in society as leaders (Altman, Rego, & Harrison, 2010). The challenges of doing this in Africa, India, and China became compelling and then overwhelming. Our path forward involved small prototype projects grounded in *design thinking* and *collaborative inquiry* (as explained below), including the stories we tell in this chapter. An emerging relational perspective on leadership development research and practice at CCL helped us think and act more interdependently and collaborate with a variety of partners and clients (McGuire, Palus, & Torbert, 2007).

From Leader-Centric to Relational Leadership

The shift from a leader-centric to a relational understanding of leadership transcends and yet includes aspects of the traditional individualist understanding. The relational view focuses on the fabric of how people connect and relate, while not at all losing sight of the learning and development of individual actors. Interdependent, connected, and more agile forms of leadership require individual development in tandem with the sociocultural evolution of shared beliefs and practices.

A challenge in developing relational leadership is that individuals in traditional roles typically "have their minds made up" about what effective leadership looks like. At the same time, traditional forms of leadership have often overreached their capacity for effectiveness in a changing world. This is a golden opportunity for individual and collective development.

Torbert depicts individual development as a life-long process consisting of increasingly complex and relationally agile stages (Torbert, 1987, 2004, 2013), building on the work of Robert Kegan, Chris Argyris, and other learning and development theorists (Argyris, Putnam, & Smith, 1985; Commons & Richards, 2003; Cook-Greuter, 1999; Kegan, 1994; Kohlberg, 1969; Wilber, 2000). At the CCL, we find this model helpful for (co-)framing and (co-)exploring "vertical" leadership development (Petrie, 2014) in an increasingly interdependent world (McCauley, Drath, Palus, O'Connor, & Baker, 2006; McGuire et al., 2007; Palus & Drath, 1995).

In Torbert's model, each stage represents a distinct epistemology (structure of logic) for relating, framing, and acting (Kegan, 1994; Piaget, 1954). These are referred to as "action logics," or as "leadership logics" when exercised in leadership contexts (Torbert, 2004). Premised on constructive-development theory, individuals mature predictably from one stage to the next stage, where one can continue to access earlier logics as necessary, but now as objects or tools within a larger and more complex logic (McCauley et al., 2006). There are potentially at least seven successive stages beyond early childhood (as popularized in *The Seven Transformations of Leadership*, Rooke & Torbert, 2005):

1. Opportunist: Wins for self in any way possible
2. Diplomat: Wants to belong and fit in
3. Expert: Focused on logic and expertise
4. Achiever: Driven by personal and team achievement
5. Redefining: Reframing complex problems in unique ways
6. Transforming: Generating organizational and personal transformations
7. Alchemical: Integrating material, spiritual, and societal transformations

Currently, most large organizations are governed by Achiever action logics, which makes sustained, inter-systemic, intentional change unlikely (Fisher & Torbert, 1991; Rooke & Torbert, 1998). The Opportunist and Achiever stages are particularly individualistic (Kegan, 1994). It is only in the last three stages (Redefining, Transforming, Alchemical) that a leader fully engages relational and potentially transformative beliefs and practices. Notice that the names themselves of the first four logic are person-oriented, while the last three logics are process-oriented, a recent evolution of the nomenclature meant to underline their relational nature (Torbert et al., 2015). An interdependent (or more accurately here, *inter-independent*) leadership culture emerges when Redefining, Transforming, and Alchemical leadership logics become central to creating shared direction, alignment, and commitment (Palus et al., 2012).

A growing body of evidence shows that organizations with interdependent leadership cultures are more agile and better able to adapt in healthy ways (Drath, Palus, & McGuire, 2010; Laloux, 2014; McCauley et al., 2008). In line with this evidence, we propose a path to healthier organizations and positive societal impact as follows (McGuire & Rhodes, 2009):

1. Increasing wisdom and maturity (i.e., post-Achiever relational logics) of one or more individual senior leaders by means of stage development and/or career succession.
2. Increasing wisdom and maturity of the leadership council (or senior team, etc.) as a whole (post-Achiever relational logics) by means of peer and social influence, spiritual inspiration, and coaching.
3. Formation and execution of wise and mature mission-based leadership strategies (plural, multi-perspectival, cross-sectoral) for positive cultural and societal advancement.

Methodologies for Cocreating Leadership Development

Two methodologies have helped us work within a network of partners and allies to cocreate leadership development initiatives in East Africa: design thinking and collaborative inquiry.

Design thinking means using the mindset of a designer to approach and solve complex challenges (Martin, 2009). Designers focus on useful solutions that are well-suited to users and their context. Design thinking allows ideas and designs to emerge from shared experiences rather than being imposed by experts (Brown & Wyatt, 2010). Key principals of design thinking are empathic immersion in the world of the user, the integration of analysis and intuition, and rapid prototyping.

As CCL framed its aspirations for extending leadership development to more parts of the world, it was easy to become paralyzed by the range of possibilities and obstacles. We collaborated with the design consultancies IDEO and Continuum to jumpstart our appreciation of design thinking as applied to social innovation.

Collaborative inquiry is a methodology for collective learning and mutual development in the face of complex challenges (Bray, Lee, Smith, & Yorks, 2000; Torbert, 1981). It is a collaborative interweaving of research and practice intended to help people shift from a Dependent (Diplomat), to an Independent (Achiever), and toward an Interdependent (Transforming) set of leadership logics (McGuire et al., 2007). Collaborative inquiry integrates three domains of research and reflection: first-person (subjective), second-person (inter-subjective), and third-person (objective) (Torbert, 2004).

A core practice of collaborative inquiry is dialogue, a form of conversation that surfaces and tests assumptions, and creates shared meaning across differences in belief and culture (Kahane, 2004). Evaluation of the impact of leadership development, and learning in general, becomes based on an ongoing multi-perspective dialogue that feeds the design process.

Developing Leadership in Eastern Africa

The CCL made an exploratory move into rural Africa in 2005 when one of our team members volunteered at an orphanage in Uganda. David (pseudonym) went to Eastern Africa expecting to help with management in the local office of Good Shepherd's Fold, an organization devoted to helping vulnerable children in a country afflicted by many years of war. He encountered widespread interest in the topic of leadership development. Every time he mentioned his day job working with leaders in America, a conversation unfolded. People would ask: "Am I a leader? Can you make me one? Where does leadership come from?" There were immediate requests for help. "Can you work with our youth to help them with self-esteem, courage, and confidence?

Can you assist our team at the office?" At this point in his own life, David was mainly driven by an Expert leadership logic and he viewed these questions as technical challenges. His naiveté was offset by his contagious energy and optimism.

Upon returning to the United States, he described the opportunities he had seen. He was met with skepticism. "What do we really know about leadership in Africa? Do we dare carry Western models into another culture?" Many of his colleagues wanted to know about the business case for expanding leadership development in Africa. Some colleagues wanted to apply their own expertise to solve the problems of leadership they could see from a distance. A few friends discussed the potential for learning and their hope of collaboration and dreamed together of what might be achieved. These included people around the organization with appetites and action logics for redefining and transforming what the experts said. This network of colleagues was able to grasp the nature of the adaptive challenges and not be distracted by the technical problems. They started building a network of allies, partners, and volunteers as an extended community of social innovators with a more interdependent leadership culture.

In 2006, a research team from CCL went back to Uganda with seed funding from a U.S.-based foundation. They adapted beliefs and practices from design thinking and collaborative inquiry — including immersion, empathic observation, interviews, group dialogue, and rapid prototyping — to learn about the indigenous view of leaders, leadership, and leadership development. A goal was to understand how ideas related to leadership translated in Swahili, Lugandan, Acholi, and other native languages. We found that people typically associated the word leadership with hierarchy, authority, and political power. Often the connotations were negative. Because of this we downplayed the terms "leader" and "leadership" and substituted a relational ontology based on social beliefs and processes that create and maintain shared direction, alignment, and commitment (Drath et al., 2008).

The team concluded that there were key ideas — *Leadership Essentials* we came to call them — that could provide bridges between leadership research and practice in the United States, and the application and development of leadership in Africa (Browning, 2006; Wakefield, 2006). These essentials were described in different ways but were always present in some form in the groups we interviewed. Our initial leadership essentials categories included *self-awareness, communication, learning*, and *teamwork*.

First, self-awareness — knowing "who I am" and by extension, "who you are" — was widely viewed as essential for anyone working in groups. Self-reflection and dialogue about social identity, in terms of one's given, chosen and core identities, became a central part of our work.

Communication (e.g., dialogue, influence, public speaking) both within and across social-cultural boundaries was an essential category. For example, workshops included reflection on the degree of candor present in the room at any time, and we explored mental models that shaped how we spoke with one another.

Individual and collective learning (e.g., education, training, knowledge) were essential to almost everyone's vision of a better future, and we engaged people around their learning styles, and the dynamics of feedback. Experiential learning modules were effective at exploring and improving the process of learning in public.

Better teamwork was always expressed as a need when we worked with intact groups. Everyone wanted to improve how their teams functioned. Simply making the time and space to talk about these questions was welcomed, and sometimes just a little facilitation was enough to make a big difference. Our own expertise took a back seat, in favor of whatever was needed in the moment. An essential idea was that effective groups create and maintain shared direction, alignment, and commitment in getting from "here" (our present condition) to "there" (a better future.) Focusing on DAC helped groups innovate new forms of leadership in context of their own challenges.

A series of workshops was codesigned by CCL and their host team at Good Shepherd's Fold Orphanage with these leadership essentials in mind. The prototype design changed with each iteration based on feedback and mutual learning. The groups intentionally engaged in creative, open, and honest conversations, with the prototype design in question as "something in the middle" of the dialogue, as an object for examination and co-construction (Palus & McGuire, 2015). Mistakes became occasions for discovery and improvement.

For example, it had been taken for granted that PowerPoint presentations would be used in these workshops. Power blackouts forced the use of flip charts. When a deck of 20 slides had to be distilled to a single flip chart in real time, some of the first compact and concise designs for Leadership Essentials began to take shape. Someone described the design requirement for a single Leadership Essential as "so elegant that you can draw it in the dirt with a stick."

Hand-scored paper and pencil self-assessment tools such as the Myers-Briggs Type Indicator were initially thought to be ideal for workshops. However, they reminded participants of the national examinations used in school, implying that responses were right or wrong rather than personal preferences. As a result, these types of self-assessment tools were replaced by simple reflection and dialogue tools without a testing format (e.g., Visual Explorer, Social Identity Explorer).

At the end of a workshop for nongovernment organizations hosted in Jinja, Uganda, the delivery team asked for reflections. One tall man from Northern Uganda leaned into the circle to speak. When he was a boy he had been kidnaped by the Lord's Resistance Army. In recent years, he had been restored to his family and was now leading a local community-based organization in Gulu helping rehabilitate other ex-LRA soldiers. He said, "Where you come from leadership is about better business. But here in Uganda this same thing you are teaching us today can save lives. These lessons about leadership can end wars and help end epidemics."

The CCL team left Uganda inspired. They also had many questions yet to be answered. Much reflection and dialogue on these individual and shared experiences ensued.

Samaritan's Purse invited the team to come to Ethiopia the following year. They wanted to apply leadership development in the southwestern corner of Ethiopia, in a region called Gambella, where there was intense conflict between the warring tribes of the Nuer and Anuar. The region was home to thousands of refugees who faced food insecurity and political instability. Aaron, a young grant writer working for Samaritan's Purse, had suggested that they include leadership development as a lever for food security by bringing together members of warring tribes. The most important outcome of the Samaritan's Purse program in Gambella was the creation of a safe learning environment for critical conversations. At the close of the program, a ceremony took place where tribal leaders placed rocks and cement to create a set of steps in a public courtyard. The steps, still visible today, stand as a touchstone reminder of a commitment to peace.

The invitation to visit Ethiopia resulted in a longer stay. Within a few years Aaron joined the CCL team to focus his efforts fully on developing leaders across Ethiopia.

Partnership with World Vision Ethiopia

Partnership is fundamental to CCL's work in East Africa. Dialogue among multiple perspectives results in mutual learning and development, new insights, and better designs.

CCL is a resolutely secular and inclusive organization with a desire for partnership well beyond our own perspectives. Our partner, World Vision Ethiopia, is a faith-based organization focused on improving the lives of children. They began their work in Ethiopia in the early 1970s and expanded their work with emergency response programs during the 1984 famine. Both parties needed to learn more about the roles of both faith-based values and secular values in relation to leadership development in Africa. Starting in 2006, World Vision and CCL staff started informally sharing insights. A steady stream of learning transfer began between these organizations with differing perspectives but with many similar values and intentions. The dialogue deepened based on shared experiences, mutual respect, and trust.

In October 2012, the top 100 managers from across World Vision Ethiopia gathered at a meeting at the Red Cross Center. The incoming National Director, Margaret Schuler, invited members of our team to facilitate a dialogue about leadership. Schuler, in her new role, observed a stagnant, underperforming organization, and expressed her passion and commitment for positive change in World Vision with transformation of the leadership culture as a key lever.

Sponsorship and funding are key strategic success factors for World Vision Ethiopia. They faced a changing funding landscape before and during this period. Sponsorship funding decreased dramatically and donor-driven grants became more competitive each year. Short-notice budget cuts became more frequent. Where the World Vision team had previously been the expected winner of certain grants, now other NGOs were proposing more creative solutions in larger consortiums to win the attention and funding from donors. The World Vision Ethiopia team was pressed to be *both* more individually responsible *and* more collaborative in order to be innovative and competitive. An environmental shift took place from a dependent context where loyal sponsorships from abroad supported World Vision, through an independent context where the local team came to expect to win grants based on reputation, and into an increasingly interdependent context where consortiums, networks, and partnerships were essential to success.

The majority of World Vision staff had been hired from church or government. Their principle identity was Christian. The other main cultural influence was government. They acquired the traditional, hierarchical leadership culture of these sources. Senior leaders were in positions of command and control, casting the vision and taking all the decisions, with junior team members waiting for instructions. Loyal employees who met the *status quo* and kept the peace in the system enjoyed a steady career progression. This was a dependent leadership culture, based in the action logics of diplomacy and expertise. Their work of humanitarian aid and emergency response had grown to fit predictable templates that were repeated year after year without innovation.

Through organizational restructuring and communications, Schuler made the new paradigm clear: Individuals were accountable for results. External and internal collaboration would increase. The idea that children are at the center of the work was re-established. This shift to children at the center was a symbol of significant transformation. The culture of the organization was starting to be redefined. Many were starting to reflect upon and reconsider their core beliefs and practices about creating effective direction, alignment, and commitment. New leaders were recruited with all this in mind.

Leadership Essentials workshops were offered to all staff members. A common language of leadership emerged and took root in each of the regions. Goals created by staff in the workshop were shared with supervisors and woven into the next performance conversations. By the end of the year, all national office and country program managers were engaged in performance conversations that included leadership competencies. Leadership development became a metric side by side with spending and operational metrics.

This redefining and transforming approach to leadership provided a means of breaking with the old way of being and doing.

Leadership Logics at World Vision

As part of collaborative inquiry, we often conduct both formal and informal assessments of the leadership cultures and leadership (action) logics of the people involved, including our own

(McCauley et al., 2008; McGuire et al., 2007). Development occurs as these cultures and logics change over time to become more adequate in facing complex and changing leadership challenges. The overall direction of such development tends to be toward more relational beliefs and practices (Torbert, 2004). In practice, leadership cultures are a mix of logics, and we try to observe tendencies and preferences as members in the mix evolve in concert.

We met Schuler in 2012 when she had just been appointed as National Director for World Vision in Ethiopia. We estimate her leadership logic in that period as that of advanced Achiever, with emerging logics for Redefining complex challenges, and with Transforming aspirations. Because of a host of challenges, she wanted to transform World Vision from a strong hierarchical leadership culture based in diplomacy, compliance, and expertise to a culture of collaboration, agility, and shared leadership.

Schuler speaks of how her own development early in her career opened her mind to her potential beyond that of simply being an expert in a field. She describes development experiences that helped her see herself in the midst of a life-long journey becoming a better leader, a better manager, a better parent, a better family member. This type of integrated self-understanding is essential to the action logic of the Achiever stage and is highly prized in Western cultures. It also provides the necessary foundation for the Redefining leadership logic, in which one's own strong (independent) identity becomes increasingly "inter-independent" with other strong identities.

When Schuler arrived, the incumbent senior team of World Vision embodied the leadership logics of Diplomat and Expert. This served them well in a politicized environment with a steep hierarchy, but did not bode well for strategic culture change. Schuler decided that it would take too long to develop the existing team toward a shared leadership logic sufficient for transformation. Her solution was to retain a few key members, and then restructure, recruit, and further develop the team she needed.

We watched as Schuler won people over to a set of more mature leadership logics. She worked hard to spend one-to-one time with her senior team members and she leveraged retreats and regular senior team meetings to practice collaboration.

Several of her revised team were strong achievers and were able to appreciate her approach of redefinition and reframing toward a more collaborative culture. However, when Schuler moved into a period of true transformation, it strained the relationship with a number of senior team members who remained traditional in their outlooks. As the bar was raised regarding redefining and transformational expectations, opportunists, diplomats, and experts felt themselves outside of the core culture and left behind. As a result, many people opted to leave the organization, and the senior team was reconfigured through a number of purposeful efforts to restructure and reduce the workforce. As the noise quieted down, the right people remained. Change was underway at World Vision Ethiopia.

Both World Vision Ethiopia and CCL have grown as a result of a partnership where collaborative inquiry and design thinking have been applied to shift and shape a culture of interdependence.

Strategic Lessons for Leadership Development from Ethiopia

We conclude by reflecting on what we have learned so far within these relationships and from these experiences, in terms of strategic advice for innovators in leadership development.

LOOK FOR ESSENTIALS

Leadership differs among cultures and so must leadership development. For example, the GLOBE project studied the cultural context of how middle managers in 62 countries recognize effective leadership (Hofstede, 1993; House, Hanges, Javidan, Dorfman, & Gupta, 2004). The attributes thus named vary across cultures according to six distinctive styles pertaining to participation, autonomy, self-protection, and so on. Leadership beliefs and practices cannot simply be imported naively from one culture to the next. *Differentiating* the unique qualities of each person and culture is a key first step in spanning boundaries, prior even to finding common ground and integrating across differences (Ernst & Chrobot-Mason, 2010).

At the same time, we now believe that there are aspects of human relationships shared among cultures that when developed toward maturity can begin to bridge different cultures and contexts. Such beliefs are contentious in an era of cultural relativism. Our efforts at collaborative inquiry in Ethiopia surfaced the term "essential" and the idea of "leadership essentials" as fruitful vehicles for identifying leverage points for leadership development. Each category of leadership essential — including but not limited to *self-awareness, communication, learning,* and *teamwork* — is adapted through design thinking and collaborative inquiry to the local culture(s) and context(s). In other words, these essentials should be adapted to the *leadership strategies* (plural, multi-perspectival, cross-sectoral) for positive healthy advancement of the larger societies and cultures (Asif & Palus, 2013).

DEVELOP BOTH INDIVIDUAL AND COLLECTIVE ASPECTS OF LEADERSHIP

The path to more relational forms of leadership lies in developing individuals as well as collective aspects such as teamwork and culture. "Individual" and "collective" can be managed in a "both/and" way as a healthy polarity (Johnson, 1992). The relational view of leadership understands that the individual role is powerful, and at the same time is always performed in the context of the whole system of beliefs, practices, and action logics (in sum, the leadership culture) that shape how shared direction, alignment, and commitment are created (Drath et al., 2008).

COLLABORATE, INQUIRE, AND DESIGN

Adapting leadership development to local contexts requires continuous learning and sustained collaboration around the building and testing of prototypes. This kind of collaborative inquiry and design thinking go beyond the independent Expert and Achiever action logics typically found in the world of consultants and academics, and require the more interdependent (post-formal) logics of transformation and alchemy. Development in this approach is mutual rather than something "done to" a subject. In simpler terms, societal health requires that we work together in increasingly wise, mature, and practically effective ways.

MAKE LEADERSHIP ONTOLOGY AND EPISTEMOLOGY EXPLICIT

How we frame and recognize effective leadership determines the nature and quality of our designs, as well as the quality of our partnerships. The relational leadership ontology of *direction, alignment, and commitment* offers a wider range of adaptive choices than the traditional, individualistic, and narrower ontology of *leaders, followers, and goals* (Drath et al., 2008). Likewise, the positive transformation of leadership capacities, aimed at improved societal health per evolving mission-based leadership strategies, requires more wise, mature, and transformative action logics (epistemologies).

Finally, let's reprise the three part developmental path for increasingly relational leadership proposed earlier in this chapter. We believe it to be true, and, it remains to be tested and adapted in any new context. We invite readers to use design thinking and collaborative inquiry and compare this path to your own situations:

1. Increase wisdom and maturity of individual senior leaders
2. Increase wisdom and maturity of the leadership council
3. Formation and execution of wise and mature mission-based leadership strategies for positive cultural and societal advancement.

References

Altman, D. G., Rego, L., & Harrison, S. D. (2010). Democratizing leadership development. In C. D. McCauley & E. Van Velsor (Eds.), *The center for creative leadership handbook of leadership development* (3rd ed., pp. 221–250). San Francisco, CA: Jossey-Bass.

Argyris, C., Putnam, R., & Smith, D. (1985). *Action science: Concepts, methods, and skills for research and intervention.* San Francisco, CA: Jossey-Bass.

Asif, V., & Palus, C. J. (2013). *Leadership strategies for societal impact.* CCL White Paper. Greensboro, NC: Center for Creative Leadership.

Bray, J. N., Lee, J., Smith, L. L., & Yorks, L. (2000). *Collaborative inquiry in practice: Action, reflection, and making meaning.* Thousand Oaks, CA: Sage.

Brown, T., & Wyatt, J. (2010). Design thinking for social innovation. *Stanford Social Innovation Review,* Winter.

Browning, H. (2006). *Leadership development cards.* Unpublished technical report. Greensboro, NC: Center for Creative Leadership.

Commons, M. L., & Richards, F. A. (2003). Four postformal stages. In J. Demick & C. Andreoletti (Eds.), *Handbook of adult development* (pp. 199–220). New York, NY: Kluwer Academic.

Cook-Greuter, S. R. (1999). *Postautonomous ego development: A study of its nature and measurement.* Dissertation Abstracts International, 60, 06B. UMI No. 993312.

Day, D. V. (2000). Leadership development: A review in context. *Leadership Quarterly, 11*(4), 581–613.

Drath, W. H. (2001). *The deep blue sea: Rethinking the source of leadership.* San Francisco, CA: Jossey-Bass.

Drath, W. H., McCauley, C. D., Palus, C. J., Van Velsor, E., O'Connor, P. M. G., & McGuire, J. B. (2008). Direction, alignment, commitment: Toward a more integrative ontology of leadership. *Leadership Quarterly, 19,* 635–653.

Drath, W. H., Palus, C. J., & McGuire, J. B. (2010). Developing an interdependent leadership culture. In C. D. McCauley & E. Van Velsor (Eds.), *The center for creative leadership handbook of leadership development* (3rd ed.). San Francisco, CA: Jossey-Bass.

Ernst, C., & Chrobot-Mason, D. (2010). Boundary spanning leadership: *Six practices for solving problems, driving innovation, and transforming organizations.* New York, NY: McGraw-Hill Professional.

Fisher, D., & Torbert, W. (1991). Transforming managerial practice: Beyond the achiever stage. In R. Woodman & W. Pasmore (Eds.), *Research in organizational change and development* (Vol. 5), Greenwich CT: JAI Press.

Heifetz, R. A. (1994). *Leadership without easy answers.* Cambridge, MA: Harvard University Press.

Heifetz, R. A., Linsky, M., & Grashow, A. (2009). *The practice of adaptive leadership: Tools and tactics for changing your organization and the world.* Cambridge, MA: Harvard Business Press.

Hofstede, G. (1993). Cultures and organizations: Software of the mind. *Administrative Science Quarterly, 38*(1), 132–134.

House, R. J., Hanges, P. J., Javidan, M., Dorfman, P. W., & Gupta, V. (Eds.). (2004). *Culture, leadership, and organizations: The globe study of 62 societies.* Thousand Oaks, CA: Sage.

Johnson, B. (1992). *Polarity management: Identifying and managing unsolvable problems.* Amherst, MA: HRD Press.

Kahane, A. (2004). *Solving tough problems: An open way of talking, listening, and creating new realities.* San Francisco, CA: Berrett Koehler Publishers.

Kegan, R. (1994). *In over our heads: The mental demands of modern life.* Cambridge, MA: Harvard University Press.

Kohlberg, L. (1969). Stage and sequence: The cognitive developmental approach to socialization. In D. Goslin (Ed.), *Handbook of socialization: Theory and research.* New York, NY: Rand McNally.

Laloux, F. (2014). *Reinventing organizations: A guide to creating organizations inspired by the next stage of human consciousness.* Millis, MA: Nelson Parker.

Martin, R. L. (2009). *The design of business: Why design thinking is the next competitive advantage.* Cambridge, MA: Harvard Business Press.

McCauley, C. D., Drath, W. H., Palus, C. J., O'Connor, P. M. G., & Baker, B. A. (2006). The use of constructive-developmental theory to advance the understanding of leadership. *Leadership Quarterly, 17,* 634–653.

McCauley, C. D., Palus, C. J., Drath, W. D., Hughes, R. L., McGuire, J. B., O'Connor, P. M. G., & Van Velsor, E. (2008). *Interdependent leadership in organizations: Evidence from six case studies*. CCL Research Report No. 190. Greensboro, NC: Center for Creative Leadership.

McGuire, J. B., Palus, C. J., & Torbert, W. R. (2007). Toward interdependent organizing and researching. In A. B. Shani, S. A. Mohrman, W. A. Pasmore, B. Stymne, & N. Adler (Eds.), *Handbook of collaborative management research* (pp. 123−142). Los Angeles, CA: Sage.

McGuire, J. B., & Rhodes, G. (2009). *Transforming your leadership culture*. San Francisco, CA: Jossey-Bass.

Nicolaides, A., & McCallum, D. C. (2013). Inquiry in action for leadership in turbulent times: Exploring the connections between transformative learning and adaptive leadership. *Journal of Transformative Education, 11*(4), 246−260.

Ospina, S., & Uhl-Bien, M. (Eds.). (2012). *Advancing relational leadership research: A dialogue among perspectives*. Leadership Horizons Series. Charlotte, NC: Information Age Publishing, Inc.

Palus, C. J., & Drath, W. H. (1995). *Evolving leaders: A model for promoting leadership development in programs*. Greensboro, NC: Center for Creative Leadership.

Palus, C. J., & McGuire, J. B. (2015). Mediated dialogue in action research. In H. Bradbury (Ed.), *The Sage handbook of action research* (3rd ed.). Thousand Oaks, CA: Sage.

Palus, C. J., McGuire, J. B., & Ernst, C. (2012). Developing interdependent leadership. In S. Snook, N. Nohria, & R. Khurana (Eds.), *The handbook for teaching leadership: Knowing, doing, and being* (pp. 467−492). Thousand Oaks, CA: Sage Publications with the Harvard Business School.

Petrie, N. (2014). *Vertical leadership development, Part 1: Developing leaders for a complex world*. CCL White Paper. Greensboro, NC: Center for Creative Leadership.

Piaget, J. (1954). *The construction of reality in a child*. New York, NY: Basic Books.

Porter, M., & Kramer, M. (2011). Creating shared value. Harvard Business Review, January−February.

Rooke, D., & Torbert, W. R. (1998). Organizational transformation as a function of CEOs' developmental stage. *Organization Development Journal, 16*(1), 11−28.

Rooke, D., & Torbert, W. R. (2005, April). Seven transformations of leadership. Harvard Business Review, pp. 66−77.

Torbert, W. R. (1981). Why educational research has been so uneducational: The case for a new model of social science based on collaborative inquiry. In P. Reason & J. Rowan (Eds.), *Human inquiry*. Chichester: Wiley.

Torbert, W. R. (1987). *Managing the corporate dream. Restructuring for long-term success*. Homewood, IL: Dow Jones-Irwin.

Torbert, W. R. (2013). Listening into the dark: An essay testing the validity and efficacy of collaborative developmental action inquiry for describing and encouraging transformations of self, society, and scientific inquiry. *Integral Review, 9*(2), 264−299.

Torbert, W. R. & Associates (2004). *Action inquiry: The secret of timely and transforming leadership.* San Francisco, CA: Berrett-Koehler.

Torbert, W. R., Herdman Barker, E., Palus, C. J., Horth, D. M., & Harrison III, S. (2015). *Transformations™ facilitator's guide.* Unpublished product, beta version, in the Leadership Explorer™ tool suite by CCL Labs. Greensboro, NC: Center for Creative Leadership.

Wakefield, M. (2006). *Essential principles of leadership development.* Unpublished technical report. Greensboro, NC: Center for Creative Leadership.

Wilber, K. (2000). *Integral psychology.* Boston, MA: Shambala.

Seeds and Plants: Local Case Studies

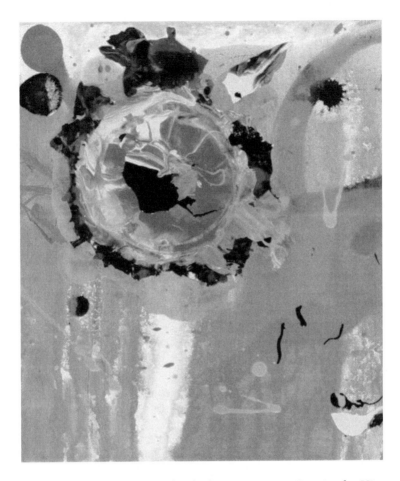

Susan Amber Gordon. *Birth of Blue Supergiant Star in the Virgo Cluster*. 2013. Repurposed acrylic mixed media on canvas, 12″×24″. Private collection

Seeds and Plants: Local Case Studies

John Eric Baugher and Karin Jironet

In 1977, Professor Wangari Maathai began planting trees in rural Kenya as a small project at the National Council of Women of Kenya that later expanded and became known as the Green Belt Movement. Nearly four decades later, tens of thousands of workers in this movement have planted over 51 million trees. When asked about the origins of her work, Maathai (2010), the first African woman to win the Nobel Peace Prize, explained that it began as a practical response to the needs expressed by rural communities in Kenya, and especially women, to secure "clean drinking water, adequate and nutritious food, income, and enough energy for cooking and heating" (p. 13). Yet in Maathai's view, there is no distinction between the practical and the spiritual. As she recounted, "After a few years I came to recognize that our efforts weren't only about planting trees, but were also about sowing seeds of a different sort — the ones necessary to heal the wounds inflicted on communities that robbed them of their self-confidence and self-knowledge" (Maathai, 2010, p. 14).

This section contains six case studies of health-affirming initiatives in local contexts in Bangladesh, Ecuador, Mexico, New Zealand, Rwanda, and the United States. We begin with this vignette of Maathai's work as it brings to light common themes across the diverse cases presented here, namely, how local initiatives can offer seeds for affirming life and healing the wounds that threaten the well-being of humanity and the wider contexts that support health and human flourishing. Before turning to the individual chapters, we use Maathai's work to explore the analogies of "seeds and plants" and the power of case study and ethnographic methods in relation to healing and the interrelated "wounds" that present in various contexts across the planet today.

The "seeds" Maathai (2010) refers to are the "core values" inspiring her work, including a love for the environment expressed tangibly in action, a respect for that which is given expressed through not wasting or laying waste to the earth's resources, a focus on individual and communal agency, a cultivation and trust of inner strength, and a commitment to the common good expressed through how one uses one's time, energy, and resources. Such seeds are the foundation of health, the source of human flourishing, or what Aristotle called *eudaimonia*, the contentment or "inner prosperity of mind that disposes one's outward actions" (Robinson, 1989, pp. 115–116; see also Dustin & Ziegler, 2007, pp. 50, 234). By "plants" we refer to *wise action* with the understanding that lofty ideals or a critique of what is not working cannot alone heal or affirm health. Just as peace cannot be reduced to a critique of war or the absence of war, so too is health not simply a revulsion toward that which is sickening, but instead is fundamentally grounded in positive actions that affirm beauty, truth, and life. We see actions as positive to the extent that they are grounded in seeing the whole, flow from clarity of purpose, and are attuned to local contexts. As Barry Schwartz and Kenneth Sharpe (2010) explain, "practical wisdom" is doing the right thing, in the right way, with the right person, in the right situation, at the right time (p. 83).

In our introduction to the section, "Air and Water: What Flows Lives," we suggest that what is required of leaders today is a continuous interrogation of our deepest held assumptions and an orientation away from self-other dichotomies toward a wider awareness of our participation in a common human journey, a view likewise affirmed by the five thoughts leaders in their interviews in the opening section of the book. Such awareness is not an abstract or theoretical orientation that diverts one's attention from the particulars of embodied experience. Instead, it is a doorway to seeing more deeply what is revealed in the particular, a process that may be quite painful.

Maathai (2010) described her grief in 2009 when her work on a fact-finding mission led her to witness a 200-year old sapele being felled by a timber company in the Congo Basin's forest. Scientists refer to this area as the world's "second lung," the Amazon being the first, on account of the large volume of carbon dioxide it inhales and oxygen it exhales (Maathai, 2010, p. 37). A representative of the timber company who was accompanying

Maathai noticed tears welling in her eyes as she witnessed the tree fall, and he assured her not to worry, since "there are millions of other trees out there in the forest" (p. 40). Such an attitude, of assuming the earth's resources are in endless supply, of valuing a living organ solely as a marketable commodity, of freely taking life to feed insatiable desires, has brought so much destruction to the planet. Mirroring these outer "ecological wounds" are what Maathai (2010) calls wounds to "our inner ecology, our soul and sense of being human," and in her view, "our first task must be to acknowledge these wounds, something that is at once simple, and, because some of these wounds are so deep, immeasurably difficult" (p. 19).

What Maathai describes can be linked to the "epistemology of the wound," the possibility ethnographic methods offer researchers to engage one's full faculties — intellectual, emotional, and spiritual — toward contemplatively beholding ambiguous or otherwise painful realities and thereby seeing beyond the controlling dichotomies of self and other, inner and outer, local, and global (González-López, 2010; see also Baugher, 2014a). The authors in this section do not use this explicit language, although each in some way points to the importance of reflexivity in our seeing and to the inherent ambiguities of the work of leaders in particular contexts. We invite readers to engage these texts with a similar contemplative sensibility. We will travel widely in this section, from poor informal settlements in peri-urban Mexico to indigenous communities in the Andes, from executive boardrooms in New Zealand to community engagement with the arts in California, from youth leadership work in Bangladesh to women's leadership in post-genocide Rwanda. Rather than approaching these readings with the attitude of the tourist — distant, removed, safely peering in from the outside — allow yourself to tarry with what comes up for you as you consider the ambiguities of leadership in such diverse contexts of the world. Read with embodied engagement, like a honeybee in a field of flowers, literally allowing yourself to enter what has budded and opened for you from these different seeds and plants offered. Ask yourself: Where do I see myself in relation to the local contexts described in each of these chapters? To what extent am I willing to allow the beauty, suffering, and truth of the lived experiences described in these chapters change my own ways of thinking, feeling, and being in the world?

In the opening chapter of this section, "The Inner Practice of Community Development: Embracing Deep Democracy in

Mexico," Patricia A. Wilson describes two participatory action research (PAR) projects in poor peri-urban communities outside of Mexico City. Wilson refers to these projects as fundamentally about "embracing deep democracy," a foundational practice for healthy communities in which "community members recognize their interdependence and shared future." Drawing on her own involvement as a change agent in these projects, Wilson invites readers to consider a fundamental question that pertains to leadership in any context: "How do we know our efforts are making a difference?"

Wilson takes us into the heart of the beast — the leader's engagement with power. Consistent with thinking that runs throughout earlier sections of this book, Wilson invites readers to rethink this foundational notion and its related practices. Grounded in her own journey beyond the poles of community development as "top-down expert planning" versus "the righteous battle of bottom-up advocacy," Wilson sees power that heals not as something possessed or held, but as an embodied practice and an emergent, inter-subjective phenomenon. Wilson leaves us with the imagery of effective leaders (including educators) as "midwives" supporting the birth of emergent seeds of health in individuals and communities. For Wilson, crucial to such transformational learning is a contemplative pedagogy "consistent with the practice" that is guided by "a vision of an empowered civil society" co-creating the future.[1]

Patricia Wilson's notion of leaders midwifing social change affirms the view of Eisler's partnership paradigm presented in the section "Air and Water: What Flows Lives" that care is central to healthful leadership and social change (see also Baugher & Ubalijoro, 2015). Carolina Bown's chapter, "Sumak Kawsay among Indigenous Women Leaders of Ecuador," likewise connects leadership with practices of care. Bown analyzes original interviews and ethnographic observations of 19 indigenous

---

[1]There is a vast literature on contemplative pedagogy that has direct bearing on the nature and challenges of leadership development and leadership practice as described by Wilson and other contributors to this book. For more general introductions to the epistemology and practice of contemplative pedagogy, see Barbezat and Bush (2014), Zajonc (2009), and Gunnlaugson, Sarath, Scott, and Bai (2014). For perspectives and practices of contemplative pedagogy in relation to community and ecological health, see Ettling and Guilian's "Midwifing Transformative Change" and other chapters in O'Sullivan and Taylor (2004).

women leaders from eight Andean communities in Ecuador to understand how these women draw on the principle of "sumak kawsay" to guide their actions as leaders of grassroots organizations. Roughly translated as "good living," this Andean principle is embodied by the grassroots indigenous leaders Bown interviewed through actions that support the health of Mother Earth (*Pachamama*), indigenous cultural sustainability, and the well-being of women and other community members. Bown articulates how caring actions that seek to preserve indigenous ways of knowing and being are not the result of "backward-looking" traditionalism, but are creative and wise expressions of adaptive leadership that valorize long-term thinking and the health and well-being of future generations.

The question of how indigenous knowledge interfaces with contemporary business practice is picked up by Jane McCann in the chapter "Kiwi Ways of Leading: How 30 New Zealand Government Chief Executives are Encouraging Healthier Cultures." For 20 years, McCann has worked as a consultant with 30 public sector Chief Executives (CEs) in New Zealand to help them address "complex, multi-generational, and interdependent problems." In this chapter, she presents some observations from her work with the CEs situated against the historical background of British colonizers' repression of the indigenous Māori and subsequent "development of a bicultural public sector and increasingly multicultural New Zealand society." Fundamentally, McCann's interest is in supporting CEs in creating a more inclusive public sector, and in this regard, she sees "storytelling" as crucial. McCann's chapter raises the question of how personal, organizational, and historical narratives could be constructed in ways that include diverse identities and ways of knowing particularly when those leading organizations have all been educated in similar Anglo-American institutions.

In the chapter "'The Arts Are Not a Luxury': The Arts as a Source of Community in California," Barbara Rose Shuler presents the Bach Festival in Carmel, California, as an example of how committed arts leadership can contribute to community building and collective renewal and learning. The Festival has been in continual existence for over 80 years, and Shuler suggests that crucial to the organization's longevity has been the current and founding leaders capacity to maintain "their status as beloved members of the community" through the formation of "authentic arts partners." Seeding such partnerships has been a commitment to the core value of inclusivity along socio-economic lines. While some practices of inclusivity Schuler describes seem to express a charitable attitude (allowing entrance to some performances based on a barter system), others suggest a degree of reciprocity, such as the formation of a management program for college seniors through which students attain on-the-job training while the Festival learns ways it can best develop to be relevant to younger generations. Max Klau and Jill Hufnagel's chapter likewise examines processes of strengthening communities through youth leadership development. The chapter "Strengthening Communities through Adaptive Leadership: A Case Study of the Kansas Leadership Center and the Bangladesh Youth Leadership Center" presents two very different projects in different parts of the world (Kansas and Bangladesh) that offer a similar conclusion — youth leadership projects may be most successful when educators withhold teaching and thereby challenge students to turn inward for "intrinsic sources of direction, purpose, and answers" (see also McGrane, 1994). Klau and Hufnagel's work affirms that transformational learning necessarily involves "opening to the unknown and a willingness to abide with the uncomfortable emotions that accompany such openness" (Baugher, 2014b, p. 236).

The epistemology of the wound is engaged deeply in the chapter "Women and Leadership in Rwanda, Emerging Transformation: The Spiritual, Social, and Political Dimensions of Transmuting Suffering," in which Éliane Ubalijoro, Bagwiza Jacqueline Uwizeyimana, and Marilyn Verghis explore what lies behind 20 years of transformational women's leadership in Rwanda following the 1994 genocide that left deep collective and individual trauma. The starting point of the chapter is traditional Rwandan spirituality, in which "feminine wisdom is embodied, deeply connected to emotions and to the nurturing and care a mother holds for her children." As the authors explain, "for a woman to stand in this wisdom, she must connect to her feeling self." This chapter, in itself, represents a movement into such wisdom, a movement more deeply into the wound, into the embodied grief of the feeling self. Ubalijoro and Uwizeyimana are both of Rwandan origin, and the chapter includes first-person accounts of the transformational power of women leaders in their own journeys of healing and becoming. One expression of Rwandan spirituality that intends toward healing is that of "good anger," a form of grieving that allows "action and vulnerability to coexist." In Ubalijoro's words, "carrying the wholeness of the murdered ones in inner places" has been essential for her to "hold trauma in an embodied way where polarities coexist."

Such "inner places" of wholeness, the source of human flourishing, ground Rwandan women leaders in the feminine and allow an outward move in the social and political spheres away from the divisive policies of 20th century colonialism and its destructive legacy toward creative ways to promote a healthy world.

Throughout our time working on this book, we became more and more aware of the many important grassroots initiatives happening around the globe, so many "seeds and plants" that could have been included in this section. Basic to ethnographic methods is the irreducibility of the case, the understanding that history and context are crucial to interpretation of meaning. With that in mind, we do not claim that these chapters are in any way representative of local initiatives across the globe, but instead they point to just some of the variety of the human effort that is taking place all over the world to preserve and further the health of individuals, communities, cultures, and the planet. All of these efforts are not yet connected with each other, raising the question of how we might work to bring into connection and cross-pollinate various local actions toward health and sustainability across the globe.

References

Barbezat, D. P., & Bush, M. (2014). *Contemplative practices in higher education: Powerful methods to transform teaching and learning.* San Francisco, CA: Jossey-Bass.

Baugher, J. E. (2014a). Sociological mindfulness and leadership education. In K. Goldman Schuyler, J. E. Baugher, K. Jironet, & L. Lid-Falkman (Eds.), *Leading with spirit, presence, and authenticity* (pp. 79–89). San Francisco, CA: Jossey Bass.

Baugher, J. E. (2014b). Contemplating uncomfortable emotions: Creating transformative spaces for learning in higher education. In O. Gunnlaugson, E. W. Sarath, C. Scott, & H. Bai (Eds.), *Contemplative learning and inquiry across disciplines* (pp. 233–251). Albany, NY: SUNY Press.

Baugher, J. E., & Ubalijoro, É. (2015). Cultivating the capacity to suffer. In International Leadership Association (Eds.), *Becoming a better leader: Applying key strategies* (pp. 117–122). New York, NY: Routledge, E-Book. Retrieved from https://goo.gl/TCSZ38

Dustin, C. A., & Ziegler, J. E. (2007). *Practicing mortality: Art, philosophy, and contemplative seeing.* New York, NY: Palgrave Macmillan.

González-López, G. (2010). Ethnographic lessons: Researching incest in Mexican families. *Journal of Contemporary Ethnography, 39*(5), 569–581.

Gunnlaugson, O., Sarath, E. W., Scott, C., & Bai, H. (2014). *Contemplative learning and inquiry across disciplines.* Albany, NY: SUNY Press.

Maathai, W. (2010). *Replenishing the earth: Spiritual values for healing ourselves and the world*. New York, NY: Doubleday.

McGrane, B. (1994). *The un-TV and the 10 MPH car: Experiments in personal freedom and everyday life*. Fort Bragg, CA: The Small Press.

O'Sullivan, E., & Taylor, M. (2004). *Learning toward an ecological consciousness: Selected transformative practices*. New York, NY: Palgrave Macmillan.

Robinson, D. N. (1989). *Aristotle's psychology*. New York, NY: Columbia University Press.

Schwartz, B., & Sharpe, K. (2010). *Practical wisdom: The right way to do the right thing*. New York, NY: Riverhead Books.

Zajonc, A. (2009). *Meditation as contemplative inquiry: When knowing becomes love*. Great Barrington, MA: Lindesfarne Books.

8 The Inner Practice of Community Development: Embracing Deep Democracy in Mexico

Patricia A. Wilson

Right now listening to you, my colleagues in different governmental agencies and universities, is an aha moment for me. I can hear that you each took in deeply the importance of working with people in this collaborative horizontal way, alongside and for the people. This work is so difficult to understand and explain. It's not an imposition of authority by government agencies ... Nor is it just about planting trees and water quality. ... I ask you all to transmit the special nature of this work and what we've learned here, including the emotions and feelings, to your agencies. This is so important. I feel this from my heart ....

With these words and feelings, the director of the Guadalupe Dam Watershed Commission outside Mexico City acknowledged the pivotal importance of the community development practitioner's relational awareness and process sensitivity in fostering healthy communities. The two dozen government professionals and educators that she was addressing had just completed a two week field experience in participatory action research (PAR) for

211

sustainable community development. They had let go of their titles, authority, expertise, programs, procedures, and plans and had begun to build trusting relationships for collaborative action. These practitioners had discovered the key to creating healthy communities: fostering interconnectedness and cocreativity in the civic arena. Not only had the two peri-urban communities changed as a result, the practitioners came out changed as well.

This chapter explores the inner practice — the thoughts, feelings, and perceptions — of the community development practitioner as change agent for healthy communities. It draws on a three year change process in sustainable development using PAR in two ecologically and socially vulnerable communities in the outskirts of metropolitan Mexico City. This ongoing project gave me the opportunity to introduce others to the role of change agent and test my own practice.

I weave together my personal experience in the two communities with that of the government professionals and educators who were introduced to participatory leadership through this fieldwork. Asking the question, "How do we know our efforts are making a difference?", I trace the relationship between the PAR experience, the changes in the practitioners' perception of themselves and their roles, and concrete impacts in the communities and institutions where they work. I conclude that the real measure of the practitioner's success is the ability to continually discern and engage the emergent next steps that call the change agent forward.

Deep Democracy, the Change Agent, and Emergence

My early approach to community development ricocheted between the heady delight of top-down expert planning and the righteous battle of bottom-up advocacy. Over the last two decades, however, my work in mindfulness, dialogue, collaborative inquiry, and action research has found a practical application in building healthy communities through deep democracy.

In deep democracy, as I have described it previously (Wilson, 2004), community members recognize their interdependence and shared future. They care about the well-being of the community as a whole, and are willing to act. This conscious interconnectedness enables distributed leadership and self-organizing change — the life-giving elements of a healthy evolving system. Fostering conscious interconnectedness in the civic arena builds deep democracy — the willingness of the individual to engage across difference, to hold the tension between conflicting values and views, and to learn from observing, listening, and acting in collaboration (Wilson, 2004).

The implications of deep democracy for community development practice can be daunting! The community development practitioner must be strong enough to let go of the accustomed role of having answers, platforms, master plans, and especially control, and instead learn to trust process and be open to possibility.

The change agent for deep democracy is foremost a catalyst. As with a tiny homeopathic intervention, the system responds to balance itself and evolve, seeking its own health and wholeness as it is capable of doing. As a practitioner, I need not know precisely what the system is capable of nor how it will unfold. The outcomes regularly exceed my expectations with results that I could never have imagined, much less engineered.

Drawing on the theory of complex adaptive systems and evolutionary systems thinking, the change agent for deep democracy views power not as a structure to be combated or deployed but rather as patterns to be shaped and created. Therefore the change agent focuses attention on opportunity, possibility, and evolutionary potential, while holding a vision of an empowered civil society actively engaged in governance through cocreative participation.

Emergence is the engine of change in complex adaptive systems. The change agent recognizes the power of emergence — the creation of new patterns that prompt the evolution of a system to its next level. "Working wikily" as some say, the change agent for deep democracy fosters self-organizing, self-regulating change in the civic arena (Box 1).

The leader or change agent for deep democracy senses what is emergent in a community in the present moment and makes space for those emergent properties to come forth. To practice at the emergent edge, the practitioner must start with existing patterns: begin where people are; start with what is possible (Westoby & Dowling, 2013). From that space the change agent builds trust, creates a new conversation, and fosters agency. A new pattern emerges, potentially self-organizing and self-replicating.

Emergence is the act of becoming, not only in the objective world but in the subjective world of identity and meaning. This

---

Box 1: Roles and Skills of the Change Agent.

The change agent for deep democracy strives to accompany the community in a process of self-organized action learning: to listen to, learn from, and work with, the community. Can she see possibility, not just problems? Can he refrain from giving the residents his solutions and instead work with them in a mutual learning process? Can she sense together with the local people what positive change is ready and wanting to emerge, to blossom forth, in that community? Can he accompany the community in identifying and taking the very next action step that would help that manifest? Can she work with the community to reflect on, learn from, and move to the next action?

Most important, can the change agent for deep democracy stay in a place of resonance, acceptance, non-judgment, and trust in the unfolding process as he works with the community? Can he keep his mind and heart open? Can she be calm and confident in the face of uncertainty, of not knowing? Can she stay in the present moment with them? Can he recognize and let go of his assumptions, of the need to know, of the need to fix or solve, of the need for a particular path or outcome?

When the change agent can see the community as a living evolving organism embedded in a larger living evolving system, he can see opportunity within apparently rigid hopeless situations.

When the change agent models these skills, attitudes, and practices, his or her simple presence becomes a force for transformation.

© Patricia A. Wilson.

---

inner dimension of emergent practice raises the following questions: Can the leader be comfortable on the generative edge of chaos? Can she dance into the chaos, through it, and back again? Can he hold the fragile tension between order and chaos, structure and flow, intention and accident, reflection and action? (Westoby & Kaplan, 2013). Emergent leadership is an embodied practice, a felt experience that causes one to question "who am I becoming?" "who are we becoming?" "what is wanting to emerge through me and us?" (Scharmer, 2008).

The Fieldwork in Peri-Urban Mexico

The Cuenca Presa Guadalupe is an ecologically rich watershed threatened by the continuing climb of urban growth and informal settlements out of the valley of Mexico and up the mountains of the watershed. Over the last 25 years, low income settlers displaced from the valley by rising costs and intensifying development have settled on the sides of steep ravines and unserviced spaces to create new lives and new communities. The once pristine creeks and rivers that flow through these ravines have become the *de facto* sewers and waste dumps for these settlements, sending the black and gray water directly into the now unusable Presa Guadalupe Lake.

The technical director of the Presa Guadalupe Watershed Commission knew that the Commission had failed in its public education campaigns and policy tools to change behaviors in the urbanizing areas. She wanted to understand these peri-urban communities better to protect the health of the watershed. Through exchanges with the sustainable community development group at the University of Texas, the director of the Commission arranged for me to work with local government professionals and educators to engage two informal peri-urban communities in participatory action learning around environmental issues that the community members themselves would identify. These professionals were under the impression they were coming to a two week classroom seminar on sustainability with a few excursions to the communities. They were in for a surprise and so was I!

Story from the Classroom: Preparing the Change Agents

I was glad that the field project in the two peri-urban communities, El Tráfico and Llano Grande, would become a medium for introducing 24 local government professionals and educators to PAR. But I did not know just how daunting it would be for them to suspend their accustomed roles as experts, authorities, decision-makers, managers, problem-solvers, instructors, and trainers.

After an overview of PAR and what to expect for the two weeks, followed by a round of introductions, I invited them to form two teams, one to work in El Tráfico and the other in Llano Grande. Their task was to propose a game plan for their first day in the field and present it to the plenary for feedback. One team came up with a top-down plan they were quite proud of to teach the community new skills on the first day! The other team fell into chaos and despair because, they said, no one was in charge of their group and it wasn't clear how their work would be evaluated!

At that point, I faced an important decision: resolve the tension in the room by stepping into the authority role they were accustomed to or create a safe space in which to experience the insecurity and uncertainty and work through it. I chose the latter. And the participants rose to the challenge (Box 2).

The workshop unfolded with daily rounds of fieldwork in the two communities in the mornings, followed by lunch, reflection, planning, and preparation at a nearby college in the afternoons. The two teams each worked through unaccustomed challenges. Not knowing each other, having no one officially in charge, nor having a clearly defined final product to aim for, they learned as they went. As I cited in Wilson (2015), one participant said afterward, "we were as naked and vulnerable as the residents themselves ...." "I was actually afraid at the beginning, it was very difficult," another admitted. "I really doubted that we would accomplish anything," expressed a third (p. 9).

When the frustration was high, I led the teams in dialogic inquiry to reflect collectively on their experiences and "become uncertain together" (Philippson, 2009, p. 29). At one point, I introduced participatory theater for each team to act out its experience. The resulting laughter was a turning point. Until then I had been choosing which team to accompany to the field each day based on their degree of uncertainty and discomfort. Afterward they began to invite me so I could see the wonderful things that were happening!

The Story from the Field: A Personal Reflection on Practice

EL TRÁFICO: LETTING GO OF JUDGMENT

El Tráfico is a community of 15,000 inhabitants founded 25 years ago as an informal settlement. Now, integrated into the urbanized area of Nicolás Romero, it is recognized and partially legalized by the municipal government.

In El Tráfico, I began to see a picture that I judged to be anything but hopeful. I saw the rigid, carefully crafted hierarchical

Box 2: A Personal Credo for Deep Democracy.

As a practitioner of deep democracy, I choose to focus on what is possible. I choose to see myself not as outside or against the system that I want to change but as an interconnected part of that evolving system. I seek to respect and understand the living elements of that system — individual and collective, human and natural. I seek to know, understand, and connect with whatever "other" or enemy (internal or external) I may perceive. I seek to care about the other and the whole, at whatever scale, from face-to-face to planetary, to see our interconnection. I seek to find my own role in fostering the next evolutionary step toward health and well-being that is wanting and able to emerge, trusting in a larger logic and wisdom to unfold. I seek attunement to that larger wisdom, a field of resonance with the emergent, and a dialogic presence with my cocreative collaborators. I am vigilant in my mental hygiene to let go of disempowering thoughts, of cynicism, despair, and condemnation.

As a change agent for deep democracy, I hold my professional and personal opinions lightly, as propositions to be tested, rather than positions to be defended or imposed. I develop my inner intuitive knowing, not just my rational analytical knowing. I value and foster collaborative inquiry and choose to create spaces for such inquiry to flourish wisely, through cycles of dialogue, action, reflection, and collaborative learning. I learn to hold the tension between competing views, to practice "not knowing," and to see the result as a fertile field of possibility. I seek to discern where my professional knowledge, my expertise, can contribute to the collective process rather than overwhelm or undermine it.

As a trainer of change agents for deep democracy, I aim to replicate and exemplify the practice of deep democracy in the classroom: self-reflection, dialogue for building shared understanding, collaborative learning and inquiry, group deliberation and decision-making, and participatory action learning. I aim to facilitate a transformative learning experience. Thus I am not a trainer at all. Rather, I create a space for the participants' own learning, action, and reflection. The critical learning is not the mastery of the methods of participatory engagement but rather the inner practice of the facilitator.

© Patricia A. Wilson.

structure of the political party in power at the municipal (county) level reaching down into the community (*colonia*) through self-serving clientelistic relationships. The party's point of leverage was the local leader Señora E, who maintained a tight control on the local community by replicating the paternalistic power structure locally.

As a result of her party loyalty, commitment to the community, and constant hard work, Señora E had won considerable municipal benefits for this relatively poor community: several paved streets, piped water twice a month for most households, a new middle school, and other amenities. The system worked — but not in the participatory horizontal way it needed to, in my opinion, to be really healthy.

It didn't take long to feel my negative opinion coloring my interactions, tarnishing my joy, affecting others on the team, making us feel rather helpless and hopeless. The rigidity of my own assessment was not serving me nor our effort at deep democracy.

I made a conscious effort to look again, to see the possibility, the potential, the spaces for change, the fluidity in what had seemed solid, dead, or moribund. As I got closer to the community, connected more deeply, and listened more closely, I saw spaciousness in the lattice work, I saw fluidity in the frozen structure, and I saw opportunity for change. I could see the hierarchical clientelistic structure calcifying on its own. I didn't need to oppose it, nor even criticize it. There was no enemy to fight, only old self-reinforcing patterns slowly crumbling from entropy, ready to evolve, already giving birth to something new. I looked for the life-giving elements, even in the very players who held the rigid top-down structure together.

With patience and hopefulness, our team of professionals, students, and myself went forward with the community and its leader. Each morning we rearranged the chairs in the meeting room from straight orderly rows facing the head table into a circle, only to find them the next morning in uniform rows again. On the fourth day, we found the chairs in a circle! That was the morning that Señora E confided to me just how tired she was from her decades of work for her party and her community.

That same day the women that Señora E had recruited for us decided themselves on their next step: making thread and yarn out of the plastic bags strewn in trash heaps and clogging the creek. A quick demonstration by one of our Mexican team members launched the women into making their own beautiful creations, since they already knew how to sew, weave, knit, and crochet. The ladies gathered plastic bags each afternoon and returned in the mornings to share the bounty and pick the colors for their designs.

As they knitted and crocheted, the women talked about themselves, their families, and their community. They came from different neighborhoods of El Tráfico, yet found so much in common. The women decided to continue gathering every Friday morning — not to please Señora E nor to get something from her — but because they saw value in getting together and were creating the value themselves.

The women wanted to involve men from the community in building a retention wall with discarded tires. Señora E chose an active party member's house for the demonstration. The next day the community was abuzz about the utility of old tires, which disappeared quickly from the creek bed and empty lots.

On our team's last day in El Tráfico, the meeting room over-flowed with people: women wanting to learn to knit with plastic and men wanting more ways to reuse tires. As the women's circle knitted, they recounted their accomplishments over the last 10 days. Teenaged girls sitting on the floor in the middle of the circle drew or wrote down what they said: the plastic bags they had recycled; the earrings, purses, shawls, and table-cloths they had made; their impact on all who saw their creations; and the ongoing circle of women they had formed (Wilson, 2015). The women's pride and sense of accomplishment was contagious and soon the men's group had come up with a plan: making fences with discarded plastic bottles, the third major contributor to the nonorganic waste stream after plastic bags and old tires. Señora E, smiling with satisfaction at the energy, warmth, and happiness in the room, told us that "something really important has shifted here over these two weeks. It will no longer be the same." Perhaps she was referring to the new sense of interconnectedness, initiative, and creativity that was palpable.

A year later, the women's group continued to meet, collect plastic bags, and sew (Wilson, 2015). They had taught their technique to many women in El Tráfico and some in other communities. A few were selling their products commercially. The women continued to meet each Friday on Señora E's patio, to talk, sew, and act. Used tires now fetched a price. Señora E was working to get a piece of *ejido* land for a community park and negotiating with the government for full legalization of land titles.

Box 3: Mindful Action Rules for the Participatory Change Agent.

Ten rules I try to work by:

1. When I'm sure I know what needs to happen next,
   I question my assumptions.
2. When I'm judgmental about what is happening,
   I question my assumptions and open my heart.
3. When chaos breaks out, I stand calm and confident,
   and wait for 30 minutes, knowing that something
   beautiful will emerge beyond what I could have imagined or planned.
4. If I notice I'm trying to control, I let go.
5. If I let ends become more important than means,
   I step away.
6. If I begin to doubt, I remember to trust in the
   collective process.
7. If things begin to flow, I know I'm meant to do this.
8. If people are praising me for my work, I know I have
   failed to make it *their* success.
9. When I feel myself wanting to tell others what to do,
   I move into inquiry with them about what's possible
   and what *they* see as next steps.
10. I remember that I am working with them to realize
    their vision, not mine.

© Patricia A. Wilson.

LLANO GRANDE: DEEP LISTENING AND STAYING CALM

Smaller and poorer than El Tráfico, Llano Grande is an informal community settled over the last 10 years. Considering it "irregular," the municipal government provides no infrastructure for water and sanitation.

Much to the surprise of our team of professionals, students, and myself a police escort followed us to Llano Grande on our first day there, under orders from the municipal government concerned about our safety. Señora L, a young leader and party member, had been the only one to receive us that morning; but as soon as the police escort showed up we heard whistles being passed from person to person throughout the community.

Shortly this early warning system produced a hostile group of people led by a rival community leader, Tomás. Carrying his machete and accompanied by tough-looking young men, Tomás let us know we were not welcome, that they would do *whatever* (poignant pause!) was necessary to defend their land and homes from us.

This could have been an excellent moment to get back on the bus and leave! Nevertheless, our team stayed and listened to the venom, bravado, and underlying fear that Tomás and his people had to spit out about how outsiders had bought up land nearby and displaced their people. Finally when Tomás and his group had nothing more to say, we asked if they would like to know why we were there. Apparently surprised by our team's calm demeanor and willingness to listen, they said yes. We said we were there to work with the community in taking a few steps closer to creating the kind of community they wanted to live in for the long term. Tomás relaxed a bit and let us go off with Señora L and about a dozen of her people who had gathered during this confrontation. In the meantime, we had sent the police away.

Was deep democracy possible in a very poor community that was fearful of losing its land and divided into antagonist factions? The participatory change agent starts with what is and looks for emergent signs of positive movement. The emergent shadow side of this community would be, of course, further division and fear. Community healing was a prerequisite for positive change, that is, conscious evolution, to occur. And that could only happen if the two factions could come together. Was that possible? We didn't know.

Señora L agreed to put the word out, with the help of our team, for a community meeting the following day to plan a community park she said that everyone wanted. A weedy stretch of sloping land with a broken swing and seesaw, the designated parkland surrounded a crumbling church whose last priest had left the year before. The church and the parkland were seen by all as neutral territory, not belonging to any faction. We gave it one more day.

The next morning, a sizeable crowd slowly gathered to participate in the park planning. But not Tomás and his people. As I talked to Señora L, someone spotted Tomás a block or so away working on a car engine. The perfect opportunity! Would Señora L see the importance of inviting Tomás to join her in the park design process? She resisted until I asked, "Would you like to take the park design to the municipal government and say,

'Here's our park proposal that some of us put together?' Or would you rather say, 'Here's our park proposal that the whole community created together?'" She walked over to invite him. Purposely none of us on our team accompanied her; if the divide between her and Tomás were to be bridged, she would have to do it herself.

We watched in silence as she walked the block by herself and talked to Tomás. The conversation lasted several long minutes. Then she turned to walk back — with Tomás! We felt we had witnessed an historic moment in Llano Grande. And we were ready to commit to working there.

Tomás and Señora L joined the park planning group just as the children were finishing their earnest presentations and the adults had begun, one by one, to present their drawings and ideas. The facilitator asked Tomás to contribute his thoughts. He offered many galvanizing ideas that showed his concern for the community. He and some of his people stayed another hour to talk informally with Señora L and her people. The barriers came down as the group found common purpose and common ground. That day a lot of healing happened in Llano Grande.

On our closing day, Tomás's people and Señora L's people gathered together at the school to review what they had accomplished over the 10 days: not only had the community come together for the first time to create a collaborative plan for the park, they had worked on garbage separation and recycling, composting, seed germination, and making trash cans for the park from recycled plastic bottles.

The reward for our team was the warmth, the smiles, the appreciation, the sincere invitation to return; their pride in what they had accomplished; and most important the ease and solidarity that we could see between Tomás's people and Señora L's people.

Eight months later, the park plan had become a reality. Sprouting a playscape made of brightly painted discarded tires, the new park was a source of community pride, cohesion, and vitality (Wilson, 2015). A year after the field workshop, the community was moving forward to measure, record, and legalize their plots.

Outcomes

The closing ceremony for the professional participants was a chance for both teams to come back together and share their personal responses to the intense experience. The responses that were shared, along with written evaluations, provided rich narrative to code and cluster. The results are described in detail in Wilson (2015). The majority of the professional participants described one or more personal, affective, or relational impacts — that is, a felt experience that somehow changed them. The following three themes emerged.

A NEW EXPERIENCE OF TEAMWORK

Some were most moved by the closely knit teamwork that had evolved: moving through the chaos and uncertainty of not knowing their teammates nor having a clear idea of expectations nor having someone in charge to tell them what to do; figuring out how best to contribute to the team effort, realizing one's own capacity to contribute and be respected; learning from each other and respecting each other; being lifted up by the strength of the team to keep coming back each day, learning from experience and moving forward; enjoying the satisfaction of teamwork; and making new colleagues and friends.

DEEPER CONNECTION WITH THE COMMUNITY

Frequently mentioned was the experience of a deeper connection with the community — valuing the opportunity to listen to community members, learn from them, work shoulder to shoulder with them, respect and appreciate them, earn their respect, and connect with them in a heartfelt way. "I could see my own niece and nephew in the eyes of the children," said one practitioner through his tears.

PERSONAL CHANGE

The most frequently mentioned theme was personal change: becoming aware of one's own assumptions, prejudices, and attitudes of superiority or disdain toward community people; learning to trust process and open to the present moment; becoming comfortable with not knowing, not being in control, nor having established procedures to follow; and letting go of the role of expert, decision-maker, or technician.

For the majority of the practitioners, the two week experience in participatory community development had touched them at the level of values, attitudes, feelings, and relationship. It had been an embodied felt experience of conscious interconnectedness. They had skated together on the edge of emergence — the

undefended openness to possibility in the moment that charac-
terizes participatory practice — and had come out changed. In so
doing, they had experienced a deeper connection not only among
themselves but also with the communities. They had experienced
deep democracy. As one agency official articulated, "The kind of
democracy many of our elected officials have promised our
nation and that we've been struggling to put forth — this kind of
democracy is what we experienced during these two weeks."

Impacts

While almost all the government professionals and educators
who participated in the workshop were deeply affected by the
two week experience in participatory learning and action, I
wanted to find out how much of that change they could carry
over into their work lives and institutional settings. Would the
old patterns overpower the new perspectives, or would the new
patterns become seeds of change? Six-month follow-up interviews
with 15 of the 24 professional participants reported in Wilson
(2015) revealed the following changes.

INDIVIDUAL CHANGE
Community relationships
The majority described noticeable changes in how they relate to,
and communicate with, people in the communities where they
work: redefining their work as supporting the community and
the projects the community defines, listening attentively to
community members, working *with* them, showing respect for
community residents and their values, and as one said, "doing
my work with love, like in Llano Grande."

Workplace relationships
Nearly half of the government professionals also expressed
having changed the way they relate to their coworkers and
employees: treating staff, colleagues, and team members with
more respect and tolerance; sharing more openly; asking for
input and feedback; relating on a more personal level; and being
attentive to others' reactions and responses.

Teacher-student relationships
Most faculty participants reported significant changes in their
pedagogy. One professor, an agricultural engineer, explained

that despite the authoritarian pedagogy of information delivery that she was trained in, she realizes the importance of engaging students in research about their own ecosystem: "The students in my soil contamination class live on agricultural lands nearby. I now engage them in doing their own field research, then we apply what they have found and learned."

Another professor recounted a similar change in her pedagogy:

> The very next course I taught after the workshop, we focused on team projects. Each team built a small retention pond at someone's home. The students learned they could build the structures easily and cheaply. Their parents saw how practical it was.

One respondent, who works in local government but also teaches at a preparatory high school in Nicolás Romero, shared this:

> The workshop definitely changed my way of teaching — transformed it literally. I now do inquiry, action, and reflection with my students to rediscover the environment in which they live. What I experienced in the workshop I'm doing with them, inside and outside the classroom. All three of my classes have received this very well. They feel listened to and respected. In one class ... they mapped every ecological problem they could find, first on the campus and then in the community. Then they visualized and prioritized their actions, just like we did in El Tráfico. There are so many actions they want to take now. I accompany them and give them whatever information sources might be helpful, and they decide what they want to do. They plan and carry out everything. I don't even do any of the arranging! We are just two weeks into the new semester and they have already organized two field trips to the municipal ecology office, ..., created a campus environmental club, and started a recycling and composting project. ... The head of the school is amazed! In 15 days we have achieved a revolution in this institution.

INSTITUTIONAL CHANGES

Most of the government respondents reported having little or no institutional influence beyond their immediate work teams or staff

(Wilson, 2015). However, institutional change has been quite significant among the two universities and one high school represented in the workshop. A professor from the local technological college, Universidad Tecnológica Fidel Velázquez (UTFV), said that his institution now realizes it had overlooked the relevance of community. "We had no relationship with local communities," said another professor, "until this workshop!" Spearheaded by the three professors who attended the field workshop, UTFV has consciously built upon the relationships started during the workshop to connect students and faculty with local communities, especially El Tráfico, and develop community-focused internships and service learning courses for students.

The changes in classroom pedagogy introduced by the high school teacher who attended the workshop not only galvanized her students to action but resulted in school-wide institutional changes. Within a year, the students' composting initiative became a one acre organic garden on the campus. The students cultivate high-value crops such as amaranth and chia seeds as well as organic vegetables. They have learned to market them and manage the business. Data from the organic produce business feeds into math, statistics, technology, and sustainable agriculture courses. The school has received news coverage and multiple awards.

The participants from the Universidad Albert Einstein (UAE) became aware of the significant difference between their accustomed community service orientation and a participatory action approach. They felt aligned with the values of PAR. One year later, during our next field-based workshop, the rector of the UAE asked for advanced training in the theory and methods of PAR for the faculty and senior students who participated in the fieldwork. In Fall, 2014, my graduate students and I designed and conducted a three month on-line course with biweekly live interactive sessions for eight faculty and students from UAE.

Upon completion of the course, UAE launched a new major in their human development program called sustainable community development (DECOS), with PAR as the primary tool of engagement. Two of the online course graduates coordinate the degree program and fieldwork. Now two years after the field workshop, DECOS faculty lead biweekly field trips with UAE students to Llano Grande and another community in the mountains, and are preparing for its second incoming class of students. These students will go on to take positions in local schools, government, business, and nonprofits.

SENSING THE EMERGENT EDGE

With these developments at UAE, the nature of my university's involvement is changing. Our yearly field workshops are no longer anchoring UAE's community engagement efforts, but rather complementing them. The annual visit of the University of Texas team in 2015 became an opportunity for the UAE faculty and students in DECOS to show us their ongoing work with the communities, ask questions, participate in coaching circles, share their insights and learning, and deepen their inner practice of participatory community development.

I sense a significant evolution in the emergent edge of our work in Mexico — a new kind of interconnection. Building upon the grounding in direct community engagement, we are now cultivating a local network of the change agents that have emerged from our field workshops and the DECOS program in PAR. Where this will lead is unclear now. We may expand the local network to elsewhere in Mexico, deepen locally through partnerships with local government and nonprofits, or build knowledge networks though horizontal exchanges with similar clusters of change agents in other countries. Just as the communities, we work in are evolving, so is the role of the University of Texas team. We look for what is possible, for what is emergent, for what is ours to do. There are no laurels to rest on nor benchmarks to measure ourselves by — just emptying to inner guidance, flow, trust, and the sense of serving something larger. The compass is deep democracy, in essence the inner experience of interconnectedness (Wilson, 2004), which serves as a guide to healing and wholeness both inside and out.

Summary and Conclusions

Regarding my own practice as a change agent for deep democracy, the experience in El Tráfico drove home the importance of being vigilant about my thoughts, particularly judgmental thoughts that close down the heart. Awareness of one's thoughts creates the opportunity to let go of a thought that is not useful before it does harm. Such emptying is a prerequisite to presencing (Scharmer, 2008), the openness to discerning what is wanting to emerge. Emptying is a practice of mindfulness, being fully present in the moment. My experience in Llano Grande reinforced the importance of deep listening. It was the deep listening that gave us the strength not to flee and trust to bring the two factions together.

The experience of introducing the 24 government professionals and educators to PAR through the workshop and accompanying fieldwork in El Tráfico and Llano Grande reinforced an important lesson for me: The pedagogy must be consistent with the practice. In this case, the temptation to resolve the insecurity of the participants by stepping into the authority role gave way to the instinctive knowing that it was better to create a safe space in which to be uncertain together. That choice allowed the participants to go through the eye of the needle and find their own resolution. They could then do the same with the community participants and experience the satisfaction of seeing results much greater and more useful than they could have planned or engineered.

Six months later, the majority of workshop participants interviewed could point to better relationships with the communities where they worked and with their teams and colleagues. Most of the educators had begun to engage their students through participatory inquiry and action.

Significant institutional changes have since been made at both universities to develop ongoing relationships with local communities. UAE sends a faculty-led team of students to Llano Grande twice a month. UTFV goes monthly to El Tráfico. UAE has hired and trained faculty to teach PAR. In late 2014, it launched a new major in sustainable community development using PAR as the primary method of engagement.

The sustainable community development group at the University of Texas has begun to focus on supporting, rather than anchoring, the efforts of the two universities in Mexico to engage local communities using PAR. Our annual field workshops are designed now to bring together the change agents for deep democracy that have emerged from our previous work there, engage them in coaching circles, and link them with similar clusters elsewhere. We continue to look for what is emergent and what is wanting to be expressed through us.

Conscious connectedness begins in the heart and mind of the individual — whether an outside change agent, a local leader, or a community participant. It sparks an inter-subjective unfolding: the transformation of identity from I to we. Like a catalytic meme, a self-replicating fractal, or a homeopathic healing agent, this transformative process can carry the emergent seed of societal or systems evolution to the next level of consciousness, caring, and creativity. Through inner practice, the community development practitioner can become present and attentive to the pulses, pressure points, and possibilities of a community, holding spaces for realignment and transformation. The community development practitioner becomes a midwife to healthy community.

Acknowledgments

I wish to acknowledge the students, faculty, public sector professionals, and community members who have participated with me over the last four years in this ongoing project of sustainable community development in the Guadalupe Dam watershed near Mexico City. I am particularly grateful to the Universidad Albert Einstein (UAE), the Universidad Tecnológica Fidel Velázquez (UTFV), and the Guadalupe Dam River Basin Commission (CCPG), and of course to my colleagues and students at the University of Texas Center for Sustainable Development and Institute of Latin American Studies. Some of the research described here was first published in *Planning Forum* (Wilson, 2015).

References

Philippson, P. (2009). *The emergent self: An existential Gestalt approach.* London: Karmac Books.

Scharmer, C. O. (2008). *Theory U: Leading from the future as it emerges.* San Francisco, CA: Berrett-Koehler Publishers.

Westoby, P., & Dowling, G. (2013). *Theory and practice of dialogical community development: International perspectives.* London: Routledge.

Westoby, P., & Kaplan, A. (2013). Foregrounding practice – Reaching for a responsive and ecological approach to community development: A conversational inquiry into the dialogical and developmental frameworks of community development. *Community Development Journal, 49*(2), 214–227. doi:10.1093/cdj/bst037

Wilson, P. A. (2004). Deep democracy: The inner practice of civic engagement. *Fieldnotes,* No. 2, Shambhala Institute. *National Coalition for Dialogue and Deliberation* [online]. Retrieved from www.ncdd.org. Accessed on August 17, 2015.

Wilson, P. A. (2015). The naked practitioner: Participatory community development in peri-urban Mexico. *Planning Forum, 16*(1), 5–17. *Texas Architecture* [online]. Retrieved from www.soa.utexas.edu. Accessed on August 17, 2015.

9 Sumak Kawsay among Indigenous Women Leaders of Ecuador

Carolina Bown

A bove 3,000 meters, the landscape of the Andes of Ecuador is breathtakingly beautiful. A deep blue sky is often the background for yellow, green, and brown mountains. When the wind blows, white plump clouds form a dense mist that can cover deep valleys in shroud in a matter of seconds. This is the highlands, home to the descendants of Incan and other pre-Columbian groups who preserve many of their ancestral traditions. They solve some disputes through indigenous justice; treat maladies with fragrant medicinal herbs; and live in their *ayllus* or groups of families connected by blood ties (Estermann, 1998). They also work the fields as their ancestors did. They mostly grow corn, lima beans, and potatoes — the staple Andean diet — which they supplement with other grains, rice, beef, chicken, and guinea pig. Within the communities, women manage a challenging workload. They take care of children, household chores, family vegetable gardens, and farm animals. However, this rural image should not be misleading. The roles of women in Andean communities are constantly being negotiated, creating a unique setting for studying leadership. With the expansion of women's grassroots organizations since 2009 and other societal changes, more indigenous women are stepping out of private spaces and holding leadership positions in rural communities (FENOCIN, 2015). When these women lead, they accomplish formal organizational goals while also promoting environments that support a healthy world. Within the Andean culture, healthy and sustainable communities are those that respect nature, provide citizens with material and spiritual resources, and are able to preserve their unique cultures for future generations.

With a qualitative approach to studying leadership, I examine in this chapter how indigenous female leaders exercise the Andean principle of *sumak kawsay*. Roughly translated as *good living*, it is a model that leads to a healthy world by encouraging a way of life that agrees with nature, social responsibility, and the well-being of individuals and communities. Based on this definition, this chapter addresses the following two questions:

1. How do Andean women understand the principle of *sumak kawsay* as guiding their actions as leaders of grassroots organizations?
2. How does leadership in this part of the world reflect the local culture, values, and practices?

Understanding the Andean Concept of *Sumak Kawsay*

At the national level, Ecuador has taken important steps regarding the recognition of rights of indigenous peoples and of women through legislation. An example is the 2008 Ecuadorian Constitution (Constitución Política de la República del Ecuador, 2008) that was ratified after the progressive leadership of some legislators and pressure from different societal groups. With a more gender and ethnic inclusive nature than the 1998 document, the 2008 Constitution purposely integrates the words *men and women* into the text and expands the collective rights of the indigenous peoples. It is important to point out that this is the first national Constitution in the world — later followed by Bolivia in 2009 — to incorporate in its text the indigenous principle of *sumak kawsay* and to legally grant rights to the *Pachamama* or Mother Earth. These additions to the Constitution are noteworthy both in content and form as they oppose the current market-oriented approach to the earth that dominates Western cultures and have been incorporated in the original Quechua (or Kichwa) language. They also share similarities with ecofeminist voices, such as Carolyn Merchant's (2008) critical assessment of a mechanistic approach to nature.

Based on the Andean notion of *sumak kawsay* integrated into the 2008 Constitution, the Ecuadorian National Institute for Statistics and Census developed *el buen vivir* [good living]. The objective of this index scale is "to inform about the population's well-being and to design public policies that are coherent with the real needs of Ecuadorians" (INEC, 2015a). Therefore, in addition to using Western instruments to measure the welfare of people — such as income level, GDP, Gini coefficient, or life expectancy — Ecuador has provided legitimacy to an indigenous model of living on a national scale through institutional initiatives that were unseen less than a decade ago.

Sumak kawsay has been explained by scholars and activists in several ways, including "a new economic and political model for society and state, and a new vision with respect to nature" (Vega Ugalde, 2014, p. 73) or "an opportunity to collectively build new ways of life as alternatives to the current Western's goals of advancement and development" (Acosta, 2012, p. 62). From an ecofeminist perspective, Magdalena León (2010) presents the idea of an *economy of care* as part of this principle that values economic diversity, solidarity, sustainable ways of production, and a subsistence economy traditionally carried out by women.

There are some well-established definitions of *sumak kawsay* in the literature, although there is no consensus on whether this principle should be understood only within the Kichwa worldview or if it is an ideal for everyone, indigenous or not (Manosalvas, 2014). Other issues are whether the concept of *buen vivir* has been "borrowed" or "stolen" from the indigenous world, if leaders and activists committed to the indigenous cause should be the only ones defining *sumak kawsay* (Houtart, 2011; Vega Ugalde, 2014), and whether the official discourse of the government has lately given preference to the Spanish term *buen vivir* over the Kichwa term (Manosalvas, 2014). Finally, Houtart (2011) points out that the activists and scholars' discourses concerning *sumak kawsay* have great room for interpretation, with a variety of connotations (p. 12). Despite the fluidity of the concept, there is agreement that *sumak kawsay* relates to societal health. Although the relationship with nature is most central, *sumak kawsay* also includes other elements, such as social responsibility, equality, solidarity, and justice.

The Ecuadorian and Andean Contexts

Before exploring how Andean women carry out leadership, we need to understand the context in which they live today. With a population of 16.1 million (INEC, 2015b), Ecuador has had its share of social, political, and economic turmoil for decades and, as a consequence, women leaders from all groups of Ecuadorian society have frequently exercised leadership in unstable conditions. After a period of eight presidents in 10 years, the election of Rafael Correa to the presidency in 2007 brought a period of relative stability. Nevertheless, his governing style has been fraught with controversy. Supporters argue that Correa's legitimacy lies in having won free elections three times and in the government's important public and infrastructure investment in roads, hospitals, and schools. His opponents point to the president's authoritarian style, limitations to an independent judicial branch of government, and restrictions to the rights to free press and free speech (Basabe-Serrano & Martínez, 2014; De la Torre, 2013). In addition, Correa's latest plans to develop a primary extractive economy are seen as a menace to the environment and to indigenous cultures. Concerns from indigenous leaders and activists are frequently expressed in social networks and media these days.

In terms of national diversity, there is a rich heritage in Ecuador, with 14 indigenous nationalities and 18 indigenous peoples officially recognized (CODENPE, 2015). As I was taking field notes and interviewing participants for this research, I witnessed many cases in which Western culture and newer technologies are present in the highlands. The following passage from my observations illustrates this phenomenon:

> When I arrived to interview Jacinta (a pseudonym), her computer was on and she was working on an Excel spreadsheet. As the president of a community-based bank that provides small loans to farmers, she spoke in Kichwa to her two children and in Spanish to me. She was wearing a characteristic Kichwa-Salasaka white blouse covered by a shawl (in this case purple, as a sign of mourning) held by a *tupu* [metallic pin] and a mid-calf long black skirt fastened by a multicolor sash. Her 22 year-old daughter — a medical student at the Universidad de Santiago de Cuba thanks to an agreement between the two governments — wore Western clothes and browsed Facebook in Spanish while speaking to her mother in Kichwa.

The example above shows how Western culture combined with the effects of migration and more access to technology are reshaping the traditional ways of living of indigenous groups. Additionally, besides having to adapt to external demands from the Ecuadorian society and the whole world, indigenous groups have historically suffered great inequality in Ecuadorian society. Indigenous women from rural communities have been especially vulnerable (Abramo & Valenzuela, 2008; INEC, 2010). They face gender and ethnic-based discrimination as well as inequities due to class, education, and language. As a result, they may not always take part in making political, economic, and reproductive decisions that affect them (Bown, 2013, p. 23). Other issues that continue to affect indigenous rural women are domestic violence, lack of rights in reproductive and sexual health, and limited access to credit, water, land, and technical and professional development (Mena, 2009).

Female Leadership in Contemporary Ecuador

Despite of the challenges mentioned above, several studies point to the important presence indigenous female leaders have had in politics during the last century. Female leaders were active in the indigenous mobilizations of the nineties (Prieto, Pequeño, Flores, Cuminao, & Maldonado, 2010), some becoming public figures at the national level when the indigenous movement was institutionalized (Picq, 2013). In their leadership positions, the women of the 20th century focused on structural changes to move Ecuador toward a multiethnic and intercultural state. Some scholars suggest that presently there is an absence of public indigenous female leaders or that they have been coopted by the government (Picq, 2013; Vega Ugalde, 2014). I argue that in the last 15 years they have continued advancing in politics, education, and business, but many are doing so at the grassroots level. By successfully leading organizations, they provide new sources of income and of knowledge about important issues — such as new laws, political rights, and sexual education — to women who live in rural areas. So, although female indigenous leaders do not have the visibility of the women of 15 or 20 years ago, they continue to enhance the lives of individuals as they exercise *sumak kawsay* in practical ways at a local level.

Cross-cultural research, such as the GLOBE study (House, Hanges, Javidan, Dorfman, & Gupta, 2004), reveals that Ecuador's profile is similar to other Latin American countries in terms of leadership attributes, identifying the charismatic/value based leadership dimension as the most desirable. Robert House et al. (2004) indicate that this leadership dimension "reflects the ability to inspire, to motivate, and to expect high performance outcomes from others on the basis of firmly held core values" (p. 14). Since cross-cultural research has been mostly restricted to urban, male leaders, it could be illuminating to investigate whether Andean women leaders possess similar accepted attributes, like those associated with charismatic leadership. The concept of adaptive leadership may be particularly helpful for understanding how Andean women lead in ways that reflect local culture, values, and practices. Drawing from biology and comparing organizations to ecosystems that can evolve and adapt, Ronald Heifetz, Alexander Grashow, and Marty Linsky (2009) define adaptive leadership as "the practice of mobilizing people to tackle tough challenges and thrive" (p. 14).

Data and Methodology

This chapter draws from a larger in-depth qualitative study that identifies new forms of leadership among women from indigenous communities of Ecuador. Using a basic interpretive and descriptive qualitative design (Merriam, 2002), data were primarily collected from semi-structured face-to-face interviews with 19 Kichwa women. The interviews included questions about their experiences as leaders in grassroots organizations, the ways they influence gender equality, and the contextual factors that affect their leadership. Data also came from document analysis and observations that served as a means of *data triangulation* by providing additional confirmatory and descriptive information about the context and role of these women in their organizations (see Denzin, 1989).

I selected the participants and the communities with a combination of *typical case sampling* — which describes what is typical of a culture to people not familiar with the setting studied — and *maximum variation* — to identify important common patterns that cut across a wide range of variation. Both are effective strategies when there is not much information about a certain population, such as rural citizens in developing countries (see Patton, 2002). I specifically sought out a sample of women from different age groups, education levels, indigenous communities, and types of organizations. Three key informants helped me in their selection: FODEPI's legal adviser, a representative of the *Kañaris* before CODENPE, and an activist and art teacher from the province of Azuay.

The 19 women leaders interviewed in 2012, 2013, and 2015 were from eight Andean communities located in seven different provinces. Some led community-based cooperatives that manufactured typical crafts, such as Panama hats or embroidered textiles, while others directed private or public organizations that offered intercultural education, health programs, or financial support. The youngest was 24, and the oldest was 60 years old. Seventeen were married and had on average two children each. In terms of education, the two older interview partners had attended primary school, six had completed high school, eight had Bachelor's degrees, and three Master's degrees. Language and dress are two of the most visible elements of indigenousness. Seventeen of the women were fluent in Spanish and Kichwa, and two spoke only Spanish. Eighteen wore their traditional attire during the interview and wore this clothing on an everyday basis.

I recorded and transcribed the interviews, and all quotations are verbatim. I then coded the interviews, observations, and documents with the computer software ATLAS.ti (Version 7). I followed Richard Boyatzis's thematic code development approach, which is a process of organizing the data by topics and themes, and coding it into categories or patterns to uncover the manifest content (directly observable in the information) and the latent content (underlying the phenomenon) and to convert them into narratives (1998). Data analysis followed the three stages of coding recommended by William Neuman (2012). Through iterative processes of open, axial, and selective coding, four major subcategories under the category *sumak kawsay* emerged "protecting the environment," "preserving the culture," "impacting the workplace," and "impacting the community."[1] These subcategories were used to respond to the two guiding questions in this chapter.

The data analysis includes coded segments from documents and observations and direct quotes (translations mine) of the women leaders' own thoughts about the Andean principle *sumak kawsay*. I am a native speaker of Spanish with extensive experience in the Ecuadorian culture, yet I acknowledge the possibility

---

[1] For more details on the coding process, see Carolina Bown (2013).

of misinterpretations in cross-cultural research. To increase the trustworthiness of my interpretations, I used techniques recommended by several qualitative researchers, including member checking, reflexivity, peer debriefing, prolonged engagement, data triangulation, and an audit trail (see Lincoln & Guba, 1985; Padgett, 1998).

Regarding the first question, "How do Andean women understand the principle of *sumak kawsay* as guiding their actions as leaders of grassroots organizations?" I noticed that the participants elaborated on different elements of *sumak kawsay*, whether they actually used those words or not. Whereas only 5 out of 19 participants (26%) mentioned the exact term *sumak kawsay*, this finding is still significant considering that the interview protocol had not been originally designed to address this theme. While for some of these women, *sumak kawsay* is basically linked to protecting the environment, for others it relates to the well-being of the communities, whether this means helping women preserve the use of natural medicine, treat alcohol dependency, or teach women about reproductive rights and managing money.

Sumak Kawsay in Ecuadorian Grassroots Organizations

Antonia, director of the Environmental Management Department of a central province in Ecuador, has two Master's degrees, a remarkable career, and a busy agenda. The night before our interview, she had received a call from a politician requesting her to explain her perspective on food sovereignty before the National Assembly (the Ecuadorian legislative branch) in Quito, the capital. While riding in the back of a pickup truck, we conducted a 90-minute interview. I asked her about her role as a leader and she gave me a detailed description. Among other topics, she spoke of the important relationship between nature, women, and the betterment of communities:

> The environment and *sumak kawsay* have to do with women. Why? Because it is we, women, who are in charge of water, the family vegetable garden, the weeding, transforming trash into fertilizer, and because we are more connected to the Pachamama, food sovereignty, climate change, and anything that affects our communities.

Since the relationship with nature is the most known component of *sumak kawsay*, it was not surprising to find an excerpt under the subcategory "protecting the environment." However, what caught more my attention was that Antonia made a connection between *sumak kawsay* and gender when referring to environmental sustainability in the province of Cotopaxi. According to her, women are the true protectors of the earth, water, and food sovereignty. Women in the community work the soil using ecologically oriented techniques, but still fear the effects of climate change. The view Antonia expresses is consistent with current ecofeminist perspectives, such as Merchant's (2008) environmental paradigm, as well as with the rights granted to the Pachamama in the 2008 Ecuadorian Constitution. Antonia communicates her concerns to community members so their traditional way of relating to the Mother Earth can subsist for future generations.

In addition to effectively attaining formal organizational goals, such as successfully running a bilingual intercultural school, a community-based bank, or a Panama hats cooperative, indigenous female leaders have a positive impact on women's lives outside the specific organizations' boundaries. Cecilia, a teacher and healer from the southern province of Loja, brought up the principle of *sumak kawsay* when discussing the use of natural medicine. Again, this reflection was not a response to a direct question about *sumak kawsay*, but to a question from the interview protocol about her role as a leader influencing gender equality. At the time of the interview, she was a representative of her community before a national organization of indigenous people of Ecuador. She was also debating about accepting a full-time teaching job in a different town:

> The notion of *sumak kawsay* has always existed among our people. The fact that we care about our well-being with spiritual and ancestral natural medicine shows that this principle has always been part of our way of life. As an auxiliary healer, because I am not a shaman, I make sure to treat malaise in a holistic way, respecting nature.

In her role as a teacher, Cecilia has a podium not only to deliver her content (social studies) but also to teach the practices of natural medicine. The *sumak kawsay* subcategory, "preserving the culture," refers to all of those leader's initiatives conducive to maintaining local traditions. Continuing the practices of holistic healing is important in their society, similar to Merchant's (2008) view on nature that favors a holistic approach to the well-being of people.

I also found examples of *sumak kawsay* through co-occurrences during the data coding process. Co-occurrences are those instances when two or more codes are linked to the same quotation or segment (Contreras, 2012). In other words, whenever a participant is talking about theme X, she is also talking about theme Y or Z. An example of co-occurrence in this research was that several portions of the interviews were coded as both *food sovereignty* and *sumak kawsay*. In contrast with food security, food sovereignty means ensuring enough to eat for citizens as well as the kind of nourishment that is aligned to each community's culture and needs. Thus, when an Andean leader provides coworkers with non-GMO seeds and plants, and another leader encourages them to preserve native plants like the mashua tuber *(Tripaeolum tuberosum)*, even though doing so may not be lucrative, they are addressing *sumak kawsay* through leadership.

Another important co-occurrence refers to the application of *sumak kawsay* in the public school setting. Tránsito, director of a bilingual intercultural school in the province of Cañar, asked rhetorically during the interview: "How can we tell our children to follow the notion of *sumak kawsay?*" to which she answered "By teaching this concept through actions." Tránsito was referring to a connection she perceived between the Andean principle and solving drinking problems: "Since addictions are a great problem here, I tell employees that alcohol or even showing up smelling like alcohol is not allowed on the school's premises. It may be a small step but it can spark a change." Tránsito believes that it is her role as a leader to guide her employees toward temperance, a reflection of healthy living. Initially I had coded her actions under the subcategory "impacting the workplace." Given the iterative nature of this research, I later recoded these initiatives under the subcategory "impacting the community" as well, since, as she stated, "in some cases arrangements were made to take her female employees' husbands to A.A. meetings." According to Heifetz et al. (2009), adaptive leadership is "specifically about change that enables the capacity to thrive" (p. 14). Tránsito began this change within the organization, by addressing the problem of alcohol dependency in every Monday meeting; however, the effects of her actions extend even beyond the organization's boundaries. From a traditional Western perspective of leadership, "this step" — as she called it — would be unexpected from a leader and rather considered unacceptable. But, in the context of the Andes, Tránsito has the community's approval to impact not only her followers but also their extended families. Similar to the concept of *democracy* in modern Western societies, *sumak kawsay* is an ideal of the Andean world that can be achieved through many actions, even if the term is left implicit by the leaders. Other initiatives carried out by Andean women that reflect the principle of *sumak kawsay* and lead to societal health are preparing women for political and leadership positions through civics classes, bringing health resources to women in their homes, participating in the literacy program "*Yo sí puedo*," and running workshops on education opportunities, nutrition, and domestic violence.

With respect to the question of how leadership in this part of the world reflects local culture, values, and practices, I found new ways of exercising leadership that flourish in grassroots organizations, but also extend beyond organizational boundaries. In effect, many of the women interviewed expressed having additional responsibilities beyond their formal organizational goals. I specifically asked them about their leadership strategies to support followers in the workplace, and many spoke about their influence in their followers' private spaces. At first, I thought that they had not understood my question; but later, during the data analysis process and by unveiling the latent content (Boyatzis, 1998), I realized that for them, there is no clear boundary dividing public and private spaces.

The following example comes from my field notes taken on a Saturday afternoon in the province of Tungurahua. The hamlet of Yatzaputzán is an isolated place high in the Andes, with no cellphone reception and the temperature barely above freezing. The day I was there, a professor of Economics and six of his graduating students from Pontificia Universidad Católica were leading a two-day workshop for members of this cooperative. The themes were budgeting and how to prepare this organization for a possible expansion. There were four men and twelve women, two of them with infants on their backs, attending the workshop. All the attendees were in a circle and alternated the abstract materials with meal breaks and *dinámicas*, or activities planned every two hours to relax participants. PowerPoint, textbooks, and a whiteboard supported the presentations by the university students and the attendees, which was clearly a cooperative approach to learning. When I asked the president of the cooperative whose idea it was to hold this workshop, she responded, "If we want to get out of poverty, we need to learn about the rules of banking." From her perspective, teaching women from a rural cooperative how to get a loan from a bank or how to create a budget is conducive to financial sustainability and it falls under the subcategory "impacting the community." Even though they have much to do at home and in the fields, this leader encourages followers to attend this two-day workshop because she believes that developing financial skills will have a positive long-term effect in the community.

Another important theme in the analysis concerns how indigenous female leaders empower other women regarding domestic abuse. According to official data, violence against women is prevalent across all provinces, educational levels, ethnicities, and age groups in Ecuador. Indigenous women are the most affected, with 67.8% of them suffering one or more types of domestic violence (INEC, 2015c). Since addressing this issue leads to healthy communities, I included those initiatives that help other women to confront this problem as part of *sumak kawsay*'s subcategory "impacting the community." When the president of a cooperative that exports Panama hats speaks, she shows that she is proud of the effect she has on younger or more timid women: "I like having my (female) peers coming to me and asking me, 'What did you do when your husband did that?' Or even asking me about what I do when my husband comes home angry." It was an emotional moment during the interview when Rocío narrated how she had persuaded a physically abused member of the cooperative to confront her spouse. She empowered her peer by telling her what to say and what to do (to grab an iron-cast pan) if the husband attempted to hit her. As an adaptive leader, Rocío considers it an obligation to promote change and, to paraphrase Heifetz et al. (2009), she tailors her interventions to the individuals involved and to the unique characteristics of the situation facing the leader (p. 10). For Rocío, to serve the community, the cooperative must support members at risk, including when the risk is at home. In other words, the well-being of their organizations, followers, and communities is interconnected for Rocío and other female leaders.

Female Andean leaders adapt leadership strategies to their local cultural context. They use, for example, *conversar* (talking things out) as a form of persuasion and mentoring. *Talking things out* helps peers to overcome shyness in public speaking or to hold leadership positions. It also helps them address problems and disputes in followers' homes. *Talking things out* is more "intrusive" than is typical in Western cultures, whereby followers expect their leaders to inquire about their private lives and to address issues such as marital life, domestic abuse, and the virtue of filial piety. A clear example of this more "intrusive" leadership style is two participants' public campaign to treat alcohol dependency among male employees as well as among the spouses of female employees. A female leader telling an employee that she has arranged an appointment with a doctor for her husband or offering to take her husband to an A.A. meeting can be an acceptable expression of leadership in the Andean world.

Conclusions

I draw two primary conclusions from this study. First, by following Boyatzis' (1998) thematic analysis, I found that the Andean concept of *sumak kawsay* — which was defined as a model that leads to a healthy world by encouraging a way of life that agrees with nature, social responsibility, and the well-being of communities — guides how Andean women carry out leadership in grassroots organizations. In addition, and opposing the current Western belief that corporations have rights as individuals, the Ecuadorian legislation favors the indigenous notion of *sumak kawsay* and grants rights to Mother Earth. Although this eco-feminist approach is aligned with Merchant's ecological view of nature, assessing the actual impact of the 2008 Constitution on the health of Mother Earth or on the lives of the communities is challenging. The innovative laws have been approved, but they are not always enforced.

Second, Andean women leaders are both similar to and different from women leaders in developed countries. Still dressed in traditional clothing that reflects their communities of origin, they connect the past with the present by encouraging followers to preserve their unique cultures, values, and practices. Heifetz et al. (2009) pointed out that "adaptation is a process of conservation as well as loss" (p. 23). By drawing on this concept of adaptive leadership in this way, these indigenous women are not backward-looking traditionalists, but wise leaders. By working under the principle of *sumak kawsay*, they promote health and sustainability by moving into the future what is most worthy and precious in their culture, benefiting the next generations. Additionally, as adaptive leaders do, Andean women "tailor their interventions" (see Heifetz et al., 2009, p. 23). When Andean women lead, they bridge spaces of the workplace and private lives and empower followers across spheres of their lives.

During the interviews, these women leaders addressed me as *compañera* [comrade] and I considered them my peers in this research endeavor. With this approach, I have helped make their voices heard in a wider context, an important outcome since these women are not typically considered formal organizational leaders. In this way, the lens of leadership studies has been turned in a new direction with a dual result: (1) the principle of *sumak kawsay* has been defined within grassroots organizations, an approximation to an emic definition, and (2) I have found new context-contingent ways of exercising leadership.

With the recent expansion of women's grassroots organizations, female leadership in rural and indigenous communities may be having a greater impact than anticipated. Therefore, governmental and nongovernmental policymakers who wish to promote positive changes in the Andean world should know that supporting grassroots organizations directed by Andean women could be an effective way to promote healthy environments in this region of the world. As an example, Ecuadorian women working in a local cooperative in the highlands earn their own income and also get the benefit of having access to information about nutrition or the new laws against domestic violence. As a result, a positive reciprocal relationship between grassroots leadership and leadership at the level of policymaking is essential for the health of these communities and our planet.

Future research on grassroots leadership among indigenous groups in Ecuador should address how the other players of Ecuadorian society, including men, urban citizens, and the government, may practice the notion of *sumak kawsay*. Investigating how the currently ratified laws regarding the rights granted to the Pachamama are impacting the health of the earth and of the communities would be of most importance.

References

Abramo, L., & Valenzuela, M. (2008). Igualdad de género y mercado de trabajo en América Latina. Latin American studies association. *LASA Forum, 39*(4), 19–21.

Acosta, A. (2012). Buen vivir – Sumak kawsay. *Una oportunidad para imaginar otros mundos*. Quito, Ecuador: Ediciones Abya-Yala.

ATLAS.ti. (Version 7). [Computer software]. ATLAS.ti Scientific Software Development GmbH.

Basabe-Serrano, S., & Martínez, J. (2014). Ecuador: Cada vez menos democracia, cada vez más autoritarismo … con elecciones. *Revista de Ciencia Política (Santiago)*, 34(1), 145–170.

Bown, C. (2013). *Indigenous and rural women leaders' support of gender equality in Ecuadorian organizations*. Doctoral dissertation, University of Maryland Eastern Shore.

Boyatzis, R. E. (1998). *Transforming qualitative information: Thematic analysis and code development*. Thousand Oaks, CA: Sage.

Consejo de Desarrollo de las Nacionalidades y Pueblos del Ecuador [CODENPE]. (2015). Retrieved from http://www.codenpe.gob.ec/index.php?option=com_k2& view=itemlist&layout=category&task=category&id=348&Itemid=469

Constitución Política de la República del Ecuador. (2008). Retrieved from http://www.asambleanacional.gov.ec/documentos/constitucion_de_bolsillo.pdf

Contreras, R. (2012). ATLAS.ti learning guide. A learning guide for participants in the ATLAS.ti introductory workshops. ATLAS.ti Training Center. Retrieved from www.atlastitrainingcenter.com

De la Torre, C. (2013). El tecnopopulismo de Rafael Correa: ¿Es compatible el carisma con la tecnocracia? *Latin American Research Review*, 48(1), 24–43.

Denzin, N. K. (1989). *The research act: A theoretical introduction to sociological methods*. Englewood Cliffs, NJ: Prentice Hall.

Estermann, J. (1998). *Filosofía andina, Estudio intercultural de la sabiduría autóctona andina*. Quito, Ecuador: Ediciones Abya-Yala.

Federación Nacional de Pueblos y Nacionalidades Indígenas y Negras del Ecuador [FENOCIN]. (2015). Retrieved from http://www.fenocin.org/informacion-institucional/quienes-somos/

Heifetz, R. A., Grashow, A., & Linsky, M. (2009). *The practice of adaptive leadership: Tools and tactics for changing your organization and the world*. Boston, MA: Harvard Business Press.

House, R. J., Hanges, P. J., Javidan, M., Dorfman, P. W., & Gupta, V. (2004). *Culture, leadership, and organizations. The GLOBE study of 62 societies*. Thousand Oaks, CA: Sage.

Houtart, F. (2011). El concepto de sumak kawsay (buen vivir) y su correspondencia con el bien común de la humanidad. *Revista de Filosofía*, 69(3), 7–33.

Instituto Nacional de Estadística y Censos [INEC]. (2010). *Las mujeres indígenas del Ecuador: Condiciones de educación y uso de la lengua en el acceso al empleo*. Retrieved from http://www.ecuadorencifras.gob.ec/estudios-socio-demograficos/

Instituto Nacional de Estadística y Censos [INEC]. (2015a). Retrieved from http://www.inec.gob.ec/estadisticas/?option=com_content&view=article&id=235& Itemid=180

Instituto Nacional de Estadística y Censos [INEC]. (2015b). Retrieved from http://www.ecuadorencifras.gob.ec/

Instituto Nacional de Estadística y Censos [INEC]. (2015c). *Encuesta nacional de relaciones familiares y violencia de género contra las mujeres*. Retrieved from http://www.inec.gob.ec/sitio_violencia/

León, M. (2010). El "Buen Vivir": Objetivo y camino para otro modelo. In I. León. (Ed.), *Sumak Kawsay/Buen Vivir y cambios civilizatorios* (pp. 105–111). Quito: FEDAEPS.

Lincoln, Y. S., & Guba, E. G. (1985). *Naturalistic inquiry.* San Francisco, CA: Jossey-Bass Publishers.

Manosalvas, M. (2014). Buen vivir o sumak kawsay. En busca de nuevos referenciales para la acción pública en Ecuador. *Íconos. Revista de Ciencias Sociales, 49*, 101–121.

Mena, C. (2009). *Proyecto equidad en el campo—Mujeres y hombres juntos para el desarrollo. Documento "Visión de las desigualdades de género y la situación de las mujeres en el país en los sectores rurales y en las organizaciones filiales de Fenocin." Prioridades para superar esta realidad.* Ecuador: Fenocin.

Merchant, C. (2008). *The death of nature: Women, ecology, and the scientific revolution.* San Francisco, CA: HarperOne.

Merriam, S. B. (2002). *Qualitative research in practice: Examples for discussion and analysis.* San Francisco, CA: Jossey-Bass Publishers.

Neuman, W. L. (2012). *Basics of social research: Qualitative and quantitative approaches.* Boston, MA: Pearson.

Padgett, D. K. (1998). *Qualitative methods in social work research: Challenges and rewards.* Thousand Oaks, CA: Sage.

Patton, M. Q. (2002). *Qualitative research and evaluation methods* (3rd ed.). Thousand Oaks, CA: Sage.

Picq, M. L. (2013). The inheritance of resistance: Indigenous women's leadership in Ecuador. In M. Becker. (Ed.), *Indigenous and Afro-Ecuadorians facing the twenty-first century* (pp.71–94). Cambridge: Cambridge Scholars Publishing.

Prieto, M., Pequeño, A., Flores, A., Cuminao, C., & Maldonado, G. (2010). Respect, discrimination, and violence: Indigenous women in Ecuador, 1990-2007. In E. Maier & N. Lebon (Eds.), *Women's activism in Latin America and the Caribbean: Engendering social justice, democratizing citizenship* (pp. 203–218). New Brunswick, NJ: Rutgers University Press.

Vega Ugalde, S. (2014). El orden de género en el sumak kawsay y el suma qamaña. Un vistazo a los debates actuales en Bolivia y Ecuador. *Íconos. Revista de Ciencias Sociales, 48*, 73–91.

10 Kiwi Ways of Leading: How 30 New Zealand Government Chief Executives Are Encouraging Healthier Cultures

Jane McCann

How do leaders promote development of a healthy, sustainable culture within a public sector system, achieving both organizational and societal outcomes? This chapter provides examples of how 30 government Chief Executives (CEs) in New Zealand are working to do this, all of whom I observed on the job over a 20-year period. These CEs chose to be observed and receive feedback, so the sample is biased toward leaders who are open to new ways of leading. They, like leaders worldwide, are facing complex, multigenerational, and interdependent problems which have no quick or easy solutions. In New Zealand, these issues arise against a historical backdrop of repression of Māori by the British and the development of a bicultural public sector and increasingly multicultural society. CEs acknowledge that the thinking of the past will not work for these problems, so they are designing new structures, engaging in new cultural practices and developing ways of operating to address such issues.

I coached CEs and leaders for years, sitting across the table, listening to their stories about how they structure systems and teams to create high-performance cultures of delivery. I listened and offered help in the form of frameworks, models, and leadership tools. And I was content. It was not until I went into their organizations and observed first-hand for days at a time what these CEs actually did that I learned about the gap between espoused theories and real experience: what we believe we do as compared with what we actually do (see Argyris, 2000, p. 5). Suddenly, I realized that they had not necessarily been doing the things they had been describing to me! No longer content to sit across the table and hear one perspective, my role shifted when I began to go into their organizations as an observer/coach and hold a mirror to their actual behaviors (see Mintzberg, 1973).

Observational data on top executives is rare in New Zealand, as it is throughout the world. I have gathered it for 20 years, while focusing on my work as a leadership coach rather than writing about it. When I heard about this book, it seemed like the right time and place to sift through my data and experiences and share it with scholars, consultants, and leaders who might be interested in learning from it.

I define a healthy organizational culture as a place where people can bring their whole being (physical, emotional, intellectual, social, and spiritual) to work, where people choose to belong, and where they can reach their potential while being physically and psychologically safe. This definition has been shaped by my behavioral and health sciences background as well as by Lee G. Bolman and Terrence E. Deal's (1991) concept of lenses or frames: the structural frame (roles and structures); the political frame (power); the symbolic frame (social, tribal, and anthropological); and the human resource frame. In addition, I have seen New Zealand leaders use the ancient Māori model of health called *Te Whare Tapa Whā* from Mason Durie (1964) who uses the Māori meeting house (Te Whare) as a metaphor, which has been adapted by many New Zealand leaders to apply to their organizational cultures. This model (which I will discuss later in the chapter) could, I believe, become the ideal culture-creation metaphor in New Zealand if it were more widely adopted, because of its grounding in New Zealand's culture and history.

The challenges New Zealand faces, like many other Western democracies, include economic and fiscal constraints, child poverty, obesity, and climate-change issues. Challenges specific to New Zealand include the structural rebuild of Christchurch City after three major earthquakes in 2010 and 2011, the settlement of Māori land claims, biodiversity risks, and pollution problems as New Zealand moves from a sheep-based economy to a dairying one (Gill, Pride, Gilbert & Norman, 2010, p.1). The New Zealand government bears much of the burden for addressing or solving these issues on behalf of its 4.5 million citizens. It employs government departmental CEs who run the Core Public Service and directly employ over 45,000 people. This Core Public Service sits within the wider state sector of government which employs an additional 180,000 people including police, teachers, defense, and health workers. These CEs recommend solutions to government by way of ministerial advice, legislation, policy, and regulatory reform. The public sector is made up of a diverse workforce: 17% are Māori, 8% are Pacific Peoples, and 8% are Asians; patterns similar to the general population. Forty-two percent of CEs are women, from a public sector pool of 60%, (State Services Commission [SSC], 2014, p. 8). Although there are a handful of Māori and Pacific CEs in the public service, I did not observe any.

These departmental CEs use varied models of organizational culture, including principles from Jim Collins' (2001) *Good to Great*, Ed Schein's (1995) primary and secondary culture embedding mechanisms, and Roger Harrison's (personal communication, 1990) three universal challenges to map out their organizational strategies and cultures:

What has worked in our past that we want to regain (honoring the history)?
What's working now that we want to retain (honoring the present)?
What have we never dared do, that if we did it would take us into the future?

The CEs know it takes at least 2–5 years for changes and new structures, systems, and practices (Schein's primary mechanisms) to become anchored into systems, processes, and behaviors, independent of people coming and going from the organization. They emphasized that culture involves the collective will and are a reflection of place and time, especially New Zealand's societal norms and values. They say that their role as leaders is to set the structural and behavioral environment and the tone of discourse, and then provide the direction forward through role-modeling behaviors that uphold shared cultural values. Their cultures reflected three histories: the organizational, the personal, and the societal histories, the latter of which I discuss now in depth.

The Impact of New Zealand's History

The importance of place, time, and societal norms in the creation of organizational culture cannot be underestimated. What works in one hemisphere, country, or cultural context may not work in another. I am therefore providing a snapshot of New Zealand's cultural history (King, 2003), plus examples of how some CEs are building upon that history. I write from the perspective of a White, European New Zealander (Pākehā), not a Māori one. New Zealand is an independent, multicultural, immigrant settler nation of islands in the South Pacific with a population mix of 70% White Europeans (Pākehā), 15% Māori, 10% Asian, and 7% Pacific Peoples. Our heritage was influenced originally by indigenous Māori and since the 1830s was shaped by British settlers (Belich, 1996). British colonization and its consequences are a large part of our heritage. The legacy of new technologies and new cultural influences, including Christianity, was followed by the then government's systematic suppression of Māori and the confiscation of their land to entice British settlers. A covenant of trust between the Crown and Māori was signed in 1840, and this Treaty, called *Tiriti o Waitangi*, is the founding document of New Zealand. The subsequent Land Wars, the near destruction of Māori identity, culture, and language, and the broken trust by subsequent governments has taken a heavy toll on the people. For example, among the things that caused great suffering, Māori children were punished for using their own language in schools until the mid-20th century. Such actions left a history of unresolved, wicked problems (Belich, 1996; Orange, 1987).

There is no one "precise history of colonialism in New Zealand, rather multiple perspectives" (Anderson, Binney, & Harris, 2014, p. 12). In *Healing our History*, Consedine and Consedine (2012) "challenge New Zealanders ... to learn our colonial history" (which has only recently been taught in schools) and "to become better informed, and support the change that values all people, regardless of cultural background" (p. 7). The process of healing is not over. Since 1975 and the introduction of the Treaty claims process, the New Zealand government has accelerated how it is addressing these complex issues — settling land claims, combined with a strong, legislative, and regulated commitment to biculturalism in the public sector, and making CEs accountable for implementing these policies. Each government department is required to create a Māori Responsive Plan or Framework, detailing how they will implement the principles of

Tiriti o Waitangi and have regard for Māori whether they be citizens, employees, contractors, or customers of government services.

These bicultural foundations have impacted the way the CEs I observed are creating their organizational cultures based on their histories, their rites, rituals, myths, legends, and stories (Schein, 1995). This bicultural history is so ingrained in me, that until it was pointed out to me by editor Kathryn Goldman Schuyler during the writing of this chapter, I, like many Kiwis, took biculturalism for granted, because it is such an integral, unconscious, positive part of our New Zealand identity, particularly in the public sector. In practice, biculturalism is a cornerstone of the organizational cultures of departments within the public sector. Each agency and CE have Māori advisors. Many of these Māori elders, men and women (kaumatu and kuia), hold second-tier decision-making roles at the CE management table. *Tikanga* (Māori customs) and Treaty education and Māori language (*Te Reo*) training is offered to government employees and the Māori language is one of the official languages alongside English and New Zealand Sign Language. All CEs were seen using Māori and English, alongside Māori spiritual practices like *Waiata* (songs that preserve the wisdom and history of the ancestors) and *Mihi* (reciting ones genealogy) on ceremonial occasions for new staff or guest welcomes, celebrations, and farewells. Waiata practice in government departments is common and a positive organizational culture creator.

Some CEs were seen holding their strategic thinking sessions on *marae* (Māori meeting grounds and houses); these are the geographic heart and spiritual hub of each Māori *Iwi* (tribe), *hapu* (subtribe), or *whanau* (family). This was another culture creation and motivational exercise by about half of the CEs observed. They put their long-term planning process in its wider cultural context and use it as a way to educate staff about the bicultural roots and history of New Zealand and the citizens they serve. This is seen by staff as a holistic approach, including the spiritual aspects of a healthy culture, and is done by the CEs in a low-key, humble manner.

The Observational Methodology

This chapter draws on observational data on 30 CEs gathered over a 20-year period from 1995 to 2015. To honor the contract of confidentially and to protect the identities of individual CEs,

I have combined the histories and practices of a number of them into each example. CEs invite me into their organizations to shadow them and their executive teams over days or weeks. I then provide them with verbal and written feedback on how they contribute to and maintain healthy cultures, as well as what they do that interferes with this. This is done at meetings, in their offices (increasingly open-plan), and occasionally by shadowing them in Parliament.

My role is to observe and then reflect back what I see — first at their executive team meetings (generalized feedback) and afterward in depth, providing one-to-one feedback and coaching using the behavioral evidence I gathered. This coaching ranges from roles as a sounding board, advisor, problem solver, or skills developer. My job is to listen, reflect, and enable them to come to their own solutions, and like their other advisors, help them create the environment and culture to solve the tough issues. My personal coaching practice includes taking time for personal reflection and silent retreats, combined with regular external supervision to test my own pattern blindness, mental models, boundaries, defensive behaviors, prejudices, biases, and assumptions.

During an observation I sit in silence, away from the meeting table — I try to be inconspicuous, and the teams report that after a few minutes they have forgotten my presence. I move silently from place to place around the perimeter of the room to get a view of each member of the team (noting the team's reaction to each speaker). I record, analyze, filter, and synthesize what I see and hear. The methodology for these observations has evolved over 20 years. Its genesis emerged from my Master's thesis (McCann, 1997) on New Zealand Public Sector CEs, using Henry Mintzberg's (1973) methodology, shadowing leaders and measuring time-use and roles, for example, meetings and desk work and then interpreting their roles: informational, decisional, and interpersonal. I added the role of risk manager role to Mintzberg's taxonomy, as this was the role most often seen in my CE research (and still is in my 2015 observations). The need for this role may be related to New Zealand's unicameral system and its small population, said to have only three degrees of separation between citizens and the Prime Minister. This means that citizens have ready access to politicians and CEs, and there is a potential for boundaries to be breeched if not managed appropriately. Because risk is managed well, New Zealand is rated number 2 on the Transparency International Least Corrupt Country Index (Transparency International, 2014), and the CEs practices of prevention, strong boundary setting, and showing no favoritism have established and helped to maintain this position.

In 2002 I shifted from recording CEs activities to observing the impact they had on their teams of direct reports, known as General Managers. I call this new method of all-team shadowing, *Leadership Impact Analysis* (McCann, 2014). It involves using a set of psycho-social filters including Bolman and Deal's (1991) human resource and symbolic lenses (p. 16), observing the non-verbals, the group dynamics, and noting the behaviors that move the agenda forward, like curious questioning, initiation, mediation, attentive listening, and inviting others into the conversation. Anti-group or blocking behaviors like withdrawing, over-talking, downloading, pontificating or lecturing (rather than questioning), posturing, or promoting divisional interests over the good of the whole are also included in the analysis. I also consider ways that I see them being courageous, based on Meron Klein and Rod Napier's (2011) Five Courage Factors which are candor; purpose (lofty audacious goals); will (to renew spirit); rigor to invent better ways; and risk taking in relationships (the courage to empower, trust, and invest rather than be self-protective).

At the end of each meeting I reflect back to the executive team on what I have witnessed, particularly any gaps between espoused culture (the rituals, rites, or stories) and the actual behaviors unfolding before me (Argyris, 2000; Schein, 1995). Because I conduct a full review of each department's strategies, values, and culture statements before each observation, I can easily observe such gaps.

As appropriate, I incorporate tools for challenging assumptions such as Chris Argyris's (2000) Ladder of Inference and Otto Scharmer's U theory (2009). These help me see and convey how leaders listen, observe, open themselves, connect to their source, and co-create.

How New Zealand CEs Encourage Healthy Organizational Cultures

Over these 20 years, the leaders whom I observed have been spending upwards of 85% of their time with people, at some form of meeting, whether formal, informal, planned, or unplanned. I concluded that leaders do and must lead at meetings, unlike Stefan Tengblad (2006), who criticized the increased need for meetings, inferring that the real work of the CE was elsewhere in his comparative Mintzberg-based study. It seems to me that if they do not lead at meetings, when do they lead?

I did not see any saints, rather hardworking, conscientious men and women motivating their teams while designing healthy organizational cultures in their agencies. I saw plenty of gaps between what the CEs said or espoused and what they did, and most were open to having these gaps mirrored back to them (this was the reason they invited me in). One or two had pattern blindness about the impact of their actions on others but modified their behaviors after engaging in some courageous conversations with me.

One example:

Lee seems to typify government CEs. The eldest of four children from a farming family, he attributes his public service ethos to his mother, a teacher, and to his grandfathers. One was a soldier, a veteran, who returned from World War II, to live with them on the family farm. His maternal grandfather Andy did not serve in the war; he was a pacifist who was imprisoned in New Zealand as a conscientious objector. Andy was later abandoned and rejected by the wider family for his lack of patriotism. The family split apart, in part, it seemed, because of how impoverished they became. The family moral dilemmas and conflict affected Lee's choice of studies: initially philosophy, then post graduate work in psychology, followed by an MBA. Lee told stories about the courageous personal stand that his grandfather took, giving this as the reason for becoming a public servant and a CE. He often says that his job is to foster an environment that creates a culture that is healthy enough to enable his teams to be frank with Ministers of the Crown, while being courageous in their recommendations (see Klein & Napier, 2011). I saw him using a variety of organizational culture building techniques from Peter M. Senge, Art Kleiner, Charlotte Roberts, Richard B. Ross, and Bryan J. Smith's *The Fifth Discipline Fieldbook* (1994), which he had studied at an American business school.

Lee's story is similar to many CEs: They are eldest children with family histories of strong moral foundations, with family role models who influenced their career choices. Many have primary disciplines in economics, medicine, policy, or law. CEs were historically recruited for their intellectual prowess, but more recently they are being recruited for their mix of high IQ and EQ, their ability to deliver results through "leadership that cultivates a sustainable, innovative culture with engaged staff and stakeholders, and who operate with integrity … imagining inspirational futures … with people and through innovation ... integrity, courage and resilience" (State Services Commission, p.1). This description, drawn from the SSC Leadership Success Profile (2013) is the expectation created by their employer, the State Services Commission. This is a tall order: almost a recipe for sainthood. I have seen them trying to act in these ways, but of course none succeed all the time.

Being Culturally Aware

All of the CEs whom I observed were university educated in New Zealand, the United Kingdom, or the United States. As Brad Jackson and Ken Parry (2008) pointed out, I have begun to perceive how the Western leadership research paradigm "excludes and marginalizes other ways of knowing (particularly Māori)" (p. 80), and I now question my own educational monocultural biases. My awareness of these issues was reinforced by McNally's thesis on New Zealand CEs (2009), in which she reiterated the view that "educational institutions have assimilated the predisposition towards the democratic individualism found in the North American culture" (p. 5). I began to see more value in Māori models of leadership that include consideration of the earth, sky, and ancestors; consensus decision making, listening, and talking until every voice has been heard; a wider spirituality; and consideration of the implications for family (*whanau*).

Both Western and Māori ways of leading and being are used increasingly by New Zealand CEs to create healthy, sustainable business cultures. From their Western university educations, they have developed approaches to leadership that refer to things like "the Kiwi way of doing things around here," "a pattern of shared basic assumptions" (Schein, 1995), and "the character and personality of the organization" (Inkson, Henshall, Marsh, & Ellis, 1986). From their growing awareness of the Māori perspective, some use Durie's (1964) *Te Whare Tapa Whā* model, originally used to describe physical public health, but adapted by CEs to their organizational culture creation. Durie (1964) described the four walls of the Te Whare meeting house as:

Taha Wairua — spiritual health and well-being. Unseen and unspoken, faith and spiritual awareness.

Hinengaro — psychological well-being, mental health, the inseparability of mind and body, expressing thoughts and feelings.

Taha Whānau — connection to family and social relationships and connections. Linking to wider social systems, belonging, sharing and caring.

Taha Tinana — physical well-being in all its forms, shelter, food, activity (p. 22).

I have seen CEs consciously or unconsciously using both ancient and modern definitions in their everyday cultural crafting practices.

An example:

One CE, whom I'll call Mary, uses many Māori practices to create and maintain her department's culture. She says it is not her role to create the culture — that it already exists through the people and history of the organization. It is her role to foster the positive aspects of the culture and direct it towards the higher societal good. Mary uses consensus decision making around her executive table. She allows the team to talk until everyone has had their say. She says this is her way of getting ownership and surfacing differences during the discussions.

She has a particularly strong focus on the physical and mental health of staff. They are encouraged to take days off when they are stressed — she calls these "preventative, mental health days." She was heard telling a general manager to "take a holiday and go to the beach before you get sick." Mary described the importance of listening in her CE role. When asked during a staff forum "What makes a good leader?" she replied that she learned the basis of leadership in her time as a volunteer on the telephones as a Samaritan (a crisis help-line) listener. "If there's one skill all leaders need it's listening — listening without judgement — allowing people to talk their way through the issues to solve our own problems." She quoted Carl Rogers (1975) "When I have been listened to, and when I have been heard, I am able to re-perceive my world in a new way ... elements that seemed insoluble become soluble ... and confusions become clear" (p. 31).

Like many CEs, Mary is an eldest child. She had a distinguished career overseas and returned home to follow her passion of social justice. Her primary disciplines were law (criminal and treaty law), to which she added an MBA from the United States. She juggles many hats and is specific about which one she is wearing when staff come to her, for example, whether it is in the role of decider, advocate, helper, advisor, coach, or listener. She's also an insightful, powerful questioner. Her most often heard questions are "What is important to you (the Minister, our clients) in this?" And "Will this make a difference?" She does this to understand the other party's values and drivers. Her rationale: If she knows these, she can honor and not violate them.

Chief Executives Leadership Practices

CEs demonstrate their culture shaping at a numerous meetings, where I saw them using meeting methods ranging from Marvin Weisbord and Sandra Janoff's future search conferences (cited in Kahane, 2007, p. 103), to story telling seminars (relating the good news stories of delivery, health, safety, or culture); using introverted and extraverted brainstorming; as well as using innovation board games and various debating techniques. They held standing and walking meetings in a variety of settings. And some, as result of their training from Adam Kahane, are using his learning journeys (McCann, 2012) to first test their own assumptions and then go to each other's teams and humbly listen and learn from one another.

SHAPING CULTURE THROUGH PEOPLE

Leaders hold meetings as their way of leading and shaping culture. Some CEs hold generational meetings, inviting various generational groups (baby boomers, Gen Y, etc.) to gather opinions about maintaining and upholding the organizational culture. Five generations were seen in many of these workplaces. Meetings are also their vehicle to lead and involve people in problem solving. CEs held large (250 plus) and small meetings with their own teams and across sectors to engage and gather options and ideas around the curly issues.

I never saw a CE giving a direct order "Do this or that!" They would be laughed at by their teams if they did. There is a delightful formal/informal way of working around the executive table, and just a little self-protection evidenced here. In a small public sector, these CEs never know which of their colleagues they may be working for next. The relationship between their direct reports (general managers) and their CE is respectful but never subservient. The CEs persuade, invite, suggest, influence, sell, and pitch ideas (non-sales selling) as Daniel H. Pink (2012) found leaders do for 40% of their time (p. 21).

These CEs seem proud to be part of a 100 year-old professional Public Service that impacts the everyday lives of all

New Zealanders and is considered to be highly ethical. They admit that they are far from perfect. They are learning, unlearning, and relearning daily how to lead in a complex, connected, ever changing, national, and international environment. By their request to be observed, they show themselves to be open to feedback and new ways of doing things. They often reflect on their own role as part of the wider system: as one said after being observed "I'm more aware of being aware." I interpreted this as the CE becoming aware of his blind spot and expanding the gap between behaviors "known to self" and "unknown to self," as the Johari window describes it (Luft & Ingham, 1955). One CE admitted that as a general manager he had been "addicted to action and loved a good crisis" as it gave him an adrenalin high. He said that after his appointment as a CE it took him several months to wean himself from this action-orientation to a more considered, solution-focused one.

The CEs seem to know their strengths and gaps as a result of getting regular feedback from staff, their employers (the SSC), their Minister, and occasionally the media, so they are open to my input about their impact, their defensive routines, or pattern blindness (Argyris, 2000). Many belong to peer learning groups, have coaches, and use reflective techniques like journaling (online or paper based).

RE-FORMING TEAMS, BUILDING TRUST, AND STORY TELLING

These CEs spent time on the process of forming and re-forming their teams as people came and went. They agreed with Schein's (1995) definition that "culture is the deepest, often unconscious part of a group, and is less visible ..." (p. 14) so they invest time to help new members learn the culture and their part within it. They help them to understand the assumptions, the norms, the unspoken rules, processes, and frameworks that the executive teams use. CEs were seen listening to each other's life stories (influences, mentors, role models) and sharing mental models from their various disciplines. They work on their team protocols (or ways of working), for example, how they will deal with conflict. They did this proactively in the cool of the moment so that the senior team had a mechanism to deal with it in the heat of the moment.

The CEs said that trust within their top team was essential to creating a sustainable healthy culture. They define trust as "behaving as expected; delivering and doing what they say they'll do; keeping promises, informing each other without withholding; putting the good of the whole before their own divisional interests" (McCann, 2010, p. 18). Trust is so important to them that when a member of their team is perceived to break trust, it often leads to a broken relationship and exit from the team or organization. This confirms Argyris's (2000) conclusion (from his ladder of inference), that data is subjectively selected about behaviors to support the conclusion "that this person is no longer loyal or trustworthy in this team" and contrary evidence is then ignored.

Sharing stories (and histories) was an important part of culture forming for some of these CEs. One CE held a two-day staff conference based solely on telling stories to each other. At the conference, teams began by sharing personal stories, then moved to stories about organizational successes and challenges, and finally shared stories about how other businesses worldwide had solved similar tough problems. It was powerful to observe how the leaders made themselves vulnerable and humble (Schein, 2013) in front of their staff who then in turn told their bosses the stories about the difficulties, the pain and pressures of delivering and working in a cost-constrained, complex, constantly changing environment. The Story Conference as it has become known, resulted in the CE and leaders making commitments to reassess workloads, which they did within a few weeks. This event has become a culture embedding success story that staff transmit to new recruits and leaders are now heard asking staff "tell me the story about that incident/problem?" Rather than "Who did it? Who is to blame?" This has opened up a whole new way of solving tough issues.

Concluding Thoughts

The wider public sector management systems that these CEs work within is a well-informed, can-do environment. The latest change management intervention, called the Performance Improvement Framework (State Services Commission [SSC], 2013), is intended to support CE's roles in creating a "good to great" culture; it is a transparent organizational review in which the results and lessons from each department is shared, with the results posted online for citizens and staff to see.

I see the CEs demonstrating intellectual rigor and personal self-discipline when faced with stressful or tough conversations around controversial issues. They invite their own staff, and those from other departments, to be involved in cross-sectoral issues and show their systems thinking skills when mapping out the probabilities and consequences on various players in different scenarios that they recommend. This ability to think systems-wide, test their own and others' assumptions, and step into the shoes of their Minister, the public, and their staff seems to be a key factor in how they model inclusiveness and create a healthy culture of intellectual debate.

Over many years, I have witnessed good, great, and bad behaviors as well as many magic moments where the CEs with passion and humility inspired their teams to deliver for a higher societal good. Referring back to my original definition of healthy cultures, I believe they could be exceptional culture creators if they actively shared some of the next practices of some of their CE peers described in this chapter, for instance using both Western and Māori models of culture creation (Te Whare Tapa Wha) and honoring all the histories that comprise New Zealand society. Departments with healthy cultures are seen as desirable employers — some staff follow good CEs from one department to another. Retention is stable, and people are involved in decisions affecting them; they report being motivated to solve difficult problems of national importance. Senior leaders are developed and trained for current and future roles by the government's Leadership Development Center and given high levels of autonomy. The CEs are doing as Pink (2009) suggests: for "21st century work, we need to upgrade to autonomy, mastery and purpose" (p. 203).

Derek Gill et al. (2010) found the health, education, and social protection within New Zealand is comparable with that of the United States, the United Kingdom, and Canada. If citizen satisfaction is any measure of a government CE's success, Kiwis rate themselves as satisfied with their own health (88%), their green spaces, forests, and environment (87%), and with their lives (87%) (Statistics New Zealand, 2013) — yet there is plenty of room for improvement. There is much more to do to get to grips with the problems facing New Zealand, and as Gill et al. (2010) suggest "Deeper system shifts may be necessary ... rebalancing the focus towards whole of system performance, supporting multiple modes of operating" (p. 47) as these CEs move from organizational leadership of their individual agencies to leaders of the wider system of the public service.

Being there in the moment with a CE as he or she faces the barrage of demands for their time, their wisdom, and their attention has taught me that there is no right way to craft a culture. No theory, model, or framework can accurately capture the nuances of the pressures and tensions CEs face on a daily basis: the sweat on their brows as they face a Parliamentary Select Committee, the twinkle in their eyes as they welcome a staff member and her child as she returns from maternity leave, or the sorrow they express as they deal with grieving families after a disaster like the recent large earthquakes. Each CE crafts culture by being inclusive in their own way — whether it's including staff and stakeholders at executive meetings; honoring different histories, generations, and cultures; respecting the rites and rituals of all; or by adapting and adopting Western and Maori models of organizational health. At their best, they demonstrate their leadership as "a sacred trust earned from the respect of those people on the receiving end," (Mintzberg, 2012, p. 221). As one CE said:

> Our job as Chief Executives … is to be the guardians of the past, deliver results in the present, and be the dreamers for the future of Aotearoa. Our task is to leave a legacy of public service that we'll all be proud of — creating a better world for our *mokopuna* (grandchildren).

References

Anderson, A., Binney, J., & Harris, A. (2014). *Tangata whenua. An illustrated history*. Wellington: Bridget Williams Books.

Argyris, C. (2000). *Flawed advice and the management trap: How managers can know when they're getting good advice and when they're not*. England: Oxford University Press.

Belich, J. (1996). *Making peoples: A history of the New Zealanders: From polynesian settlement to the end of the 19th century*. Auckland: Penguin New Zealand.

Bolman, L. G., & Deal, T. E. (1991). *Reframing organizations: Artistry, choice, and leadership*. San Francisco, CA: Jossey-Bass.

Collins, J. (2001). *Good to great*. London: Random House Books.

Consedine, R., & Consedine., J. (2012). *Healing our history: The challenge of the treaty of waitangi*. London: Penguin Books.

Durie, M. (1964). *Whaiora: Maori health development*. Auckland: Oxford University Press.

Gill, D., Pride, S., Gilbert, H., & Norman, R. (2010). *The future state*. Institute of Policy Studies Working Paper No. 10/08. School of Government, Victoria University, Wellington.

Harrison, R. (1990). *Personal communication*. Wellington, New Zealand.

Inkson, K., Henshall, B., Marsh, N., & Ellis, G. (1986). *Theory K.* Auckland: David Bateman Ltd.

Jackson, B., & Parry, K. (2008). *A very short, fairly interesting and reasonably cheap book about studying leadership.* London, United Kingdom: Sage.

Kahane, A. (2007). *Solving tough problems: An open way of talking, listening, and creating new realities* (2nd ed.). San Francisco, CA: Berrett-Koehler Publishers.

King, M. (2003). *The penguin history of New Zealand.* Auckland: Penguin Books.

Klein, M., & Napier, R. (2011). *The courage to act: Five factors of courage to transform business.* Norwood, MA: Davies-Black Publishing.

Luft, J., & Ingham, H. (1955). The Johari window, a graphic model of interpersonal awareness. *Proceedings of the western training laboratory in group development.* Los Angeles: University of California, Los Angeles.

McCann, J. (1997). *A day in the life of a chief executive: Real-time use of six chief executives in the New Zealand public service.* Unpublished Masters thesis. Massey University, Palmerston North, New Zealand.

McCann, J. (2010). How they trust at the top. *Human resources – HRINZ conference 2010 proceedings*, HRINZ, Wellington.

McCann, J. (2012). *Learning journeys. Product sheet.* Wellington: McCann Consulting Ltd.

McCann, J. (2014). *Leadership impact analysis. Real-time observation and coaching for chief executives and senior teams. Product sheet.* Wellington: McCann Consulting Ltd.

McNally, B. (2009). *Executive leadership in New Zealand: A monocultural construct?* Lower Hutt: The Open Polytechnic of New Zealand.

Mintzberg, H. (1973). *The nature of managerial work.* New York, NY: Harper and Row.

Mintzberg, H. (2012). *Managing.* San Francisco, CA: Berrett-Koehler Publishers.

Naumann, R., Harrison, L., & Winiata, T. K. (1991). Te Mana o Te Tiriti: The living treaty. Auckland: New House Publishers Ltd.

Orange, C. (1987). *The treaty of waitangi.* Wellington: Bridget Williams Books.

Pink, D. H. (2009). *Drive: The surprising truth about what motivates us.* New York, NY: Riverhead Books.

Pink, D. H. (2012). *To sell is human: The surprising truth about moving others.* New York, NY: Riverhead Books.

Rogers, C. (1975). Empathic: An unappreciated way of being. *The counselling psychologist, 5*(2), 2–10.

Scharmer, C. O. (2009). *Theory U: Leading from the future as it emerges.* San Francisco, CA: Berrett-Koehler.

Schein, E. H. (1995). *Organizational culture and leadership: A dynamic view.* San Francisco, CA: Jossey-Bass Publishers.

Schein, E. H. (2013). *Humble inquiry: The gentle art of asking instead of telling.* San Francisco, CA: Berrett-Koehler Publishers.

Senge, P. M. (1990). *The fifth discipline: The art and practice of the learning organization*. London: Random House.

Senge, P. M., Kleiner, A., Roberts, C., Ross, R. B., & Smith, B. J. (1994). *The fifth discipline fieldbook*. London: Nicholas Brealey Publishing Ltd.

State Services Commission. (2013). *Leadership success profile*. Wellington: State Services Commission, New Zealand Government.

State Services Commission. (2014). *Human resource capability in the New Zealand State Services*. Wellington: State Services Commission, New Zealand Government.

Statistics New Zealand. (2013). *New Zealand in profile*. Wellington: New Zealand Government.

Tengblad, S. (2006). Is there a "New Managerial Work"? A comparison with henry Mintzberg's classic study 30 years later. *Journal of Management Studies*, 43(7), 1437–1461. doi:10.1111/j.1467-6486.2006.00651

Transparency International. (2014). Transparency International Least Corrupt Country Index. Retrieved from https://www.transparency.org/cpi2014/results

11

"The Arts Are Not a Luxury": The Arts as a Source of Community in California

Barbara Rose Shuler

Т
he arts do live continuously, and they live literally by faith; their names and their shapes and their uses and their basic meanings survive unchanged in all that matters .... They outlive governments and creeds and societies, even the very civilization that produced them. They cannot be destroyed altogether .... They are what we find again when the ruins are cleared away.

Katherine Anne Porter, Collected Essays (p. 457)

Many believe that a community that neglects art imperils its welfare and risks losing its soul, while others, particularly in the United States, consider art as a luxury and unnecessary expense. Filmmaker Richard Attenborough (1994/2015) spoke to this tension in his maiden speech to the House of Lords in Britain in 1974:

The crucial difference must lie in what we call "soul" and creativity. From the very earliest of times, the arts have been an instinctive essential of our humanity. They are a miraculous sleight of hand which reveals the truth, and a glorious passport to greater understanding between the peoples of the world .... The arts are not a luxury.

They are as crucial to our well-being, to our very existence, as eating and breathing …. The arts are for everyone — and failure to include everyone diminishes us all. (n.p.)

As Attenborough said, art is critical to our existence, and failure to make it accessible for everyone weakens us all. We humans engage one another through art and enrich our lives through art. We evolve our understanding of the visible and unseen worlds through art, exercise the essential muscle of our imaginations by creating art, and, according to cognitive science, even develop new capacities and connections in our brains through the disciplines of art (e.g., Jensen, 2001).

As an arts writer and artist, I have witnessed how music, theater, dance, visual arts, and other creative forms can generate positive change in individuals, communities, and wider cultures. This chapter presents the Carmel Bach Festival as a living example of how the arts can contribute to a healthy society both through the intrinsic value of art and through the capacity of committed arts leadership to build community. I write out of deep personal knowledge of the Bach Festival, having lived most of my life in the Monterey Bay area, where I have served as a journalist for Monterey Peninsula newspapers and radio stations for decades. This Festival has survived for 80 years — a long time for any contemporary organization — through its model of community involvement, participation in education, and artistic excellence. This approach is found increasingly in North American and European cities (Culture Case, 2015), and it brings well-being and collaborative empowerment to the regions it serves. The quality of life in the Monterey Bay area has benefited greatly through the Bach Festival, particularly in the face of the influence of tourism in the region over the past half century.

The Carmel Bach Festival: A Prototype of a Local Arts Organization

The Carmel Bach Festival presents an annual summer festival of music and ideas in Carmel-by-the-Sea (Carmel), a town in the U.S. state of California, about 90 miles south of San Francisco. The intention of the Festival is to "celebrate the works, inspiration, and ongoing influence of J. S. Bach worldwide by immersing audiences in a festival experience integrating music, education, and ideas, and by meaningful community engagement throughout the year" (Carmel Bach Festival, 2015b). The Festival attracts musicians and audiences from around the world who come to Carmel in July for two densely packed weeks of concerts, recitals, master classes, lectures, open rehearsals, and special events, many of which are free and open to the public. It is respected internationally, and, in addition to the summer event, the Festival collaborates year-round with the surrounding communities through various programs and initiatives. The Carmel Bach Festival was founded in 1935 by two women who envisioned it as a means of nourishing the arts in a community they loved, and that is has survived over the past 80 years is quite remarkable, since many civic organizations that were once vibrant have declined or disappeared in recent decades (see e.g., Putnam, 2000). Yet the Festival has not only survived, it has endured several difficult periods and succeeded in recruiting executive leadership from across the United States and artistic leadership from Europe, enhancing both its renown and financial viability.

The enduring success of the Festival rests on two strong pillars established by the founders. The first is the exemplary music performed by virtuoso conductors, musicians, soloists, and choruses. The second is the participation of people from the region who generously donate their time, skills, and even their homes. Of course, as a not-for-profit organization, it also depends on the financial support of individual donors, businesses, grants, and fundraising events. But the Festival continues to rely on a large corps of volunteers from the community to provide the critical support that allows such an ambitious enterprise to thrive on a relatively modest budget.

A team of over 200 volunteers work year-round, serving in a wide range of areas, such as office administration, board service, ushering, ticketing, artist transportation, hospitality, and participation in the volunteer chorus. Among those who offer their services and talents to the organization, there exists a spirit of camaraderie and sense of accomplishment in being part of an endeavor that brings people together for inspiration and enjoyment in support of great musical art. Their enthusiasm is picked up by family and friends, who then often join the volunteer corps, and it also generates interest in the business community, which contributes time, skills, and goods. While the music of Johann Sebastian Bach strikes many as being something of the past, the way that the Bach Festival builds on and shares this music is a story of leadership, community, and inclusion in the present.

Brief History: Changing the Community Through Arts

The Carmel area was an intriguing place for women and leadership in the early 20th century. The Festival's original founders were two creative women with tremendous initiative in creating an institution that has survived through many changes in local and national priorities and funding. Dene Denny and Hazel Watrous moved to Carmel in the 1920s from San Francisco, where they had cultivated connections with important artists of the time across all major disciplines — visual, theatrical, literary, and musical. In those days, Carmel attracted artists, writers, poets, dramatists, and actors of greater and lesser talents, along with residents who appreciated the arts and relished the cultural identity of the town. Life partners as well as professional collaborators, during the 1920s, Denny and Watrous became home builders and designers, cultivating respect for their artistic sensibilities and their capacity to implement them (Gordon, 2014, p. 72). As local historian David Gordon described in his biography of Denny and Watrous, they were then able to use the community's own energy and creative vitality to lift Carmel to a new level of creative collaboration. By the time the Festival emerged, the women had earned reputations in Carmel as cultural leaders. Their community relationships interconnected well with their artistic enterprises.

Based on newspaper accounts from the period, Gordon explains how Denny and Watrous worked with the community from the start of the conceptualization of the Festival. As he described in an interview with me, these two women "knew that the people of the region wanted this before they knew it themselves. They also understood the importance of first generating excitement about the project, then providing the tools, help, and guidance to accomplish it. Then they let the community take credit for creating it." Central to their leadership was maintaining their status as beloved members of the community and in turn involving others. As Gordon explains, even after becoming a professional organization under Maestro Sandor Salgo, the Bach Festival never let go of its community roots.

Denny and Watrous coalesced the performing arts in the area in a number of ways. They founded the Carmel Music Society in 1927, the oldest continuing classical music nonprofit in the state of California. In 1929 they opened a centrally located gallery as a cultural center for exhibitions, lectures, music concerts, and theatrical performances. They established The Troopers of the Gold Coast at the First Theater in neighboring Monterey, California's oldest theater. In the midst of the Great Depression in the early 1930s, the Denny-Watrous Gallery offered a series of open rehearsals for a new orchestra organized with the help of Michael Penha, who at that time was the principal cellist with the San Francisco Symphony. Musicians from the region joined the professionals for this Monterey Peninsula Orchestra in what became the basis for the Carmel Bach Festival. The intention behind all this activity was not simply to entertain audiences, but to "change the community through music" (Gordon, 2014, p. 177). Open rehearsals and community interest culminated in the "1935 Summer Series and Bach Festival," a four-day celebration of Bach's 250th birthday. Top professional instrumentalists and vocal soloists joined the new orchestra. This critically acclaimed event launched the annual summer Bach Festival, which has steadily grown in stature and scope since then.

Current Leadership: Local Vision and Broad Background

The arts are not a luxury; they are a necessity.

Debbie Chinn (personal communication, May 13, 2015)

I met the current executive director of the Carmel Bach Festival, Debbie Chinn, through my association with the Festival. A national recruiting process that involved the Board of Directors and the Festival's arts leaders brought Chinn in from the Philadelphia Orchestra Association, where she provided strategic guidance toward the implementation of the orchestra's 2012 China Residency program, a five-city concert tour of China, that served as the kick-off to the 40th anniversary of President Nixon's historic visit to China. Prior to that, she was the Managing Director of California Shakespeare Theater in the San Francisco Bay Area and Managing Director of Center Stage, the State Theater of Maryland. Chinn has dedicated her career to building healthy communities through innovative and creative partnerships in the arts. Like Denny and Watrous, Chinn may be described as a multi-artistic visionary with a passion for innovation, helping as many people as possible thrive through the arts. She brings a background that includes leadership positions with professional theaters and with major symphony orchestras in Maryland, New Jersey, and California, and she has frequently been invited to serve as a grant panelist and to adjudicate program proposals for the National Endowment for the Arts (NEA). She is a fervent champion for arts and education funding, having testified at the legislative level, also in Maryland, New Jersey, and California. She specializes in organizational assessment, strategic planning, fundraising, program planning, volunteer management, board and staff development, and special events.

Chinn is passionate about arts and arts management and knows how to create and lead a strong and effective administrative team. I have observed Chinn's leadership style to be one of tolerance, respect, and working in an ensemble toward shared goals. She believes that cross-disciplinary knowledge is crucial to excellent arts leadership. A cornerstone of her leadership philosophy is that arts administrators must have experience in the artistic side and that artistic directors likewise benefit from stepping into administrative shoes on occasion. She imagines that when enough people are empowered by art, they will behave more tolerantly toward each other, dissolving discordant mindsets that weaken us as individuals and societies.[1]

Chinn leads the local Festival as well as professional organizations related to the arts. As the former president of the Association of California Symphony Orchestras (ACSO), Chinn (2015a) believes that practical questions about finances must be "counterbalanced with a focus on the core essence of what an arts organization should do to transform and enrich society" (p. 2). For her, the Carmel Bach Festival "is not about the financial bottom line but about a more crucial net asset, which is measured by how our communities are strengthened, included, and engaged by virtue of having an authentic arts partner" (Chinn, 2015a, p. 2). An example of what Chinn means by an authentic arts partner is the Virginia-based Barter Theater that was also founded in the 1930s and thrived through its relationship with the community. During the Great Depression, one man had the vision that the

---

[1]All quotes and information about Chinn are from three interviews with me that took place in May, June, and August, 2015, unless otherwise indicated.

community would be able to afford the price of admission to see a play if it came in the form of produce from farms and gardens of the region, as barter. The price of admission at that time was 40 cents or an equivalent amount of produce. All the seats filled quickly as four out of five Depression-era theatergoers paid their way with vegetables, dairy, and livestock. The result of this barter system was that the people who came felt a special kinship with this theater that offered them a spiritual and artistic home during those challenging years. A deep connection and trust was forged with their community. The theater now produces shows on a year-round basis with a budget of over $6 million. For select performances, they still accept food donations for an area food bank for the price of admission (Chinn, 2015a, p. 2).

Chinn and her staff manage over a dozen programs designed to involve people in the music and creative life of the Festival, many of which she has inaugurated. Chinn indicated that she created these community programs, because "We believe that all people have a right to express themselves through art and to have accessibility to the transcendent beauty of the music, and we aim to build an even more inclusive and welcoming environment in which people see themselves reflected in art." She and her staff, along with British conductor and artistic director Paul Goodwin, bring people together from diverse socioeconomic backgrounds to work side by side in an atmosphere infused with the great music of Western civilization. These human connections have sustained the organization and serve as an example of how arts leadership can create empowering partnerships for the well-being of communities. As Chinn (2015b) explained

> When we convene for a Carmel Bach Festival experience, which many describe as a 'renewal of the spirit,' we know that for just a brief moment in time, the garish edges of the world are softened, the noise of the world abates, and conversational discourses are muted. We find ourselves transported to a moment which the Japanese refer to as *Ichigo-ichie*, meaning 'one time, one meeting' — a gathering whose exact nature can never be fully replicated and thus should be cherished. (p. 3)

For Chinn, honoring the ideals of the founders involves taking risks and moving beyond comfort zones into new creative ventures. With J. S. Bach always at the heart of the Festival, each music director has found fresh and original ways to present the music and ideas, inspired by the composer and his powerful influence on the world. With this same unconventional spirit, Chinn has been working toward being a more authentic and inclusive partner to the surrounding communities by breaking down barriers, perceived and real, and forming meaningful, lasting relationships with diverse constituencies.

Community Engagement: Programs, Initiatives, and a New Concert Hall

The musicians and staff members of the Festival have created and managed a variety of hands-on programs and activities working with youth and adults during the Festival month and during the year. The majority of these programs concentrate on young people. Festival musicians also tour to senior centers and community centers with special programs for adults and families who are unable to attend Festival performances in the concert halls. Such projects show how arts organizations work with local community groups to involve diverse populations in the arts and nourish healthy communities. Descriptions follow of some of the main projects, through which Chinn partners with local community groups.

For over ten years the Festival Youth Chorus has operated as a chorale ensemble for high school vocalists in the three-county area around the Monterey Bay, offering the opportunity to sing with a professional orchestra and chorale in major works. The Youth Chorus also presents its own concert series and community concerts during July. Participants are eligible to take master class sessions from members of the Festival's professional chorale, a rare opportunity in this geographical area for high-school-age singers. Symphonie Constant, a recent Youth Chorus member, described how the experience has "inspired me to keep reaching for my dream. Music means everything to me. I want to become a musician and share music with other people, especially around the world" (Carmel Bach Festival, 2014, n.p.). Constant entered college in Fall 2014 as a music major.

The Festival also joined with Rancho Cielo Youth Campus in Salinas, a major city in the neighboring agricultural region with a large Hispanic population. Founded by a former superior court judge who witnessed the tragic cycle of law-breaking and incarceration of many young people of the city, Rancho Cielo serves as an alternative to jail for young, first-time lawbreakers. He envisioned Rancho Cielo as an effective alternative to help keep first offenders from becoming repeat offenders, as it is proving to be. Among the Festival connections with the youth of Rancho Cielo, each year members of the Festival's youth chorus travel to Salinas to perform for and spend time with them. Rancho Cielo's CEO Susie Brusa (2015) noted,

> Many of the youth that we have the privilege of working with are severely underserved. We try to expose them to all kinds of arts, allowing them to try them on and to expand their minds. The most important part of that is for those who find various sessions interesting to reconnect them with our society, engaging them in ways so that they want to continue their education .... Without our collaboration with the Bach Festival, we would not be able to bring this kind of music to our students. (n.p.)

According to Chinn, these students are now engaging in conversations about the music, what they like or don't like, and how it moves them or doesn't. The interactions have inspired some of them to pick up instruments again that they had previously cast aside, to find both comfort and meaning. Patricia Escobar, a Rancho Cielo senior, described how music had become for her "that one friend that we have that's always going to make us feel better. I love listening to music now! It helps you go through life. I'm really glad that they taught us that there's music that can make you feel good and do good" (Carmel Bach Festival, 2015b, n.p.).

Since 2010, Festival musicians have worked annually with the students of Youth Orchestra Salinas (YOSAL) through a workshop and a collaborative community concert. YOSAL is an El Sistema-inspired music program (Carmel Bach Festival, 2015a, n.p.), a free music education program that originated in Venezuela, which gives impoverished children a free classical music education and, with it, opportunities for living fuller, more creative lives. The YOSAL students have the opportunity to work closely with the musicians of the Festival and to travel to Carmel to hear the concerts with other patrons.

The Festival started a partnership with the local California State University Monterey Bay, creating an arts management fellowship program for college seniors to receive on-the-job experience and training with professional staff and to provide the Festival with community ambassadors from this age group. For

Chinn, "investing in the next generation of artists and nonprofit arts administrators" in this way is a two-way learning program. While the college seniors gain additional skills to enhance their school curriculum, the Carmel Bach Festival learns how it needs to develop to be relevant to a younger demographic. The Fellows teach the Festival staff what resonates with their peers so that the organization is able to adapt its marketing and messaging approaches accordingly. "I am equally interested in reaching the parents of these college students, who are in the prime audience bandwidth for us," said Chinn. "I envision that within a short five years, we will have a robust alumni group comprised of Fellows who will continue to advocate for the Carmel Bach Festival as we start to strengthen and build our audience ecology."

Another significant contribution the Festival has made to the community was inspiring the creation of an acoustically excellent performance hall, Sunset Center. In the early days of the Festival, Denny and Watrous arranged for performances to be held in the large auditorium of Carmel's Gothic-style high school. When a new school was built, the original building turned into a full-time multi-use facility and performance venue called Sunset Center, which suffered from troublesome acoustics and other problematic factors. When the Festival's former conductor Bruno Weil declared the acoustical problems to be insurmountable, the citizens of Carmel raised the funds for a thorough renovation of the aging facility. Local residents who witnessed this transformation saw how, once again, good will, wise leadership, and community involvement made this possible. Sunset Center now stands as a gem of a concert hall — a source of great community pride and enjoyment.

From Exclusion to Inclusion Through Art

Art is an irreplaceable way of understanding and expressing the world .... Art addresses us in the fullness of our being — simultaneously speaking to our intellect, emotions, intuition, imagination, memory, and physical senses .... Art awakens, enlarges, refines, and restores our humanity.

Dana Gioia (2007, n.p.)

The legacy of Denny and Watrous and the Carmel Bach Festival is one of infectious joy and generous love of the arts. Former Music Director Bruno Weil called this "the Carmel spirit." In interviews with him through his years of directing the Festival, he often said nothing like it existed in music festivals in Europe. The Carmel Bach Festival is inextricably linked with Carmel's identity as an American nexus of art and music. A profile in the *Carmel Pine Cone* (the local newspaper) of 1948, quoted by Gordon (2014), captures this quality instilled by the founders:

> They have integrated art into the community life; brought it out of the cold-air priest craft which too often surrounds it, in which the initiates talk down to the layman; and they have done it without a concession to mediocrity. Open rehearsals for Bach chorus are one example of their nearness to community living. This is the key to the pattern they have woven with the years, in Carmel and far beyond its environs, bringing fine art warmly, closely, to the least informed and those most informed. (p. 298)

History reveals that the arts are indispensable in human life. An example of a whole society renewing itself through art under nightmarish circumstances is documented in the film, *The Singing Revolution* (2006), which shows how music sustained the Estonian people during the WWII years of Nazi occupation, helping them to maintain the Estonian language and their sense of culture. Music was so important in their struggle to restore their national independence that it became known as the Singing Revolution.

In the United States, once-mandatory arts education programs have been systematically removed from public schools over the past several decades. Sadly for many millions of young people, this means the arts may seem a luxury indeed, unaffordable unless parents have the financial means and inclination to provide this education outside of school. I have conversed with adults who perceive the arts as too expensive, elitist, complicated, or inaccessible for other reasons. The story of the Carmel Bach Festival shows how it is possible to involve the broader community in vibrant, enlightening artistic experiences as a way of developing interest in and access to the arts and their community for people of various ages and backgrounds.

Chinn's own dream of making the arts accessible to everyone relates directly to challenges she faced in her youth. "I grew up in a very homogeneous community where, except for my brother, I was the only person of color in my school, and I still recall the memory of being taunted and picked on. It was very lonely experience." She continued, explaining how she eventually "found acceptance in drama class and in choir. We were a bunch of misfits coming together to do a piece of work and we were all equal in that regard." While making art with others in this diverse group she realized that the bullying had disappeared, her self-confidence had risen, acceptance and joy had replaced the isolation, and a clarity about the arts being at the center of her life's calling began to emerge.

For over a quarter of a century, I have watched the Carmel Bach Arts Festival expand its reach and influence, thriving in a setting that enjoys a historical identity as a haven of culture and arts. The experience of hearing timeless masterpieces and especially of being part of the ensemble performing this music can lift individuals out of their personal identities into an ineffable space of transcendence for a few moments. The ultimate message of the Festival is that rejuvenation of many kinds occurs — social, spiritual, emotional, and physical — when individuals and communities come together with the shared purpose of creating beauty, joy, renewal, and learning.

A strong legacy of the founders of the Festival has been its endurance for eight decades. Like a blossom that keeps unfolding, the festival has continued to grow both in its enrichment of the local community and its international stature. Nowadays, we live in a world dominated by fast action, tautly structured business plans, and expectations of quick profit turnarounds. An important lesson given by the Festival lies in the wisdom of an organization taking the time in the beginning to build a dependable foundation grounded in shared values with the communities it serves.

References

Attenborough, L. R. (1994/2015). Maiden speech to the House of Lords in Britain (abridged). *BBC Arts*, March 20, 2015. Retrieved from http://www.bbc.co.uk/programmes/articles/5MQF1rfs0xfG0fMMpcBKjfb/remembering-the-arts-attenboroughs-emotional-appeal

Brusa, S. (2015). *Carmel Bach festival, 78th season, community engagement (video)*. Retrieved from www.bachfestival.org

Carmel Bach Festival. (2014). Community engagement film (not released). Available from Carmel Bach Festival archives, Carmel, CA.

Carmel Bach Festival. (2015a). *Community engagement*. Retrieved from www.bachfestival.org

Carmel Bach Festival. (2015b). *Mission and vision statement*. Retrieved from www.bachfestival.org

Chinn, D. (2015a). President's message. *ACSO (Association of California Symphony Orchestra) News*, p. 2.

Chinn, D. (2015b). *Carmel Bach festival program book: Bach, Bohemia and beyond*. Carmel Bach Festival, Carmel, CA.

Culture Case. (2015, May 5). *Models of community engagement in arts and culture*. Retrieved from www.culturecase.org/research-category/community-engagement/

Gioia, D. (2007). Commencement address. *Stanford News*, June 17. Retrieved from http://news.stanford.edu/news/2007/june20/gradtrans-062007.html

Gordon, D. (2014). *Carmel impressarios: A cultural biography of Dene Denny and Hazel Watrous*. Carmel, CA: Lucky Valley Press.

Jensen, E. P. (2001). *Arts with the brain in mind*. Washington, DC: Association for Supervision & Curriculum Development.

Putnam, R. D. (2000). *Bowling alone: The collapse and revival of American community*. New York, NY: Siman and Schuster.

Trusty, J., & Trusty, M. C. (2006). *The singing revolution*. Estonia: Mountain View Productions.

12

Strengthening Communities through Adaptive Leadership: A Case Study of the Kansas Leadership Center and the Bangladesh Youth Leadership Center

Max Klau and Jill Hufnagel

How is it possible to strengthen entire communities through leadership development? What does it look like to develop leadership capacity both in individuals and across an entire state? A country? In this chapter, we explore the creation and development of two institutions exploring an innovative approach to these questions: the Kansas Leadership Center (KLC) and the Bangladesh Youth Leadership Center (BYLC). Both organizations use the adaptive leadership model developed at Harvard's Kennedy School over the last 30 years, alongside the dynamic case-in-point teaching methodology (Green, 2011; Heifetz, 1994). And both are engaging in large-scale leadership development intended to catalyze positive transformation not just at the level of individual participants, but also at the level of entire cities and even nations. Both KLC and BYLC seek to strengthen the civic health of their communities by growing the circle of citizens who are actively engaged in addressing communal challenges in creative and effective ways; it's an approach that results in communities that are more resilient, connected, self-aware, and empowered. For this reason, these two organizations represent important examples of how the theory and practice of leadership development might be harnessed to create healthier communities.

Large-Scale Leadership Development as a Response to a Changing World

At this early moment in the 21st century, a growing body of literature suggests that the social world is becoming less hierarchical and more networked (e.g., Brafman & Beckstrom, 2006; Kellerman, 2012, 2015). From this perspective, individuals in positions of formal authority are believed to have comparatively less power than they had in the past, while ordinary citizens have comparatively more power. This transformation is occurring across all sectors, including government, business, non-profits, education, social movements, and global geopolitics. Leadership scholar Barbara Kellerman (2015) described this change as "not specific to any single individual or institution, any group or organization. Rather, it is distal, general" (p. 4).

In today's world, it is possible, for example, for a college student to write a software program that allows music fans to share music files in a manner that disrupts the entire music industry or for an ordinary citizen to craft an online petition that gains millions of signatures in a matter of hours. These actions would have been unthinkable a generation ago and are examples of a shift in power away from a small number of individuals with formal authority and towards masses of individuals with a new capacity to create significant change. As Ori Brafman and Rod Beckstrom (2006) wrote:

> Decentralization has been lying dormant for thousands of years. But the advent of the Internet has unleashed this force, knocking down traditional businesses, altering entire industries, affecting how we relate to each other, and influencing world politics. The absence of structure, leadership, and formal organization, once considered a weakness, has become a major asset. Seemingly chaotic groups have challenged and defeated established institutions. The rules of the game have changed. (p. 8)

Kellerman has provided useful insight into exactly how those rules have changed. In *The End of Leadership* she wrote:

> [L]eadership and followership have continued to evolve ... from what they were into something quite different. More nations now are democracies as opposed to autocracies. There is less respect for authority across the board — in government and business, in the academy and in the professions, even in religion. Power and influence have continued to devolve from the top down — those at the top having less power and influence; those in the middle and bottom having more. (2012, pp. xvii–xix)

This decentralized, vastly networked world represents a new and historically unprecedented context with implications for both the theory and practice of leadership. Developing leaders capable of addressing important challenges in this new context is an important frontier of innovation for the leadership development field.

Implicit in this new context is a logic difficult to refute: In a world in which both individual and collective citizens have relatively more power and influence while formal authority figures have relatively less, one can no longer look to a small cohort of "leaders" — those in formal positions of power at the top of organizational hierarchies in business, government, and beyond — to tackle the world's toughest problems. It is questionable whether that small cohort ever had the power necessary to tackle vital public problems like educational or income inequality, environmental sustainability, or containing runaway healthcare costs. It is certain, however, that they have less power today to unilaterally address these challenges than they have ever had in the past. For this reason, a compelling case can be made that the most important public challenges can only be addressed through the collective action of vast numbers of citizens who are both willing and able to step up and work for change.

Adaptive Leadership as an Approach to Communal Transformation

Adaptive leadership provides both a theory of leadership and a practice of leadership development particularly relevant to this rapidly changing context. The model distinguishes itself from other leadership theories that emphasize traits, styles, or skills of individual leaders, or that highlight the importance of tailoring efforts to specific situations or circumstances (for an overview of these theories, see Peter Northouse, 2015). Rather, it is grounded in two theoretical distinctions that speak directly to the nature of the contextual change described in the literature.

First, adaptive leadership distinguishes between *technical* and *adaptive challenges* (Heifetz, 1994). *Technical challenges* are challenges in which the nature of the problem is clear, and people already have in their repertoire a set of responses capable of effectively addressing that challenge. *Adaptive challenges*, on the other hand, are often unclear and complex, and people do not currently have a repertoire of effective responses. This focus on the nature of the challenge being addressed — as opposed to the characteristics or skills of individual leaders — is fairly unique among leadership theories, and it provides a framework that illuminates the nature of the rapidly changing context described earlier. Although individuals may possess a wealth of technical expertise and useful experience, any attempt to exercise leadership in this rapidly changing and highly networked world presents at least some element of an adaptive challenge. Having this language and conceptual framework allows people to talk and think about current leadership challenges in useful and productive ways.

In addition, adaptive leadership distinguishes between *authority* and *leadership*. *Authority* is understood to be a formal position of power (the CEO, President, teacher, etc.); *leadership* is an activity — not a role — and it can be exercised by anyone in the system. It is defined as the attempt to move a group to address an adaptive challenge. Ronald Heifetz notes that people often conflate the terms "authority" and "leadership," perpetuating an implicit assumption that only individuals in positions of formal authority can exercise leadership. Given the fact that history is full of individuals like Rosa Parks or Mahatma Gandhi who exercised tremendous leadership without positional authority, this theoretical distinction generates understanding of the rapidly emerging new reality of how leadership and change actually occur in the world. It has a particular relevance given the evolving context within which leadership occurs today.

Equally important, adaptive leadership includes an innovative pedagogical approach to leadership development that helps individuals understand this emerging reality and learn how to effectively create change in this evolving context. Known as *case-in-point*, it is an approach with roots in T-Groups, a form of psychological training in which a group learns about human relations by exploring the real-time dynamics of the group. Similarly, the case-in-point method uses the dynamics in a classroom as the primary text for learning about leadership.

In this method, instructors use their authority in a very powerful, dramatic way to create what is experienced by participants as an authority vacuum. They seek to create and hold a space for participants, but then provide neither lecture-style teaching nor Socratic questioning. Rather, they stand silently at the front of the room and wait for things to happen. Before long, participants begin expressing their confusion and discomfort, and instructors invite participants to reflect on those real-time classroom dynamics to generate learning about leadership. Almost instantly, participants are challenged to question their own unexamined dependencies on authority figures for direction and answers and are invited to diagnose the adaptive challenges present in the classroom itself. In time, participants awaken to greater levels of awareness of the ways they themselves collude to preserve a comfortable, safe *status quo*, and begin to understand their own very real power to influence the emergent dynamics of the class.

It is an empowering space for participants, as they are able to influence events and make things happen in ways that they usually can't in traditional classrooms, but it takes a great deal of skill to create and hold a space like this. Case-in-point is built on a core paradox: It is an empowering, non-hierarchical space created through strong use of hierarchical authority. As a pedagogical approach, it is effective at developing those individuals who are willing and able to effectively exercise leadership in the networked context described earlier. After all, it is one thing to learn about leadership in a classroom that retains a traditional hierarchical relationship between instructor and students; it is another to have opportunities to attempt to exercise leadership in a classroom that mirrors the higher levels of freedom, influence, and voice inherent in the real-world context rapidly evolving beyond the classroom walls. (Readers eager to learn more about case-in-point are invited to review Chris Green, 2011; Sharon Parks, 2005).

Case Studies on Two Continents

In this chapter, we present case studies of two organizations currently using the adaptive leadership model as an approach to large-scale leadership development. Both the KLC and the BYLC are engaged in provocative, innovative efforts to answer some timely and important questions: *What if we gave everyone access to leadership development? What if these experiences were provided for individuals at the grassroots and on the front lines, and not just for the elite, or those already privileged and powerful? How might we create healthier communities by supporting as wide a circle of citizens as possible to become more empowered, effective, and engaged in the work of civic leadership?* One of these organizations is making this happen in the American heartland, and the other works in a rapidly developing nation in Southeast Asia. Together they provide important case studies regarding the promise and the challenge of using leadership development as an approach to promoting positive social change.

THE KANSAS LEADERSHIP CENTER

The KLC was established by the Kansas Health Foundation in 2007 as a way to add significant value to the leadership development work undertaken by the Foundation since its early days (Ed O'Malley, personal interview by Jill Hufnagel, January 9, 2015 is the source for data on the KLC). As they engaged in a state-wide listening tour and examined more closely various leadership efforts in action, the Foundation began to realize that the work being done at the community level was only as good as the capacity of the individuals from the community actually engaged in that work. That realization was the kernel of thought that led to the creation of KLC. In short, they posited that by developing the leadership capacity of large numbers of engaged citizens operating on the front lines of efforts to promote positive health across Kansas, more progress would be made. Funded by a core operating grant from the Kansas Health Foundation, KLC's mission is to foster civic leadership for healthier Kansas communities; the organization's vision is to be the center of excellence for civic leadership development.

Since opening its doors, nearly 4,000 people have participated in KLC programs. KLC's evaluation efforts have focused on post-program reports from alumni. In one study, 88% of alumni stated that they had made progress on leadership challenges, 85% reported that KLC ideas had made an impact on their daily work, and 80% said that they use what they've learned from the KLC. Although no formal external evaluation of impact has been undertaken to date, alumni report that the training and development they experienced at KLC builds their capacity to advance the various initiatives they are working on across the state (Kansas Leadership Center: Survey Report, October 2014).

BANGLADESH YOUTH LEADERSHIP CENTER (BYLC)

The story of the BYLC begins with founder Ejaj Ahmad's encounter with Ron Heifetz's adaptive leadership model (Heifetz, 1994) as a student at Harvard Kennedy School (E. Ahmad, personal interview by Max Klau, January 10, 2015 is the source for data on the BYLC). The course was a revelation for Ahmad. Upon graduating from the Kennedy School in 2008, the then 27-year-old Ahmad chose to move back to his home in Bangladesh to launch an organization focused on teaching adaptive leadership to the youth of Bangladesh. In just a few years, Ahmad grew BYLC from a struggling start-up, with only $10,000 in seed finance, to a thriving non-profit with a national profile providing hundreds of young people with leadership development experiences annually, while engaging the public, private, and non-profit sectors of the country to support this work.

BYLC is the country's first leadership institute, working to bridge socio-economic and religious gaps in society by uniting youth from diverse backgrounds, equipping them with leadership training, problem-solving, and team building skills, and engaging them in community service and active citizenship. BYLC's vision is to create a poverty-free Bangladesh driven by the next generation of home-grown leaders. To date, over 2,200 high school, college, and university students have graduated from 30 different programs run in Dhaka and Chittagong, the two major cities in the country. Collectively, they have logged more than 30,000 hours of service in the community.

A key element of BYLC's work is the way it builds bridges across populations of young people that are usually highly segregated in daily life. Bangladesh is a country with three distinct educational systems: English medium (where classes are taught mostly in English), Bengali medium (where classes are taught in the language of Bengali), and Arabic medium (Madrassas following a religious curriculum). The BBLT program unites students in equal proportion from each of the three educational systems, creating a rare space in the civic life of Bangladesh in which young people from these systems come together to learn and practice leadership together in a substantive way.

In 2014, BYLC commissioned an external impact assessment study with the Research and Evaluation Division of BRAC, an award-winning NGO, on its signature *Building Bridges through Leadership Training (BBLT)* program. BBLT is a two-and-a-half-month long after-school leadership course that has graduated more than 450 students — aged between 17 and 22 — over the course of 12 programs delivered in the last six years. Preliminary findings from the BRAC study (Islam & Khatoon, 2014) showed that BYLC's programs have had positive impact on participants. The study found that compared to peers who had applied to BYLC programs but had not enrolled, program graduates demonstrated higher levels of creativity, critical thinking, and problem-solving skills. They were also more likely to perceive leadership as an activity, rather than a quality an individual is born with, and possessed more knowledge about leadership activities such as public speaking and ways to mobilize people effectively.

BYLC has also had an impact on the policy and public spheres in Bangladesh. BYLC produced a report presenting the results of a survey of youth perspectives on various matters, making sure that young people have a voice in public affairs. Other leadership programs such as the biennial Youth Leadership Summit bring together hundreds of youth from all over Bangladesh along with a constellation of senior leaders from the world of politics, business, the media, and the non-profit sector. In the 2014 Summit, BYLC hosted 500 college and university students and 50 speakers for three days of leadership training, inter-generational knowledge sharing, and networking. While the exact impact of these efforts is difficult to measure, there can be no doubt that BYLC is elevating the profile of youth voice and youth empowerment in the civic life of Bangladesh.

Examples of Impact

Both KLC and BYLC aspire to develop participants into active and engaged citizens who are willing and able to take personal responsibility for transforming their own communities. In the section above, we shared general evaluation data from both programs in an attempt to present an overview of what both programs understand about their impact on participants. In this section, we present specific cases of ways that program participants have worked to create change upon completing the programs. Through these individual examples, we can gain a deeper insight into the ways that individuals and communities are transformed by these programs.

BYLC: INDIRA RAHMAN'S JOURNEY

Indira Rahman was a participant in BYLC's ninth session of BBLT, which began in October 2013 (Afrin, 2014). She lived in Dhaka and attended an English medium high school. She rarely encountered students from other school systems, and thought that the BBLT program was an exciting opportunity to connect with a more diverse group of peers. As a participant in BBLT, Rahman encountered the theoretical distinctions that are central to the adaptive leadership theory. She was challenged to question her unexamined assumption that leadership meant being in charge and was pushed to develop her abilities to diagnose the presence and nature of adaptive challenges in her own community.

After encountering these ideas, Rahman and her peers were required to put these ideas into action. A few weeks into the program, she was placed on a diverse six-person team that was tasked with developing a "Leadership in Action" project. Together, they would have to identify an adaptive challenge in their own community of Dhaka and then develop and implement a program designed to address that challenge. They chose to focus on the Tejgaon Industrial Area of Dhaka city and engaged in a process of connecting with community members there to better understand local needs. They learned that the majority of children in that neighborhood were in need of quality educational programming and supports that could prepare them effectively for the Bangladesh primary school exams in math, English, Bengali, and science. Rahman and her fellow BBLT participants decided to create a service project called *Road to School* that would address this need.

From November 3 to December 29, Rahman and her colleagues recruited 40 students in the 5−12 years age range and provided them with classes five days a week for about 5−6 hours a day. It was a major commitment by a group of Bangladeshi teens to provide needed services to Bangladeshi children who were just a few years younger than themselves.

The formal BBLT program is only two-and-a-half months long (it ran from October through December). When the formal program ended, Rahman and her colleagues were faced with a choice: Just walk away, or find a way to keep *Road to School*

going despite the fact that they had already fulfilled their requirements for BBLT. With Indira taking the lead, they chose to
continue the project.

They had to make changes to keep things running. They
began to teach classes only on weekends, as sustaining the
five-day-a-week model was too much, given their other responsibilities. But *Road to School* flourished through several unexpected
successes. They received a $1,000 grant from a mini-project
competition organized by the Meridian International Center and
sponsored by the U.S. Department of State that allowed them to
bring in permanent teachers to run classes with the children three
days a week. The staff at BYLC provided ongoing coaching and
support as Indira maintained her commitment to *Road to School*
years after graduating from BBLT.

Rahman continued trying to sustain the program even as she
completed her own studies and applied to college. When she was
accepted to study in the United States at Franklin and Marshall
College in Lancaster, Pennsylvania, she was thrilled by the news
but struggled to find a way to make *Road to School* sustainable.
She began her studies in 2014, and even while in the United
States stayed focused on her efforts to keep the program going in
some meaningful way. In March 2015, Rahman was thrilled to
learn that *Road to School* had won the 2015 Kathryn W. Davis
Peace Prize, worth $10,000, that would allow her to continue the
work of the organization in the summer of 2015.

So Rahman will once again return to serve the children of the
Tejgaon neighborhood for the summer months. With this level of
funding, she has the resources to pilot new programming focused
on teaching English as a second language and information
technology to students older than twelve.

The journey of launching and sustaining *Road to School*
has been so impactful that Indira has decided to launch a second
initiative called *Youth Walk Bangladesh* (YWBD), which is
focused on supporting other youth leaders who — like her —
created social change projects as "Leadership in Action" initiatives
during BBLT and now want to keep their programs running.

Although Rahman does not have any formal evaluation
results to share, *Road to School* has now worked with hundreds
of children, and she has seen students enroll in school who might
otherwise not have and others who are still in school who were
at a high risk of dropping out without the additional support
provided by *Road to School*. The commitment to working for
positive change that was sparked in Indira at BBLT has become

an enduring, sustainable flame. The ideas and opportunities she encountered in her BYLC experience played a central role in inspiring her efforts to strengthen her own community. Indira says, "Too often, we wait for 'someone else' to provide all the solutions. But at one point, you realize that there is no 'someone else' in society. There is only one 'someone': you. Leadership starts with you."

KLC: ADDRESSING POVERTY IN GREENWOOD COUNTY

Leadership & Faith Transforming Communities is one of the many programs offered by the KLC (Hancock, 2014). As the name suggests, the program is focused on bringing together members of local faith-based congregations and organizations to build their capacity to address communal challenges. Jan Stephens was one of several congregants from the First United Methodist Church in Eureka, Kansas who attended the program and went home with a deepened commitment to step up and work for positive change.

After encountering the adaptive leadership model, Stephens and her colleagues returned home and began seeking to diagnose local problems. While their church had always been committed to serving those in need, the group had a new level of motivation to find practical, effective approaches to make that happen. Eureka is located in Greenwood County, and Stephens knew that the county had unusually high levels of poverty: 18% for the county, compared to 13% for Kansas overall. Stephens and her fellow participants decided to experiment with efforts to address this communal challenge.

They decided on a program that would provide children with a place to play games and eat breakfast on days when school started late, allowing parents not to miss work on those days. The group wasn't sure how it would work, but this is the approach they learned from the KLC: Don't sit around passively waiting for someone else — authorities, experts, superheroes — to swoop in with the resources and answers required to solve pressing problems. *Try something* — from wherever you are in the system — and learn all you can from whatever happens. And then try something else informed by those lessons, until eventually you experiment your way into an approach that in some way effectively impacts the adaptive challenge you seek to address.

The morning program was launched with enthusiasm, but quickly sputtered. Stephens tried to gather the group of KLC alumni to refocus their efforts, but everyone was so busy that they struggled to find a time to connect. It was also difficult to engage fellow congregants who had not attended the KLC training and were not as fired up about trying to exercise leadership in the same ways. Despite the good intentions of the alumni group, it was proving difficult to make anything meaningful happen.

After months of struggling, the KLC alumni group heard about a small group of four families who had recently broken away from another local church to form a new congregation, the Flint Hills Community Church, grounded in a deep commitment to serving the poor. The two groups met to discuss their shared commitment to addressing poverty, and things finally came together. The passion and commitment of the Flint Hills group was the missing element that gave the initiative the energy it needed to begin to grow and flourish.

The two groups began to partner in their efforts to implement the program and recruit volunteers, and that collaborative effort has begun to pay off. As of the spring of 2015, the program engages clergy and congregants from every church in town. "I've lived in Eureka for 40 years," Stephens says, "and we have people come who I've never seen before. People without networks come."

Adaptive Leadership as an Approach to Strengthening Communities

These examples illuminate the impact this approach has on participants. The encounter with the theoretical framework and case-in-point pedagogical experience provided by the adaptive leadership model awakens in participant new consciousness around their own very real ability to begin addressing critical challenges in their own communities. The message is that people do not need to spend years accumulating expertise and experience before creating change; they can start where they are, with whom they are, right now. As a result, children in an impoverished neighborhood in Dhaka began receiving educational support from local teens still in school themselves, and impoverished citizens of Greenwood County, Kansas began receiving meals and childcare provided by fellow citizens eager to be of service. The promise of adaptive leadership as an approach is that it has the potential to awaken an ever growing circle of individuals to feel both responsible for and capable of undertaking related efforts intended to strengthen their own communities.

One of the benefits of focusing on these two organizations is that they provide an opportunity to explore the similarities and differences in undertaking this work in dramatically different contexts. KLC is immersed in the American heartland, working with adults in a highly developed Western nation; BYLC operates in Southeast Asia, working with young people in an emerging Eastern country. Given the considerable differences across these contexts, it is reasonable to wonder whether meaningfully different issues emerge in the encounter with the adaptive leadership model across these highly distinct communities.

It is perhaps surprising to find that the responses to this model are, for the most part, extremely similar in Kansas and in Bangladesh (per information in the interviews cited previously). In both contexts, participants find it profoundly uncomfortable to be in spaces in which authority figures are not simply providing direction and "answers" as expected. They are challenged by the clear evidence in the room that they themselves operate with often profound degrees of dependence on authority, and grapple with the implications that the theory and practice of adaptive leadership has for their own deeply held but largely unexamined archetypes of what leadership is and looks like.

Despite the considerable social, economic, age, and religious differences, participants in Bangladesh and Kansas seem to experience similar learning journeys upon their encounter with the adaptive leadership model. In both institutions, participants respond initially with anger and frustration when they experience a formal authority figure (in this case, the instructor), who does not provide direction and answers as expected. They report feeling discomfort — often profound — at having to spend extended periods of time grappling with uncertainty and ambiguity. Over time, however, they build their capacity to remain in that space, and deepen their ability to look inward for their own intrinsic sources of purpose and meaning. They also gain skills and insights regarding how they can effectively influence events in a complex, dynamic social system that mirrors the levels of freedom, empowerment, and voice that characterize the emerging context beyond the classroom walls.

By the end of the course, the vast majority of participants in both Kansas and Bangladesh report feeling empowered by the model, and also challenged by the need to look inward to find direction from their own internal sources of purpose and meaning. And in both cultures, there are always a minority of individuals who do not find the experience to be valuable or helpful; it is just too confusing and disconcerting an experience to be useful.

There are, to be sure, some differences across these programs. It is not the same, for example, to question one's relationship to authority as an 18-year-old starting out in life, as compared with doing so as a middle-aged Executive Director of a large non-profit. But the experience of discomfort, struggle, and deepened insight into both self and human relations is present — and surprisingly similar — in both youth and experienced professionals.

The similarity of this learning journey across such disparate cultures suggests that many people may operate with largely unexamined mental models of leadership that are surprisingly universal and increasingly misaligned with the rapidly evolving networked context. At some level far below conscious awareness, it seems that individuals across the world may operate with the assumption that to be a leader, one must be an individual holding a formal position of authority. Embedded in this assumption is the belief that those authority figures are solely responsible for finding the answers to complex challenges, and — by virtue of their positions — have sufficient power to unilaterally address those complex challenges. Based on the experiences at both KLC and BYLC in teaching adaptive leadership, it seems that these beliefs are widespread, powerful, and comforting; they keep the rest of us from having to step into the breach to confront the uncertainty and disequilibrium that are hallmarks of addressing adaptive challenges. In these two case studies, the dynamic, experiential way in which participants learned to engage with their own implicit beliefs and their emerging agency appears to move participants from resistance to possibility. Ultimately, stepping into such a place of possibility is both the aim and the power of adaptively framed large-scale leadership development. The experiences of these two organizations give reason to believe that these desirable leadership development outcomes can be achieved with similar efficacy in diverse cultures, working with very different participant populations.

Closing Thoughts

In opening this chapter, we argued that the world of the 21st century is becoming interconnected, interdependent, and networked to a degree unprecedented in human history. At its core, we see this new context representing a transformation in the relationship between individuals and authority. In a simple hierarchy, authorities have considerable power while the grassroots are relatively powerless; in a network, the power that authorities have to control events is markedly constrained, and the power of other individuals to influence the system is dramatically expanded. This appears to create an entirely new context that is rich with new risks and remarkable possibilities.

The experience of these two institutions illuminates a frontier of innovation for the leadership development field. Although the world is changing rapidly, many people are blind to the degree to which their way of being in the world reflects beliefs and assumptions that are limiting and increasingly outdated. As they continue to depend upon authorities in problematic and disempowering ways, they resist looking inward for intrinsic sources of direction, purpose, and answers. As a result, too many wait passively for others to "solve" our problems and are unaware of the agency and potential we each have to create positive change in ourselves and our own communities.

The promise of large-scale leadership development is that it strengthens communities by continually growing the number of citizens who have a genuine and accurate awareness of their own very real power to make change. Communities grow healthier when more and more individuals shift from being passive participants to becoming actively engaged citizens who feel responsible and empowered to confront communal challenges. As this circle of active citizens grows, these communities become more resilient, creative, responsive, and proactive in their efforts to address their own challenges and promote their own strengths. It's an approach to promoting community development that goes beyond providing participants with new ideas or helping them to develop new skills and competencies. Rather, it is about transforming their ways of being in the world at a level that goes deeper than behaviors and knowledge, allowing them to see situations, communicate with each other, and engage with challenges and opportunities in ways that become leadership for healthy communities. We believe that adaptive leadership has the power to unleash such a profound level of transformation, awakening an ever growing circle of citizens who recognize the truth of this statement by American writer Henry Miller (1941): "No man is great or wise enough for any of us to surrender our destiny to. The only way in which anyone can lead us is to restore to us the belief in our own guidance" (p. 122).

Acknowledgments

The authors are grateful for the support of Ed O'Malley and Michael Matson from the KLC and Ejaj Ahmad from the BYLC. The thoughtful insight and generous feedback from these individuals were essential in ensuring the accuracy of these two case studies.

References

Afrin, S. (2014). Author of a new road. *Dhaka Tribune*, July 14. Retrieved from http://www.dhakatribune.com/tmag/2014/jul/14/author-new-road

Brafman, O., & Beckstrom, R. (2006). *The starfish and the spider: The unstoppable power of leaderless organizations*. New York, NY: Penguin Books.

Green, C. (2011). *Case-in-point: A taxing and transforming leadership education art form*. Retrieved from http://kansasleadershipcenter.org/sites/default/files/cip_final_sglpage.pdf

Hancock, S. C. (2014). Giving hope. *The Journal*, 6(2), 52−60. Retrieved from http://issuu.com/kansasleadershipcenter/docs/summer_2014_journal_final

Heifetz, R. (1994). *Leadership without easy answers*. Cambridge: Belknap/Harvard University Press.

Islam, Z., & Khatoon, F. (2014). *How the BBLT graduates applied their learning in their lives: An assessment of building bridges through leadership training program of BYLC*. Unpublished Working Paper, Impact Assessment Unit, Research and Evaluation Division, BRAC.

Kansas Leadership Center. Kansas Leadership Center: Survey report. TCC Group, October 2014.

Kellerman, B. (2012). *The end of leadership*. New York, NY: Harper Collins Business.

Kellerman, B. (2015). *Hard times: Leadership in America*. Stanford, CA: Stanford University Press.

Miller, H. (1941). *Wisdom of the heart*. Norfolk, CT: New Directions Books.

Northouse, P. (2015). *Leadership: Theory and practice*. Thousand Oaks, CA: Sage.

Parks, S. D. (2005). *Leadership can be taught: A bold approach for a complex world*. Cambridge, MA: Harvard Business Review Press.

13 Women and Leadership in Rwanda, Emerging Transformation: The Spiritual, Social, and Political Dimensions of Transmuting Suffering

Éliane Ubalijoro, Bagwiza Jacqueline Uwizeyimana, and Marilyn Verghis

The year 2014 marked Rwanda's 20th anniversary commemoration of the 1994 Genocide against the Tutsi during which close to one million people were killed and an estimated 500,000 women and girls were raped in over 100 days. While the violence was brutal for all, women and girls were particularly targeted (Gervais, Ubalijoro, & Nyirabega, 2009). In contrast to these gruesome statistics, Rwanda today has the highest rate of women parliamentarians in the world. What is behind 20 years of women's leadership during a period of national reconstruction after deep collective and individual trauma? How can one move forward after being subjected to such collective trauma? How does society move forward? What kind of leadership toward a healthy society could one hope for in the aftermath of the Rwandan genocide?

In traditional Rwandan spirituality, feminine wisdom is embodied, deeply connected to emotions and to the nurturing and care a mother holds for her children. For a woman to stand in this wisdom, she must connect to her feeling self. As Donna Kate Rushin wrote in her 1981 poem, *The Bridge Poem* (Rushin, 2015), each woman's journey is to be the space that links our fears, weaknesses to our inner feminine power. Only when we hold these polarities are we able to own our true self and be of service to the world.

As Rwandan women leaders have worked to face the depths of their own pain, suffering, and victimhood, they have created spaces for their fellow Rwandans to do likewise with courage, inquisitiveness, compassion, and passion. Central to both this inner work and work with others has been bringing to light what was scapegoated and repressed as a healing force for those who have been oppressed. As Arthur Colman and Éliane Ubalijoro (2012, p. 135) wrote, "If we identify scapegoating as the collective analogy to ignoring the shadow in the individual, then bringing the scapegoating process to the surface is a powerful way to heal society." This chapter will explore how women in Rwanda have worked at healing society as a way to tend to their own wounds.

We explore the role of women's leadership in catalyzing and influencing collective action in reshaping post-genocide Rwanda through stories of individual women leaders, and the collective action of women leaders organizing to enact change together. It would not be possible to capture the breadth of Rwandan women's agency over the last 20 years in one chapter, and instead, this chapter seeks to convey through selected stories the essence and spirit of the collective action of women in Rwanda to help heal a nation. Among the countless leaders that have redefined the role of women and girls in post-genocide Rwanda, we have chosen stories that are also deeply personal for us (all three of the authors have spent time in Rwanda and two are of Rwandan origin) so that this chapter might continue our bond with these women and contribute to our own healing. Concepts of posttraumatic growth, feminine wisdom, and continuing bonds to Rwandan spirituality will guide this exploration. In this chapter we narrate representative leadership stories of women in Rwanda in relation to our own personal journeys of emerging posttraumatic growth in the context of continuing communal bonds and a sense of self that is embedded in a legacy of struggle and collective healing. The following two sections are written in first person singular in this co-authored chapter. Through our *individual* and *collective* voices we explore the dual nature of voice, both deeply existential and personal (the "feeling self") *and* collective, linked to the feminine wisdom in Rwandan spirituality.

Holding onto the Legacy of Rwanda's Women Peace Builders
by ÉLIANE UBALIJORO

Louise Mushikiwabo, Rwanda's current minister of foreign affairs, was working in Washington, DC in 1994 when her brother, a prominent opposition leader, his Canadian wife, and their two teenage children were murdered during the genocide. In her memoir, Mushikiwabo (2006) traces the roots of the genocide from colonial times to the events that led her home after so much loss. Her analysis shows how eugenics was introduced as a tool to divide and rule when Rwanda became part of German East Africa in 1884. The same policies continued through Belgium protectorate, to the formative years of Rwanda's independence from 1962 to 1994 in ways that shifted power but reinforced ethnic division and tensions (Langford, 2005). Through colonialism, racial and ethnic identities were politicized in divisive ways that furthered the colonizer's end and continue to shape Rwanda's contemporary politics. In 1925, Rwanda became the small administrative section of Ruanda-Urundi, attached to Belgian Congo. In 1931, the institutional reduction of complex pre-colonial Rwandan society by the implementation of mandatory identification cards of citizens over the age of 16 stating ethnicity politicized identity in an unprecedented way (Mamdani, 2000, 2001, 2002). In her memoir, Mushikiwabo takes us into Rwanda's past as she pieces together her own family history and honors the lives of the loved ones she lost.

In the last 20 years, I have drawn strength from a legacy of Rwandan women leaders like Mushikiwabo, some born in Rwanda, some born in exile, a diverse group of women whose lives and work express a creative compassion that embraces all Rwandans, a commitment to community even at the risk of one's own life, and a profound courage to see and create opportunities for individual and collective healing in the face of devastatingly deep trauma. Two of these women are Agathe Uwilingiyimana and Aloysia Inyumba. Uwilingiyimana and Inyumba represent the two sides of Rwandan women working to bridge the politicized identity divide that has been Rwanda's legacy for nearly a century: Rwandan women who grew up in Rwanda (like Uwilingiyimana) and those (like Inyumba) who grew up in exile moving together toward the unity of a people split through colonization.

On April 7, 2014, I stood in the Amahoro Stadium in Kigali as the 20th commemoration of the genocide took place. In the preceding three days, I had attended the Kigali International Forum on Genocide under the theme "After Genocide: Examining Legacy, Taking Responsibility." During the forum, I remember sitting and listening to a recounting of how Agathe Uwilingiyimana, Rwanda's first and to date only female prime minister, was raped with a Fanta bottle before being killed with her husband. She was killed to prevent her from speaking on national radio after the plane carrying then President Juvenal Habyarimana was shot down and all aboard were killed. Her intended message never reached Rwandans and the radio was taken over by the Interahamwe extremists and used to spread hate speech. I had met with her the year before in 1993. She had been in Montreal and I had given her a letter for my father. Two decades later as I listened again to the brutal details of how her life had ended, I was struck by how vivid I held the memory of meeting her and the hope she seeded in me for Rwanda's healing.

During her tenure as prime minister, Uwilingiyimana worked tirelessly to lead a transitional government that would bring peace to Rwanda following three years of civil war. Prior to becoming prime minister, she was Rwanda's first female minister of education. In this position, she provided educational scholarships based on merit, eliminating a quota system based on ethnicity. Throughout her career she faced political pressure and oppression, but as a visionary and transformative leader she challenged divisionary extremists and strove to establish a fair and just society, in which all citizens shared equal rights. For her commitments, Uwilingiyimana was regularly targeted by the genocide propaganda, often portrayed in cartoons as a whore in bed with other moderate politicians, many of whom would also be executed during the genocide (Maier, 2012–2013).

After assassinating Uwilingiyimana, extremists used national radio to divide the country, spreading messages of fear, dehumanizing and inciting hatred toward all Tutsis and political moderates as enemies of the State that required elimination. Agathe Uwilingiyimana's legacy lives on through the work Rwandans have been doing over the last 20 years to heal and rebuild a deeply traumatized nation. Agathe was one of the first people killed in the 1994 genocide because of her belief in national unity and equal rights to all Rwandans. Her work continues to be honored through *The Agathe Innovative Award Competition* initiated by the Forum for African Women Educationalists (FAWE) to support educational and income-generating projects to improve the prospects of African girls. As a founding member of FAWE, she would be proud of the partnership the organization formed 20 years after her death with the MasterCard Foundation. The goal of the partnership is to educate 1,200 Rwandan girls to prepare them for careers in Science, Technology, Engineering, and Math through a $17.4 million initiative for Rwanda and Ethiopia. Part of remembering Uwilingiyimana is holding the brutality of her last hours and the years of slander she endured as she worked so diligently for peace. Yet the deeper truth of her life is not what was done to her, but the legacy of her leadership and work for peace. I likewise remember a simple conversation with her in my city of adoption, an inner place I carry that holds her quiet, diligent, focused energy. In her presence, I could feel her dedication for peace, the overwhelming details that she patiently tackled and carried on her shoulders that needed to be tended to in her political work. She embodied a combination of focused energy, humility, grace, and perseverance that I could easily imagine flowing with others to vision, bridge, communicate, and act on the changes that Rwanda needed to embrace to bring peace.

I hold in me the memory of meeting Uwilingiyimana, of giving her a letter for my father. This simple encounter, the sharing of time and space, the passing on of a letter, reminds me that I hold in me memories of this vibrant leader alongside knowledge of her horrific death. In me, the light of who she was will continue to shine as a testament of the essence of the peacemaker who believed in a whole undivided Rwandan people. Carrying the wholeness of the murdered ones in inner places has been an essential opportunity to hold the trauma in an embodied way where polarities coexist. In my body, I hold memories of those lost. I hold images of hope, building anew, destruction, and horror. In my heart, I cry for the suffering that was inflicted, I rage for dehumanization that was perpetrated. I touch the resilient passionate energy of those who have and continue to work to bridge conflict, transmute suffering and I connect to the beauty, terror, vibrancy, and fragility of life. Identifying language that allows growth and validates the reality that deep trauma isn't something that we recover from but a struggle with highly perplexing situations aligns with Richard G. Tedeschi and Lawrence G. Calhoun's (2007) notion of "posttraumatic growth" as well as Howarth's (2000) exploration of "continuing bonds." Rwandan women leaders in the last 20 years have anchored themselves in corporeal memory of loved ones to grow personal strength and the capacity to relate with others while nurturing "new possibilities, spiritual change, and appreciation of life" (Splevins, Cohen, Bowley, & Joseph, 2010, p. 266). Whether nurtured by memory of those lost or a dream of a better tomorrow, Rwandan women continue to move through the trauma of rape, physical mutilation, dehumanization, and the horror of the murder of loved ones.

A crucial dimension of healing in post-genocide Rwanda has been the return to the country of many Rwandan women who grew up in exile. These women have been pioneers in Rwanda's transformation over the last 20 years in all sectors of Rwanda's socio-politic-economic life. One woman who symbolically represents this new feminine energy in Rwanda is Aloysia Inyumba. When I first met her, I was struck by her commitment to the children of Rwanda. Inyumba was born in Uganda in 1964 after her father had been killed in Rwanda and her family fled a wave of ethnic massacres. As a young girl in a refugee camp, her dream was always to return to her homeland, a dream she realized in the leadership role she later took in the Rwanda Patriotic Front (RPF) working to allow the return of all Rwandan refugees. Inyumba was the first Minister of Family, Gender, and Social Affairs after the genocide. At the time, Rwanda's population was composed 70% by women. Hundreds of thousands of children had been orphaned. In 2007, she was nominated as one of the 21 women leaders of the 21st century in honor of her tireless efforts to empower and support vulnerable women and orphans. Inyumba never lost hope that she could be an agent in the rebuilding and reshaping of her country since her childhood. After her own journey back to Rwanda, she encouraged other women in the diaspora to return home while also encouraging Rwandans to adopt genocide orphans. Sadly, she passed away in 2012. Messages from political, community, and religious leaders as well as celebrities were written in remembrance of her efforts to rebuild Rwanda and her capacity to inspire compassion. Her journey through exile to Rwanda represents the journey of many Rwandan women leaders who came to Rwanda as adults to become local change makers in a land that had been inaccessible before 1994. Inyumba represents the dream of the returnee enacted, an important part of Rwanda's journey toward healing.

Tikkun Halev/Tikkun Olam: Creating the Conditions for Posttraumatic Growth
by JACQUELINE UWIZEYIMANA BAGWIZA with ÉLIANE UBALIJORO

I (Jacqueline) lived and studied for over four years (2008–2013) in the Agahozo Shalom Youth Village (ASYV) in Rwanda founded by Ann Heyman, an American woman of Jewish faith born in South Africa. ASYV is a residential community located in the eastern province of Rwanda for youth who were orphaned during the 1994 Genocide and after. The ASYV community includes 32 family settings, each comprised of a family mother, big brother or big sister, and 16 sisters or brothers. In August 2013, I moved to Canada as a MasterCard Foundation Scholar at McGill University. Before studying at Agahozo, the first 18 years of my life held one constant: deep insecurity. Heyman modeled ASYV after a youth village called "Yamen Orde" that was built in Israel in the 1950s for the Jewish orphans of the holocaust. Based on the Yamen Orde experience, she believed that transformational healing for Rwandan youth could occur as long as they were given the opportunity to ground their hope in the future. Orphans at ASYV have the space to strive for academic excellence while grieving with dignity, without pity or judgment.

ASYV's philosophy is grounded in the Jewish principles of Tikkun Halev ("repairing the heart") and Tikkun Olam ("repairing the world"). This philosophy was introduced to us in our first two years at ASYV. In our communal life, hope for a better future and dream making were central in our discussions. Arts and sports reinforced this in an embodied way by enlivening spirit and nourishing the desire to live a purposeful life. We started expressing our dreams and aspirations for the future we want and articulating our past experiences in a safe, contained way. I started painting when I arrived in ASYV, because I realized that it was the only thing that I could do to create my own happiness while expressing my inner self and explain to others the future I wanted to live. These activities helped me understand the process of self-discovery and self-healing that I was opening to. Painting changed me. It gave my life meaning and value as I started envisioning my future life in painting and putting on canvas the parts of me I could not articulate in words. Tikkun Halev enabled me to feel agency: to touch the creativity and curiosity in me that had grown dormant when my life was all about survival. To my surprise, two of my paintings were auctioned in an ASYV fundraiser in 2012 for $300,000 in a lot with paintings from two other students. As we all developed the urge to communicate what was in our hearts through art and sports, we were able to contribute in different ways to our village's sustainability and in the process become change makers for our own community. In this way "repairing our hearts" contributed to "repairing the world."

We learned Tikkun Olam by engaging in acts of kindness for others that reinforced our agency in creating a more just world. Ann used to tell us that our life is like a line made of past, present, and future, and when this line breaks in the past, there is a need for someone to help mend it in the present so that hope for the future can re-emerge from solid ground. Many of us had no memories of our parents, with no or little knowledge of our family lineage, and this broken line was mended by the community Ann created for us. She consistently told us that starting the village was only the beginning and the only thing she could do, but the big task of Tikkun Halev, of repairing hearts, was ours to take part in for life. Tikkun Olam activities every week consisted in community service in the neighboring areas around the village. These acts include repairing the destroyed houses or the kitchens of widows, cultivating land for them, buying mattresses or other furniture for them, helping in the health center, and teaching English in primary schools. The experience of Tikkun olam sparked the realization that many people lived with far more suffering and poverty than we had known. Tikkum Olam projects made us put aside what we saw as our problems to see how we can be of service to the world. Every semester, we would fundraise within the village to buy materials we would need for the Tikkun Olam projects of the year.

Through communal support, we were able to share our personal experiences within our 32 families, which contributed to the process of self-healing. The communal learning experience opened our minds and hearts in ways that continues to create opportunities for us to discover and develop our talents. During an interview, Ann stated "the kids could have not done any better without a feeling of a meaningful connection and belongingness to a group of people whom they share the same experience" (http://www.asyv.org/). After her untimely death in January 2014, Ann was honored in Rwanda and mourned by ASYV students and alumni in the same way a loving mother is remembered. After four years in ASYV, my class graduated, and we all left the village for university. We could write e-mails to our grandmother Ann, as we called her. When I got my scholarship to McGill University, she sent me an e-mail congratulating me and promising me that she would visit as much as she could. She was very proud of me, and I could feel her joy as if she were my blood parent. Ann made sure we knew that even though we had left the village, she still cared about us and we would always be part of the ASYV family. She passed away three weeks before she had planned to come visit me for the first time at McGill University.

ASYV could not have been a success without the commitment, love, and passion of Sifa Nsengimana, the first Rwandan woman that Ann met when she was working to establish the village. Sifa was an advocate and human rights activist. She had been a voice for the voiceless, especially for those who suffered during the atrocities committed in Darfur, Sudan in 2006. As a Rwandan woman who grew up in exile in the Democratic Republic of Congo, Sifa's childhood experience was in a foreign country. Her experience seeded responsibility and desire to fight against injustice. At an early age, she realized that facing injustice of any kind required her to cultivate exceptional courage and determination. She shared with us the inspiring story of her own struggle with growing up in exile and how she overcame these tribulations. Nancy Adler (2007, p. 426) asserts that "courage transforms wisdom, which is knowledge of what is true and right, into a meaningful action." Sifa's early dream and involvement in human rights activism was rooted in a desire to lead toward sustainable health beyond her family's and her own early wounding from living in exile. Sifa became the first director of ASYV, where she mentored many of us. Her embodied transmutation of her own suffering through positive action was a source of feminine wisdom grounded in Rwandan spirituality for all the youth she inspired at ASYV. Ann's and Sifa's vision was always to help us find our way, by maximizing our full potential. Sadly, Sifa died in a car accident in late 2012 just a month before our graduation. Both Sifa and Ann are remembered as authentic leaders and mother figures able to help a younger generation dream and pursue the direction of their dreams. They both worked to bring out our "salient innate capabilities" (Ayman, 1993) and our "hidden talents and potentials."

Before we were taken in by ASYV, we were all orphans, many living on the street or in equally hopeless situations. Our courage came from the ASYV mothers who opened our eyes, hearts, and minds in order to see the world differently by transforming our grief into courage. My family mother, Mama Any, told us one day "each one of you holds your beloved ones inside of yourself, and because of that you should always strive to contribute to the greater good so their legacies can be expanded through your lived life." As Mama Any encouraged students to hold deceased ones in inner worlds, she was teaching us to transmute our suffering. By making our loved ones part of our outward social realities through honoring their legacies, we cultivated a healing spiritual connection to them. This practice of altering and continuing the connection to lost ones has been described in new models of grief research as a very effective way to cope with loss while adapting to change in an integrated way. This social validation of past trauma and present life allowed new dimensions and possibilities to be strived for that did not sever the connection to the deceased (see Howarth, 2000; Klass, Silverman, & Nickman, 1996). ASYV students could believe that success would not only bring happiness but would build on the positive legacy of lost ones and a nation's healing, thus deepening the Tikkun Halev and Tikkun Olam practices.

Mama Any was more than an advisor or motivator to us; she created a space where mouthing "mama" allowed an embodied loving response where emptiness and darkness had been. Before ASYV, I had never called anyone "mama." In my first few weeks in the village, I kept by myself, sitting quietly in the corner of our house because I never liked being where other people were chatting. Mama Any would be moving all around checking on everyone. One day she found me in my corner and then came to me and told me a Rwandan proverb that translates "holding on to sorrow won't kill you but it will nurture darkness in your heart; you are so beautiful when you smile so go and join others." I discovered that I looked beautiful when I smiled. The idea that I might be beautiful had never occurred to me.

One day during a family time, Mama Any told us "you have lost your family and relatives but you have us today. You are my daughters and I love you all as much as I love my Nicole" (her only surviving daughter out of five children). Even though we have lost our beloved ones, we still have our own life and future. She would encourage us to create our own happiness as a practice to live strong vibrant lives. She would sit us down and talk to us about how she survived hardships and brutal losses during the genocide. We were too young to have any memories but her memories gave me a space to trust in her, in life. And my fondness for her grew. Mama Any encouraged us to own the destiny of our lives and let people know that we are living a purposeful life. She would say "aho kubabara, ni mugire umujinya mwiza" which literally means "instead of being sad, have good anger," with the understanding that your sadness will only attract pity from others, whereas "good" anger will allow you to work through your suffering and succeed in your mission of honoring the legacy of your lost families. This preference for "good anger" over what would be bad or destructive action or sadness is grounded in Rwandan spirituality. This traditional wisdom for societal healing enables action and vulnerability to coexist, instead of allowing numbing or anger to take over and open a door to impulsive aggression. The many words of encouragement and motivation we got from Mama Any resonated to me with what Tedeschi and Calhoun (2004, 2007) call "posttraumatic growth." With the family mothers' support, we learned to use our grief to accelerate positively our desire of making a step forward and owning our destiny, present and past. Tikkun Halev and Tikkun Olam also favored transmuting suffering by ensuring as much as possible all our energy was used toward good deeds and right action for the world and our own selves. New memories of positive empowered action fueled by good anger of past trauma created new inner spaces for youth at ASYV.

This "permanent embodiment of grief" allowed us to transmute our suffering and to mourn without shame (Pendleton, 2009, p. 334). What stays in the shadows can be scapegoated and humiliated. The communal and spiritual dimensions of "repairing the heart" and "repairing the world" made space for contained vulnerability and compassion. This brought light to the broken heart spaces, sweeping away shame. I remember on the night of the 18th commemoration of the Genocide in 2012, Grand-mère Augusta (the eldest of the village mothers so we honored her by calling her Grandmother in French) telling us "don't live in sadness and grief in your heart but rather have courage and motivation which will enable you to accomplish your loved ones' unfinished tasks. Avoid any anger that may restore hate but rather make decisions toward progress, and your progress will be an inspiring example to others." Though that night was for mourning, we gained strength by encouraging each other and reminding each other that we have a lot to accomplish in the short time of our lives. Mama Augusta's words told us that our beloved ones left an unfinished mission, and we are responsible to take it to completion for them and for our success will always be a great honor to them. We began to clothe the nakedness of our hearts, raw from hopelessness and disappointment, in humanity with the love of the women leaders of ASYV.

Transmuting Suffering and Inequality into Hope and Opportunity

Connecting with the embodied emotions of anger, rage, and sadness has been critical to Rwandan women's journey of posttraumatic growth. The Latin origin of emotion, *emovere*, means to stir or agitate. Emotions as energy in motion can be used for good or evil. What type of action will this stirring produce? Touching anger without taking it to aggression has encouraged a connection that can be cultivated in the present and honors the deceased loved ones. The traditional wisdom in the concept of "good anger" allows "reinforcement for the emotions, thoughts and spirit" felt by the bereaved (Bagalishya, 2000, p. 341). It also incites behavior that supports growth while letting go of blame and retribution. Traditional proverbs in Rwanda convey symbolic representations that encourage emotional literacy and reflection for growth. Growing up with the gift of Rwandan elders, benefiting from these sayings was passed on as spiritual food, in the same way as actual nourishment is essential to physical growth and thriving. Drawing on the ancient tradition of using proverbs to pass on wisdom, family mothers at ASYV reconnect youth who lost their parents and other loved ones with the collective wisdom that has been part of Rwanda's spiritual fabric for centuries. Such reconnection promotes social harmony and is in line with the intent of Tikkun Halev/Tikkun Olam, of repairing hearts and the world. Ann Heyman's intention of mending the pain of Rwanda's youth was grounded in her Jewish faith and skillfully aligned with the collective wisdom of Rwandan proverbs used by ASYV mothers to bridge the fractured past of the youth with indigenous imagery to repair hearts and Rwandan society more broadly.

Women leaders in Rwanda have worked to heal their own trauma in ways that have helped transform society. Rwandan women have actively lobbied after 1994 for gender justice through new legislation on inheritance, on the matrimonial regime, and on the punishment of acts of violence committed against women and children to increase women's agency tremendously. The recently established National Gender Policy, for example, is mainstreaming gender into local policies, programs, and government budgets (Gervais & Ubalijoro, 2013, p. 67). Prior to 1994, women and girls could not inherit property or open a bank account without the authorization of a male family member. Women in Rwanda are constructing their own worlds, inner and outer, bringing "their own meaning for those worlds and their own self-identity within those worlds" (Giddens as cited in Howarth, 2000, p. 130). All of the women described earlier are transmuting their own suffering without disconnecting from their grief through contributing their skills and life experience toward the work of building societal and planetary health.

Finding a Sense of the Self Through Drumming as a Collective Healing Activity

Change fundamentally involves modifying behavior through culture. Rwandan women are working through culture to vision new ways of being. Drumming in Rwanda is a sacred form of music. Ingoma Nshya broke with Rwanda's long held tradition of drumming being reserved to men by creating Rwanda's first women drumming troupe. Ingoma Nshya deeply embodies a communal transmutation of suffering for posttraumatic growth and builds on traditional feminine wisdom of continuing bonds and the use of "good anger" in a novel way for Rwandan women. Many of the women of Ingoma Nshya are genocide orphans, survivors, and widows from all sides of the conflict. Ingoma Nshya has created a new space for women to gather, transform their suffering, and bring forward their dreams into sweet success. They have toured around the world and have also created a social venture in the South of Rwanda where the National University is located producing and selling ice cream from local produce. Through this social venture in partnership with Jennie Dundas and Alexis Miesen from Brooklyn's Blue Marble Organic Ice Cream Shop, the women of Ingoma Nshya have been able to include non-women drummers into a joint venture that helps fund the organization, contributes to transformation of local agricultural produce, and creates additional nonagricultural jobs for women locally. This transnational connection of women was ignited following a meeting between Kiki Katese, founder of Ingoma Nshya and Dundas where both committed to working together to arouse joy and catalyze new economic opportunities for women in Rwanda.[1]

All the women leaders described continue to "bring hope to seemingly hopeless situations, not because rational analysis allows them to conclude that evil can or will be superseded, but rather, because it is human to have hope" (Adler, 2008, p. 10). This spirit of transmuting suffering is present in each case. The capacity to cultivate creative endeavors has been central to Rwandan women's journey to help heal the country away from divisive policies. The Rwandan women leaders and the organizations that have been described are glimpses of the collective efforts grounded in the feminine to move away from the divisive policies that tore their country apart over a century and embody remembrance and move forward in new ways to promote a healthy world.

References

Adler, N. J. (2007). Organizational metaphysics: Global wisdom and the audacity of hope. In E. H. Kessler & J. R. Bailey (Eds.), *Handbook of organizational and managerial wisdom* (pp. 423–458). Thousand Oaks, CA: Sage.

Adler, N. J. (2008). I am my mother's daughter: Early developmental influences on leadership. *European Journal of International Management*, 2(1), 6–21.

Ayman, R. (1993). Leadership perception: The role of gender and culture. In M. M. Chemers & R. Ayman (Eds.), *Leadership theory and research: Perspectives and directions* (pp. 137–166). New York, NY: Academic Press.

Bagalishya, D. (2000). Mourning and recovery from trauma: In Rwanda the tears flow within. *Transcultural Psychiatry*, 37(3), 337–353.

---

[1]The adventure of Ingoma Nshya's ice cream shop creation and the healing work that is being birthed have been captured in the documentary film *Sweet Dreams* (http://www.sweetdreamsrwanda.com/film/).

Colman, A., & Ubalijoro, É. (2012). Transmuting suffering: A leadership and advising perspective. In C. S. Pearson (Ed.), *The transforming leader: New approaches to 21st century leadership* (pp. 130–139). San Francisco, CA: Berrett-Koehler Publishers.

Gervais, M., & Ubalijoro, É. (2013). Productive remembering for social action and change: Exploring memories of the aftermath of the 1994 Genocide through the voices of Rwandan Women. In T. Strong-Wilson, C. Mitchell, S. Allnutt, & K. Pithouse-Morgan (Eds.), *Productive remembering and social agency* (pp. 61–74). Rotterdam: Sense Publishers.

Gervais, M., Ubalijoro, E., & Nyirabega, E. (2009). Girlhood in a post-conflict situation: The case of Rwanda. *Agenda*, *70*, 13–23.

Howarth, G. (2000). Dismantling the boundaries between life and death. *Mortality*, *5*(2), 128–138.

Klass, K., Silverman, P. R., & Nickman, S. L. (1996). *Continuing bonds: New understandings of grief (death education, aging, and health care)*. New York, NY: Routledge, Taylor & Francis Group.

Langford, P. (2005). The Rwandan path to genocide: The genesis of the capacity of the Rwandan postcolonial state to organize and unleash a project of extermination. *Civil Wars*, *7*(1), 1–27.

Maier, D. J. (2012–2013). *Women leaders in the Rwandan genocide: When women choose to kill* (Vol. 8, pp. 1–20). UNIversitas, Essays, Studies, and Works. Retrieved from https://www.uni.edu/universitas/article/women-leaders-rwandan-genocide-when-womenchoose-Kill

Mamdani, M. (2000). Indirect rule and the struggle for democracy: A response to Bridget O'Laughlin. *African Affairs*, *99*(394), 43–46.

Mamdani, M. (2001). Beyond settler and native as political identities: Overcoming the political legacy of colonialism. *Comparative Studies in Society and History*, *43*(4), 651–664.

Mamdani, M. (2002). When victims become killers: Colonialism, nativism, and the genocide in Rwanda review by: Jeanne Koopman. *The International Journal of African Historical Studies*, *35*(2/3), 462–464.

Mushikiwabo, L., & Kramer, J. (2006). *Rwanda means the universe: A native's memoir of blood and bloodlines*. New York, NY: St. Martin's Press.

Pendleton, M. (2009). Mourning as global politics: Embodied grief and activism in post-aum Tokyo. *Asian Studies Reviews*, *33*(3), 333–347. doi:10.1080/10357820903153731

Rushin, D. (2015). The bridge poem. In C. Moraga (Ed.), *This bridge called my back, writings by radical women of color* (4th ed.). Albany, NY: State University of New York Press.

Splevins, K., Cohen, K., Bowley, J., & Joseph, S. (2010). Theories of posttraumatic growth: Cross-cultural perspectives. *Journal of Loss and Trauma: International Perspectives on Stress & Coping*, *15*(3), 259–277. doi:10.1080/15325020903382111

Tedeschi, R. G., & Calhoun, L. G. (2004). Posttraumatic growth: Conceptual foundations and empirical evidence. *Psychological Inquiry*, *15*(1), 1–18.

Tedeschi, R. G., & Calhoun, L. G. (2007). Beyond the concept of recovery: Growth and the experience of loss. *Death Studies*, *32*(1), 27–49. doi:10.1080/07481180701741251

14

A Living, Healthy World: Implications for Thought and Action

Kathryn Goldman Schuyler, John Eric Baugher, and Karin Jironet

O ur fundamental goal as an editorial team is to open up dialogue about developing healthy organizations in a healthy world. We want people to focus on this in their lives and work: Our hope is that none give up out of fear that it is unrealistic or romantic to seek to create healthy organizations and a healthy world, but rather should find this aim practical, philosophically coherent, wise, and very urgent. As an editorial team, we have heard and integrated many voices, diverse experiences, and types of knowing in the journey that takes solid form in this book. In closing, we wish to reflect on the themes that we introduced here, contemplate the action implications, and invite you to continue the conversations and start new ones.

How can we, as a body of human beings around the planet, with an almost unthinkable diversity of cultures, life interests, opportunities, and struggles, co-create a world that is a good home to all? As we said in the introduction, we picture "a home in the full meaning of the word: a place that we think of with love, that gave us birth, and where those we love reside." It seems so impossible a task, and yet so fundamentally part of how we

312 KATHRYN GOLDMAN SCHUYLER ET AL.

would like to define what it means to be human nowadays. Grounding this exploration in the thinking of five noted social scientists (Margaret Wheatley, Otto Scharmer, Ed Schein, Robert E. Quinn, and Peter Senge), we aim to generate a shared sense of common constituents of organizational and societal health. We are building on our earlier volume in the Building Leadership Bridges series, *Leading with Spirit, Presence, and Authenticity* (Goldman Schuyler, Baugher, Jironet, & Lid-Falkman, 2014). That book focused more on the inner development of leaders and this one has been designed to complete the arc — going from inner development to impact in the world.

Starting the Dialogue: The "Ground" and Further Nourishment

Remembering the voices of the five thought leaders, what echoes for us on the editorial team? What is etched in our thinking? We recall phrases that we won't attribute to specific authors, but let remain unlabeled in order to resonate more openly in our minds and yours.

As a leader, you have to start with yourself.

Health comes from the word for "wholeness" which comes from the word for "holiness."

All of these influential social scientists focus "*on leaders as people who are able to 'host others' well-being' — to create conditions for wholeness and integration — to nourish collective wisdom and action.*" All speak of the importance of starting with oneself. All are constantly interested in learning and making a difference in others' lives.

Health is always a question of "Whose health?"

They address the importance of not leaving out anyone — or other life forms — when we consider health and wholeness. This is not just people located in rich, "developed" countries or who have the privilege and good fortune of holding "higher" social positions around the world. More than we anticipated, all of the interviewees speak to the fundamental interrelatedness of health and the sustainability of life on planet earth. Organizational health, at this point in history, is understood to be interdependent with sustainability of the ecosystem in which we reside. At very concrete levels, these social scientists and those whom we invited into the discussion in part two of the book all regard societal health as deeply interconnected with ecosystem health, the health of all human beings, and of all living beings. Such alignment around universality is an emerging force in the world.

People are now like these very tired little donkeys, who are already carrying much too much weight and have no interest in it.

What goes on, on the edge of the system, in these places that exceed everyone's expectations?

Some of our interviewees focus more than others on those who manage to excel despite the odds, whereas others seem almost viscerally aware of the suffering of many, whether in "developed" nations or those left out entirely on the margins, who have not entered into any kind of trajectory of meaningful development. All focus on how leaders can support everyone's thinking about what is needed to generate and sustain healthy organizations and societies.

What really matters is how the people in the organization make sense of their own day-to-day work ....

Leaders can do the most good in creating an organiza-tion that is healthy by creating the conditions for people to come together and be thoughtful again. We need a way of thinking about leadership that's compatible with the systemic nature of the problems.

We see their words and actions incorporating a deep care for people and life on the planet, combined with clear thinking about action and measurement to ensure movement. In the variety of their approaches, we see what systems thinking refers to as *requi-site variety*: the importance of matching the complexity of the system in our attempts to manage or refine it.

The second part of our book brings in additional varied viewpoints. Riane Eisler explores how it impacts thinking and perceptions to look at all of human history and today's situation in terms of the difference between *domination* and *partnership* approaches to social interaction. John Eric Baugher, Walter Osika, and Karl Henrik Robèrt enable us to look at the science behind *sustainability* in the context of the shift in moral will needed for any significant change to take place. Karin Jironet helps us reflect on the nature of *ethics and leadership* in the context of the foremost organization for *global governance*, the United Nations. Samuel G. Wilson allows us to reflect on the critical question of how we can *assess progress*, since at this time so much continues to ride on what may be considered a rather primitive measure: the GDP. And Charles J. Palus, Steadman Harrison III, and Joshua J. Prasad take up the challenging task of *bridging the "gap" between conceptual thought and action*, through their case study of how their organization has been developing new, more relational approaches to leadership in Africa.

From Conceptualization to Action

The interviews ground our and your thinking in the most current views of some of the leading social scientists who have influenced thinking on this topic for decades. From these interviews, we distilled the following themes as core for a possible emerging model for organizational and societal health:

- *Wholeness.*
- *Interdependence/relatedness.*
- *Inclusion/inclusivity.*
- *Removing toxins/rebalancing.*
- *Emergence.*

These themes are foundational for conceptualizing the health of systems. We believe that such an emerging model is useful for discussing health at all levels of organization, from teams, to departments, to whole organizations, and even to communities and societies. We see these themes not only in the interviews with Wheatley, Scharmer, Schein, Quinn, and Senge, but also in the chapters that bring in additional perspectives — the nourishment provided by *Air and Water: What Flows Lives.*

For the *Seeds and Plants: Local Case Studies* — the living examples of actions to create healthier communities and organizations — while we chose to let the authors of the case studies define health for themselves so as to have a more grounded approach, we see many of these themes in their experiences around the world. Our big question here is how can leaders, educators, policy-makers, and consultants contribute to even more cross-pollination across change and action research projects?

How can we move beyond a myriad of inspiring initiatives scattered around the globe to interdependent experiments in change? How can collaborations develop that don't rely on heroic leaders in command and control style, but that use skillful leadership to embrace grass-roots people and ideas, and also assess and learn from successes? The relational leadership that Palus, Harrison, and Prasad discuss in their chapter and that Baugher and Jironet elucidate in their introduction to Part III is an essential element to such learning. The hope that we developed about the possibility of generating such an essential type of health has been reinforced by the Paris Agreement, negotiated at the December 2015 United Nations Climate Change Conference, COP 21, to reduce the effects of global warming.

Finally, the following questions are designed to make this emerging model practical. As a leader, researcher, or consultant seeking to foster healthy organization, can you see how to build on these questions, so as to have a comprehensive way of moving toward health and discussing health with others engaged in comparable endeavors?

- *Wholeness. How whole do we feel our organization to be? What do we see or feel that leads us to say this?*
- *Interdependence/relatedness. In what ways do people with different roles depend on one another mutually? What do we depend on, as an organization? What and who depends on us? What happens when these interdependencies are weakened?*
- *Inclusion/inclusivity. Who lives on the margins in our system? Do we include them in reflecting on health or ignore them? Do we consider them to be "less important"?*
- *Removing toxins/rebalancing. In what kinds of situations do we lose balance, as an organization? What do we mean by "losing balance"? What creates toxicity in our system? What processes do we have for seeing and removing it? Who pays attention to this? How do we care for those who attend to the toxic aspects of our organization?*
- *Emergence. How do we take time to think? And to think about our thinking? How do we slow down to sense what is emerging? How do we create such pauses collectively and explore what others see and sense? What do we do with such new kinds of "data"? How do we give it form? How do we validate our perceptions and sensing?*

In Concluding

This book is an appeal to dialogue. We in the editorial team have experienced this first hand through the many substantial contributions of our authors. In forming this book together over two years, the notion of dialogue has earned new significance. We have come to believe that dialogue does not simply mean talking about things or exchanging views: It means experiencing the reality of the people who create the words.

And, precisely this grasping into the dark for what might have formerly emerged only in a discourse that each us may have reserved for late night talks with a loved one, now, via Skype, in our sharing as a team of people who have never met face-to-face, manifests in the form of conscious realization of what dialogue really is about. It means to listen: to take in the thought, the experiences, and the "life" of the other. In the process of this engagement it became abundantly clear to each one of us — Kathryn, John, and Karin — that only by continuously examining ourselves and the nature of our listening could we create the kind of book we wished to. It is not as easy as it seems to bring together the voices of people who have never met, from different countries, different life experiences, and different disciplinary training. Going from thinking and acting alone to trusting the wisdom of the group while retaining individuality requires new learning. To operate simultaneously from a sense of the social field and from our own skills, training, and instinct is not easy in professional functioning.

There is a voice appealing to humanity today that speaks of vitality, creativity, embeddedness in nature, and health, as well as the individual faculty of choice. It seems that the illusion of collective responsibility for the state of the world — state, government, global institutions at large — has dispersed and that in its place, sole responsibility assumed by individual actors now counts in creating a healthy world. Yet such "sole responsibility" needs to come from a sensing of the vast social fields in which we participate, so that each is responsible for action, yet no one becomes the lone, individualistic hero. Individual conduct cannot be excluded from the equation. Who you are as a leader, big or small, what you do, how you interact with your peers, how you create dialogue — these factors matter more than they ever have when it comes to establishing health in the world today.

Let us take a moment and share the voice, the call for a greater humanity, and invite you to take part in this voice. Where are we in developing the capacity of our human community to shape its future? Whose health are you working for? Who and what do you (and your organization) depend on? How do you care for them — and do you? If you become quite still, what voices within you, from your own margins, can offer wisdom? We are available to continue the dialogue with you. "It is an imperative of the voice," says Karin. "Cultivate the capacity to bear witness to suffering, not knowing in advance the end result," says John. "To find your place in this, go somewhere new and listen. Then find another place, and another ...." says Kathryn.

With sincere appreciation,
Yours faithfully, the editors,
Kathryn Goldman Schuyler
John Eric Baugher
Karin Jironet

Reference

Goldman Schuyler, K., Baugher, J. E., Jironet, K., & Lid-Falkman, L. (2014). *Leading with spirit, presence, and authenticity.* San Francisco, CA: Jossey Bass/ Wiley.

About the Contributors

As the Leader of the Alliance Party of Northern Ireland from 1987 to 1998, **John, Lord Alderdice** was one of the key negotiators of the Irish Peace Process, including the historic 1998 Good Friday Agreement. In 1996, he was appointed as one of the youngest ever life members of the British House of Lords (the upper chamber of the UK parliament) and after the Good Friday Agreement he was also appointed the first Speaker of the new Northern Ireland Assembly, serving until 2004. From 2005 to 2009, he was President of Liberal International, the organization of some 120 liberal political parties all around the world, and from 2010 to 2014 was Chairman of the Liberal Democrats in the House of Lords. His life combines public leadership with a deep interest in the human mind. He was a consultant psychiatrist and psychotherapist for over 20 years until he retired in 2010 and took this experience into working on fundamentalism, radicalization, and terrorism where he is a recognized international expert. He is currently a Senior Research Fellow and Director of the Centre for the Resolution of Intractable Conflict, at Harris Manchester College, University of Oxford, and Chairman and Director of the Centre for Democracy and Peace-Building based in Belfast. He has been the recipient of many honorary doctorates, fellowships, and international prizes for his work in understanding and addressing politically motivated violent conflict around the world.

John Eric Baugher completed his PhD in sociology at Tulane University in 2001. He is currently a Visiting Associate Professor at the Department of Sociology and Anthropology at Goucher College in Baltimore, MD. His recent publications include contributions to the fields of contemplative pedagogy, end-of-life care, bereavement, and leadership studies. He is coeditor of *Leading with Spirit, Presence, and Authenticity* (Jossey-Bass, 2014).

Carolina Bown received a PhD in Organizational Leadership from the University of Maryland Eastern Shore, and she is a Senior Lecturer at Salisbury University in Maryland. Her research interests focus on female leadership and indigenous communities in Latin America. Bown has presented her work at the International Leadership Association (ILA) and at the Latin America Studies Association (LASA), in which she is a member of the Ecuadorian Studies Section.

Riane Eisler is President of the Center for Partnership Studies and internationally known as a systems scientist, attorney working for the human rights of women and children, and author of groundbreaking books such as *The Chalice and the Blade: Our History, Our Future*, now in 26 foreign editions, and *The Real Wealth of Nations: Creating a Caring Economics*. Dr. Eisler has received many honors, including honorary PhDs and peace and human rights awards. She lectures worldwide, with venues including the United Nations General Assembly, the U.S. Department of State, Congressional briefings, universities, corporations, conference keynotes, and events hosted by heads of State.

Kathryn Goldman Schuyler, PhD, is Professor of Organization Development and Organizational Psychology at Alliant International University. Her research and writing focuses on organizational health and sustainability, leadership development, and the experience of being present. As an organizational consultant, she has worked with major corporations as well as not-for-profits, supporting leadership teams on strategic change, culture change, and team development. Among her publications are two books, *Inner Peace—Global Impact: Tibetan Buddhism, Leadership, and Work* and *Leading with Spirit, Presence, and Authenticity*, plus many book chapters and articles. Dr. Goldman Schuyler draws on her training as a sociologist and Feldenkrais Practitioner to teach and write about embodied learning, having led a program for adults with moderate to severe neuro-motor challenges for the past 14 years. She lives with her husband, a computer scientist and composer, in San Francisco.

Susan Amber Gordon was born and raised by an artist and psychoanalyst in NYC. Amber has had lifelong exposure to cultures and art unfettered by geographical boundaries. She transforms thoughts and feelings into 2D and 3D brilliantly colored artworks. In addition to living life on the edge, her education includes a BA from Barnard College, Columbia University and extensive art studies in New York and the Washington, DC, area. Her work has been exhibited from Louisiana to DC; she now lives in the Del Ray neighborhood of Alexandria, Virginia.

Steadman Harrison III is the Mission Director and CEO for Global Outreach International and a global champion for the democratization of leadership development. In this and in his prior roles at the Center for Creative Leadership, he has supported human development across all sectors with a special focus on government and NGOs in the America, Europe, Middle East, Africa, and Asia.

Jill Hufnagel, PhD, L.P.C. is a Consultant with Cambridge Leadership Associates and the former Associate Director of the Batten Leadership Institute. Practiced in case-in-point teaching, Jill delivers leadership programming around the globe built on capacity development and possibility thinking. Jill holds a PhD in English and women's studies; she trained at UVA Darden's Graduate School of Business and Harvard's Kennedy School, and is a licensed professional counselor.

Karin Jironet, PhD, Executive guide and Jungian psychoanalyst works with senior leaders and executive teams within large companies and organizations. Specialized in the dynamics of transitions, she applies a psycho-spiritual approach which creates clarity and prompts creativity while uniting diverse components pertaining to individual- and group transition. Jironet is an internationally published author of books and articles on leadership and organizational development. She works internationally out of offices in Amsterdam, the Netherlands, and Rome, Italy.

Max Klau, EdD, is Vice President of Leadership Development at City Year, an education-focused nonprofit that engages young adults of all backgrounds in a year of full-time service focused on keeping students in high-need schools in school and on track. He received his EdD from the Harvard Graduate School of Education in 2005, with a focus on youth civic leadership education. He lives in Natick, Massachusetts.

Jane McCann, MBS is a New Zealand business woman and management consultant. For the last 20 years, she has shadowed and coached Chief Executives and their teams in real-time. Her observational methodology called *Leadership Impact Analysis* holds a mirror to behaviors and identifies the gaps between what leaders say and do, identifying their blind-spots and biases. Jane, @CEsCoach jane@mccann-consulting.co.nz, also consults in Australia, Hong Kong, and the United Kingdom.

Walter Osika is a physician specialized in cardiology and psychiatry, Head of Medicine at the Stress Clinic and Director at the Center for Social Sustainability at Karolinska Institutet, Stockholm, Sweden. He is interested in contemplative science and social sustainability and lectures on mental training, virtue ethics, and compassionate entrepreneurship. He has authored many scientific articles and books. In his leisure time, he enjoys family life, music, art, hiking, and kayaking.

Charles J. Palus is a Senior Fellow and faculty member in Research, Innovation & Product Development at the Center for Creative Leadership. As a collaborator in several cross-disciplinary research groups he studies, teaches, writes about, and develops leadership. He is cofounder and global director of CCL Labs, a community-based innovation laboratory with a long line of products including Visual Explorer.

Joshua J. Prasad is a graduate student in Organizational Psychology at Michigan State University. He is passionate about how psychology can improve organizational function such as how personality can inform job placement, and qualities that promote success at the undergraduate level. He holds an MA in Psychology from Wake Forest University and a BS in Brain, Behavior, and Cognitive Sciences from the University of Michigan.

Robert E. Quinn, PhD, is Professor at the Ross School of Business of the University of Michigan. He is one of the cofounders of the Center for Positive Organizational Scholarship. His best-selling book, *Deep Change*, has sold over 100,000 copies, and *The Best Teacher in You* won the Ben Franklin Award, as the best education book for 2015. Dr. Quinn has 35 years of experience consulting with major corporations and government agencies and is a fellow of the Academy of Management and the World Business Academy.

Karl-Henrik Robèrt is a physician, former head of the Division of Clinical Hematology and Oncology, Huddinge Hospital, and founder of The Natural Step. He is Professor of Strategic Sustainable Development at Blekinge Institute of Technology in Sweden. His research and advice on the linkage between ecology, economy, and technology earned him the Green Cross Award for International Environmental Leadership and the Blue Planet Prize — "The Ecology Nobel." He is the chairman of the International Research Alliance for Strategic Sustainable Development.

Otto Scharmer, PhD, is cofounder of the Presencing Institute, and founder of the MIT IDEAS Program, the GIZ Global Leadership Academy, and the Global Well-being and Gross National Happiness Lab. He has worked with governments in Africa, Asia, and Europe and led leadership and innovation programs at corporations such as Daimler, Alibaba, ICBC, Eileen Fisher, Google, and PwC. Dr. Scharmer holds a PhD in economics and management from Witten-Herdecke University in Germany. In 2015, he received the Jamieson Prize for Excellence in Teaching at MIT.

Ed Schein, PhD, has been a prolific researcher, writer, professor, and consultant. Perhaps best known for his work on organization culture, he was on the faculty of MIT's Sloan School of Management for many decades after earning his PhD in social psychology from Harvard. His clients have included Digital Equipment Corporation, H-P, Apple, Motorola, Exxon, Shell, BP, Con Edison, and many other corporations and agencies around the world. Besides numerous articles in professional journals, Dr. Schein has authored 14 books, including most recently *Helping* (2009) and *Humble Inquiry* (2013).

Peter Senge, PhD, is Senior Lecturer, MIT, and Founding Chair of the Society of Organizational Learning (SoL), a global network of people and institutions working together for systemic change. He is the author of *The Fifth Discipline: The Art and Practice of the Learning Organization*, coauthor of *Presence* and more recently, *The Necessary Revolution*. The *Journal of Business Strategy* named him as one of the 24 people who have had the greatest influence on business strategy in the 20th century. Dr. Senge has a Master's and PhD from MIT.

Barbara Rose Shuler is a writer and broadcaster who has covered the arts for over 30 years for media on California's Central Coast. For many years, she was an on-air radio personality producing and hosting classical music radio programs. For 22 years, she hosted a talk program on public radio interviewing writers, artists, scientists, and public figures on diverse subjects. She lives on the Monterey Peninsula, California, where she continues her active participation in the performing arts scene as well as other aspects of the community.

Éliane Ubalijoro is Professor of Practice for public-private sector partnerships at McGill University's Institute for the Study of International Development. Her research interests focus on innovation, gender, and sustainable development. She is the Founder and Executive Director of C.L.E.A.R. International Development Inc., a consulting group harnessing global networks for sustainable systems development. Dr. Ubalijoro is a signatory of the Fuji Declaration. She chaired the 15th International Leadership Association Annual Global Conference in 2013, bringing close to 1,000 leadership scholars and practitioners to Montreal. She has a 2014 TEDx talk on "Reimaging the World from Scarcity to Prosperity."

Bagwiza Jacqueline Uwizeyimana is a MasterCard Foundation Scholar at McGill University from Rwanda. She is studying Anthropology and International Development Studies. Her research interests are related to African women agency, arts, and leadership. She has presented her artwork at international conferences. In her presentations and exhibits, she uses auto-ethnography and depicts solutions through "Art as Healing" to describe growing up in post Genocide Society to address the challenges young Rwandan women still face. She has given various conference presentations on this at McGill and Tufts University.

Marilyn Verghis is an undergraduate student at McGill University studying international development, economics, and women's studies. Her research interests are related to multicultural and postcolonial feminism and critiques of globalization and international development. She is a student activist who presently serves as the Vice President for the education portfolio of the McGill African Students Society as well as the Students Society of McGill University Equity Commissioner, working on social justice activism at McGill University, the Montreal community, and across the Canadian student and diaspora student community.

Patricia A. Wilson, Professor at the University of Texas Graduate Program in Community and Regional Planning, is a faculty associate at Lozano Long Institute of Latin American Studies and UT Center for Sustainable Development. She holds a B.A. in economics from Stanford and a PhD in planning from Cornell. Co-author of *Development from Within: Facilitating Collective Reflection for Sustainable Change* (2008), Dr. Wilson teaches participatory approaches to civic engagement and community development.

Samuel G. Wilson, PhD, is an academic psychologist and Director of the Swinburne Leadership Institute at Swinburne University of Technology. He is co-convener, with Paul Kosempel of the Sustainability Leadership Learning Community of the International Leadership Association. His research focuses on lay beliefs about, and expectations of, leadership across government, business, and civil society, with a view to understanding the nature and the practice of leadership for the greater good.

Margaret Wheatley, EdD, writes, speaks, and teaches how we can accomplish our work, sustain our relationships, and willingly step forward to serve in this troubled time. She is cofounder and President Emerita of The Berkana Institute, an organizational consultant since 1973, a global citizen since her youth, and a prolific writer. She has authored eight books, including the classic *Leadership and the New Science* (1992), and, most recently, *How Does Raven Know?: Entering Sacred World | A Meditative Memoir* (2014). Her articles may be downloaded free at her web site: www.margaretwheatley.com

Index